THE RHETORIC OF VIOLENCE AND SACRIFICE IN FASCIST ITALY

Mussolini, Gadda, Vittorini

The Italian fascists under Benito Mussolini appropriated many aspects of the country's Catholic religious heritage, such as ideology, mysticism, and ritual practices, to further their political goals. One concept that the fascist regime utilized as part of a core strategy was that of "sacrifice." In this book, Chiara Ferrari looks at how the rhetoric of violence and sacrifice was used by the Italian fascist regime throughout the interwar years to support its totalitarian project and its vision of an all-encompassing bond between the people and the state.

The Rhetoric of Violence and Sacrifice in Fascist Italy examines speeches by Mussolini and key literary works by prominent writers Carlo Emilio Gadda and Elio Vittorini and their influence on the body politic. Through this investigation, Ferrari demonstrates how the idea of sacrifice functioned in relation to objectives of fascist discourse, such as averting an impending national crisis, promoting collaboration among social classes, and the forging of a social contract between the state and the people.

(Toronto Italian Studies)

CHIARA FERRARI is an assistant professor in the Department of Italian Studies at New York University.

CHIARA FERRARI

The Rhetoric of Violence and Sacrifice in Fascist Italy

Mussolini, Gadda, Vittorini

UNIVERSITY OF TORONTO PRESS
Toronto Buffalo London

© University of Toronto Press 2013
Toronto Buffalo London
www.utppublishing.com
Printed in Canada

ISBN 978-1-4426-4567-7 (cloth)
ISBN 978-1-4426-1393-5 (paper)

Printed on acid-free, 100% post-consumer recycled paper with
vegetable-based inks.

Toronto Italian Studies

Publication cataloguing information is available from Library and Archives
Canada.

This book has been published with the aid of a grant from the Humanities
Initiative at New York University.

University of Toronto Press acknowledges the financial assistance to its
publishing program of the Canada Council for the Arts and the Ontario
Arts Council.

Canada Council
for the Arts

Conseil des Arts
du Canada

University of Toronto Press acknowledges the financial assistance to its
publishing program of the Canada Book Fund.

Contents

Acknowledgments

Several friends and colleagues deserve my heartfelt thanks for their support in things both critical and practical at various stages during the preparation of this manuscript. I am especially indebted to Maria Luisa Ardizzone, Virginia Cox, David Forgacs, John Freccero, and Jane Tylus. I am deeply grateful to Barbara Spackman for nurturing this project from its very inception and for showing me along the way that it was possible and necessary to question fascism again and in new ways. Her guidance, inspiration, and incisive criticism have been simply invaluable.

During fall 2009, a New York University Goddard Fellowship supported a semester of much needed quiet time to work on revisions of the last two chapters. I am also thankful to the Humanities Initiative at New York University for providing a grant-in-aid of publication subsidy.

Finally, Ted Perlmutter's cooking, computer assistance, and tireless editorial and critical advice have sustained my soul as well as my writing. His love and encouragement have been a vital source of nourishment at all stages of the manuscript's preparation. To him I dedicate this book.

An earlier version of chapter 1 was published in *The Italianist* 23.1 (2003): 123–49 (www.maney.co.uk/journals/ita; www.ingentaconnect.com/content/maney/ita) and is reprinted here with permission.

THE RHETORIC OF VIOLENCE AND SACRIFICE IN FASCIST ITALY

Mussolini, Gadda, Vittorini

Introduction

In April 1924, Benito Mussolini remarked with satisfaction that the fascist *legioni nere* (Black Legions) of Imola had in the past made him the gift of a sword inscribed with Machiavelli's motto *Cum parole non si mantengono li Stati* (Not by words are States maintained).

The irony of the all-too-literal gift was probably not lost on the Duce. Even in its more refined book version, Sir Niccolò's advice never travelled very well in public, and, when given to the powerful, his infamous little tome had ended up more quickly on night tables than displayed on coffee tables. But flattery is hard to resist, and the fascist "prince" promptly fell *cum parole* on the rhetorical sword that he had received. Marking the self-ascribed importance of the Machiavellian motto for his political vision would be nothing less than the publication in the journal *Gerarchia* of Mussolini's own "Preludio al Machiavelli" (Prelude to Machiavelli), an essay he originally wrote as foreword to his university thesis on the Florentine statesman.

Perhaps in a faint attempt to sidestep the rhetorical corner he was painting himself into by using lots of words to honour a motto that called for few, if any, he pointed out that his "Preludio" contained a "scarsa bibliografia" (meagre bibliography). If words were impossible to avoid in making his political vision public, footnotes, at least, he could discard. The inscribed sword would fall on those marginal and annoying references that might problematize or interfere with the totality and closure of his main body of discourse. A futile gesture, to be sure, for as soon as the footnotes were eliminated, the main body would be confronted – from within, rather than from the margins – with its own inescapable limitations, which included *lack* of word limitation. That his verbose "Preludio" was, in a sense, becoming a giant footnote to Machiavelli's text, did not discourage the Duce from further elaborating on the meaning of the words *Principe* and *Stato*:

> La parola Principe deve intendersi come Stato. Nel concetto di Machiavelli il Principe è lo Stato. Mentre gli individui tendono, sospinti dai loro egoismi, all'atomismo sociale, lo Stato rappresenta una organizzazione e una limitazione. L'individuo tende a evadere continuamente. Tende a disubbidire alle leggi, a non pagare i tributi, a non fare la guerra. Pochi sono coloro – eroi o santi – che sacrificano il proprio io sull'altare dello Stato. Tutti gli altri sono in istato di rivolta potenziale contro lo Stato.[1]

> The word Prince should be understood as State. In Machiavelli's conception the Prince is the State. While individuals, driven by their egoism, tend to social atomism, the State provides an organization and a limitation. The constant tendency of the individual is to stray. He tends to disobey laws, to avoid paying taxes and making war. Few are those – heroes or saints – who sacrifice their own self on the altar of the State. Everyone else is in a potential state of rebellion against the State.

Mussolini's gloss of Machiavelli is clearly aimed at placing himself in the shoes of the prince or, if you will, in the Italian "boot," so that he can bolster his representational claim to embody the state. His impatience with those little footnotes "clinging to the main body" suggests that controlling the discursive economy of the new fascist Italy would be crucial in determining how the masses would be brought into the state. Placing limits on those egotistical individual feet inclined to wander off in disparate directions would be the chief mission of the new totalitarian state and the basis of its political and social organization. The difficulty of the task, however, was clearly evident to Mussolini, whose pessimistic remark on human nature highlighted the scale of the project he was embarking on: "Few are those – heroes or saints – who sacrifice their own self on the altar of the State. Everyone else is in a potential state of rebellion against the State."

It was a remarkable assessment, indeed. Not only did it provide a measure of the Duce's unbridled ambition, but most importantly, it pointed to the fundamental principle that would guide his regime in the following twenty years: to have "the few," heroes or saints, ready to sacrifice themselves on the altar of the state, become "the many" citizens of fascist Italy. Nobody would be left too far from the sacrificial altar, since lack of propensity to approach it voluntarily signalled the individual's potential for rebelling against the state. To maintain his state, the modern "prince" would have to make sure that sacrificial propensity became synonymous with being a fascist. The *uomo nuovo* (new man) that the regime strived to promote as a model for "the many" would, above all, incorporate the sacrificial characteristics of "the few": self-effacing heroism and constant readiness to serve the nation would be the benchmarks of ideal fascist behaviour.

If the propensity, or readiness for sacrifice was considered an essential trait that every fascist subject should display, actual physical sacrifice clearly had to be reserved for the few. Literal sacrifice on a grand scale would have led to the rapid extinction of the new fascist man and consigned the Duce to a rather lonely *ventennio*, as the regime's twenty-year tenure is known. The rhetoric of sacrifice, however, had no such dire implications and was used unsparingly by the regime throughout the ventennio to support its totalitarian project and its vision of an all-encompassing bond between the people and the state. Repeated introduction and narrative dramatizations of a sacrificial scene were fundamental to the regime's ability to sustain a revolutionary ethos beyond its early movement phase and to its efforts to create a fascist subject who would view self-abnegation as a necessary component of fascist identity.

This book analyses the specific uses to which sacrificial discourse was put during fascism and its afterlife in key literary texts by prominent Italian writers of the ventennio. It examines how sacrifice functioned in relation to other elements of fascist rhetoric, such as the frequent reiterations of an impending national crisis, of the need for collaboration among social classes, and the forging of social contact between the leader and the people. Through an analysis of Benito Mussolini's speeches and other fascist texts, I show how the formation of a fascist "new man" – a principal goal of the regime – was grounded in the voluntary sacrifice of individual voice and the acquisition of a collective "echoing" voice by the fascist subject. The literary texts I examine are similarly concerned with the mechanisms of social integration of individuals and groups in the emerging mass society and with how these "voices" would be refashioned and repositioned in a collective, national whole. I show how the sacrificial economies at work in their writings enable a complex operation of recoding fascist discourse itself.

Despite its ubiquitous deployment by the fascist regime, sacrificial rhetoric has not been properly dissected, and no sustained critical analysis on the subject has appeared to date. In the past two decades, a resurgence of studies on Italian fascism has produced numerous analyses of the relationship between culture and ideology (see, e.g., Ben-Ghiat 2001, Bonsaver 2007, Gori 2004, Lazzaro and Crum 2005, Nerenberg 2001, Pickering-Iazzi 1997, Pinkus 1995, Schnapp 1996, Spackman 1996, Stone 1998, and Witt 2001),[2] leading to a general reassessment of the importance of rhetoric and public discourse under fascism. In particular, Spackman's analysis has shown how previous approaches that characterized fascist rhetoric as "empty verbiage" – the regime's smokescreen to obscure tangible misdeeds – has not furthered our understanding of how large segments of the population came to share fascist ideals. Although a critical reappraisal of rhetoric and culture during fascism has produced valuable studies of the mechanisms of consensus from a wide variety of perspectives, the literature in the areas of sacralization and spectacularization of politics under fascism has paradoxically reintroduced some of the critical pitfalls and blind spots of the earlier "empty rhetoric" approaches – a limitation particularly evident in the works of Emilio Gentile (*The Sacralization of Politics in Fascist Italy*, 1996),[3] Mable Berezin (*Making the Fascist Self: The Political Culture of Interwar Italy*, 1997), and Simonetta Falasca-Zamponi (*Fascist Spectacle: The Aesthetics of Power in Mussolini's Italy*, 1997) that have underscored the "emotive" and "non-rational" resonance of rituals and spectacles deployed by fascism while eschewing textual analyses.

The rhetoric of sacrifice continues to occupy one of the largest and most conspicuous blind spots of the sacralization/spectacularization paradigms. Scholars have frequently placed sacrifice alongside the many fascist appropriations of "words" from the linguistic field of Italian Catholicism. Lumped inside the voluminous and opaque container labelled "religious rhetoric," sacrifice has been viewed as part and parcel of the terminological veneer that the regime used to present itself as a secular religion and to infuse its nefarious activities with the mystique and power of the sacred. While not disputing the regime's efforts to capitalize on the deeply embedded and culturally resonant linguistic field of religion, my analysis moves beyond relegating sacrifice to the contextual bin of secular religion. The question that I pose, then, is not whether the fascist rhetoric of sacrifice had its roots in, or attempted to infringe on some of the terrain traditionally occupied by the Catholic Church. Certainly, fascist rhetoric was harkening back to that tradition and trespassing on that field as much as it could while still maintaining an official line of separation between church and state. Rather, my aim is to read sacrificial rhetoric in its textual applications – to trace the specific discursive uses both of the term and the broader concept of sacrifice during the ventennio. To do so requires investigating how such deployment functioned in conjunction with other elements comprising fascist rhetoric, that is, how sacrifice was linked to such notions as crisis, social class, social contact, and the voice of the labouring body. I ask: what kind of ideological "scene" or "scenes" emerge when a sacrificial logic dominates a particular text? Through which discursive devices was sacrifice put in the service of fascist ideology?

Often derided as bombastic, Mussolini's speeches, in fact, illustrate how sacrificial rhetoric was used to displace and deflect potential class conflict by emphasizing the need to eliminate differences within the nation. As the displacement of conflict was never far removed from its reintroduction, the two moments of violence and peace were held in close discursive proximity, bound together, as it were, by the repeated rhetorical dramatization of a sacrificial crisis and resolution.

The concept of sacrificial rhetoric is equally relevant to the literary texts I examine. The writings of two authors not identified as explicitly fascist (but who initially harboured fascist sympathies), Carlo Emilio Gadda and Elio Vittorini, reveal similar preoccupations with defining which social classes should be constitutive of the Italian nation and of delineating whose voices should be heard and whose should be suppressed. Their work is particularly useful for understanding the populist aspects of sacrificial rhetoric exploited by the regime as they make opposite criticisms of the fascist modality of integrating the lower social classes into the Italian state. Gadda's anti-populism and Vittorini's populism informed their conflicting narrative representations of Italian social structure. The regime's exploitation of the mechanisms of social inclusion and exclusion, rather than fascism itself, would be problematic for the two authors as they struggled to come to terms with the changing landscape of mass society under the dictatorship. Understanding these critiques also enables one to shed light on their relationship to fascism during the ventennio and their effort to distance themselves from it in the postwar period.

The analyses of literary and political texts complement each other. Gadda's and Vittorini's efforts to describe which parts of the fascist body politic should have their purity preserved point to the tensions that Mussolini's efforts at incorporation of the lower classes into the state were trying to overcome.

Chapter 1, "Discursive Ritual and Sacrificial Presentation: The Rhetoric of Crisis and Resolution in Fascist Italy," examines the performative aspects of Mussolini's rhetoric of crisis and resolution and argues that such aspects are best understood when viewed through the logic of a sacrificial crisis.

In 1925, Mussolini delivered the speech "Discorso del 3 gennaio" (Speech of 3 January) in response to the political crisis that followed the murder of the Socialist leader Giacomo Matteotti. An analysis of this famous speech traces the rhetorical configurations that allowed Mussolini to present himself as a sacrificial victim by staging the substitution of his body with Matteotti's body. The performative and ritual dimensions of the speech enabled Mussolini to stage the formal inauguration of the fascist regime and continued to play a crucial role in the fascist rhetorical articulation of crisis and resolution throughout the ventennio. The dramatization of anti-fascist forces as specular doubles to fascist entities characterized critical speeches delivered during commemorative occasions, such as the 1932 celebration of the tenth anniversary of fascist rule (*Decennale*), and at times of national uncertainty, such as the 1939 "Discorso del 23 settembre" (Speech of 23 September) that confirmed Italy's temporary neutrality in the European conflict. The range in time – 1925, 1932, and 1939 – as well as the range of contexts speaks to the centrality of sacrificial discourse to Mussolini's rhetorical repertoire.

Understanding the ritual and performative logic underlying the contradictory images of Mussolini's public persona is key to assessing the Duce's charismatic dimension and its relation to popular consensus. By analysing recent scholarly contributions that discount such logic, the chapter illustrates how such omission has far-reaching consequences for a critical evaluation of the historical experience of fascism and for understanding the discursive mechanisms of ideological production.

By providing a detailed analysis of the deployment of rhetorical devices in these three speeches, I can shed light on the complex interaction of the sacrificial field with other thematics. Indeed, it is the ubiquity of this that points to its centrality in fascist discourse.

Whereas chapter 1 focuses on the rhetorical strategies that allowed Mussolini to constantly redeploy and recharge the moment of violence as a way to resolve political crises, chapter 2, "Sacrificial Turns and Their Rhetorical Echoes," focuses on the Duce's more "benign," if not less dangerous, side. I examine how Mussolini's goal of establishing direct contact with the Italian masses without the intervening mediation of speech led to the prescription of a paradoxical discursive style of rhetorical suppression, where the bond between the people and the leader would be defined as the sharing of a linguistic void. The sacrifice of words was deemed a crucial step in forging a new collective fascist voice that would displace friction among social classes by codifying a linguistic behaviour of selfless expression.

The fascist new man would have to imitate the Duce's style of "labouring in silence," an activity construed as the sacrifice of one's voice, as the constant, tireless effort to renunciate/reduce one's words. Social contact would eliminate the need for words, communion replacing communication in the bond between Mussolini and the Italian people. The structure of the *discorsi-dialogo* (speech-dialogues), or *prese di contatto* (forging contacts), as Mussolini liked to characterize his countless public speeches, was to reflect such logic of rhetorical suppression and, paradoxically, reproduce it with every rhetorical performance. The mechanical canned answers from the crowd that regularly punctuated such speeches were not elicited as voices but as disembodied echoes of the Duce's words, returned to him as confirmation of his capacity to comprehend the people. A *voce unica* (voice in unison) was said to characterize such "dialogues," establishing an echoing circuit between the Duce and the people.

The voice of the fascist subject was simultaneously elicited and denied. Specifically, it was elicited as a sacrificial, self-denying voice that bounced back – echoed – the master's voice. Through the sacrifice of one's voice, the new man could acquire mastery of a fascist discursive style, and the ability to performatively exchange subject/master positions with the Duce. This relation of exchangeability was also reinforced by the frequent Mussolinian claims to be the faithful servant of the people, always working late into the night for the benefit of the nation and, of course, to provide the chief example of laborious submission. Mastery of a fascist identity required, first and foremost, the acquisition of one fundamental skill: labour in silence. The collective *voce unica* of the fascist nation would not tolerate the potentially dissonant voices of individual labourers, or even worse, those of labour organizations affiliated with specific social classes.

Although the regime did not seek to eliminate the economic class structure, it strove to deflect potential class conflict by emphasizing the harmonious cooperation of different social classes in the attainment of national goals. Cooperation would be fostered by closer interaction among groups, particularly between constituencies representing physical and mental labour, or what Mussolini called "accorciare le distanze sociali" (reducing social distance). Reducing social distance did not mean that the fascist state favoured eliminating class-based economic differences; it meant, rather, that these differences should not count in ideological terms. They would be there, and yet, effectively displaced – sutured, as it were – in the equalizing act of sacrificial giving to the nation. As the only body sanctioned to speak, the organic state would mirror, unify, and recirculate the "voice of the people," erasing background noises or other disturbances to the Duce-masses echo-chamber.

This ideological suture, however, did not appear entirely seamless to two prominent literary figures of the ventennio. The question of which social classes a collective, national voice should represent – and which it should exclude – preoccupied the writers Carlo Emilio Gadda and Elio Vittorini. They shared a deep concern with the new "proximity" of social classes that fascism promoted and articulated through sacrificial displacement and, in particular, with the mechanisms that facilitated social inclusion of lower strata of the population into the state. They differed sharply in their view of the masses. Gadda's anti-populism became a crucial referent of his narrative representations of Italian society. Vittorini's populism was no less fundamental to his journalistic and literary production. As I argue in chapters 3 and 4, Gadda's and Vittorini's respective discursive positioning of the Italian masses in relation to fascism sheds light on an important function of sacrificial discourse during the ventennio: its usefulness and adaptability as a rhetorical field for describing the relation between parts and whole and naturalizing the desired outcome as if it had stemmed from properties of the body. The mechanisms of social class mobility (and, of course, its interdiction) within the nation, were often articulated by linking the function of specific social classes with the corresponding parts of the physical body. Prioritizing those functions and identifying their hierarchical order for the proper organization of the national whole involved excluding, and often forcefully expelling, problematic parts.

In chapter 3, "Gadda's Sacrificial Topographies," I examine just how problematic some of those parts were for Gadda and what kind of textual control he attempted to exert over them. I argue that in his novel *La cognizione del dolore* (*Acquainted with Grief*) (1938–41), the portrayal of sacrificial mothers (mothers whose sons died in war) as gatekeepers of social exchange (verbal and sexual) constitutes a counter-narrative that masks the novel's obsession with other labouring bodies. The household servants are depicted as the source of incoherent and obscene voices that constantly trespass the norms of propriety and, ultimately, threaten "to bring down the house." These "other bodies" are Gadda's real concern and bone of contention with the regime: fascism's invitation of the previously excluded masses of workers into the totalitarian state. The figure of the sacrificial mother with her bodily resemblance to the town's bell-tower that summons the multitudes, stands in the novel as fascism's "whorish" appeal to the lower classes. The dangerous entry of "lower parts" into the national body is the image that Gadda's novel insistently reproduces and simultaneously displaces by drawing a narrative topography of open sites.

Another famous work by Gadda, *Eros e Priapo* (*Eros and Priapus*) (1967), affords a further opportunity to clarify the relation between sacrificial figures and "lower parts" that governs the narrative of *La cognizione*, as well as providing an insight into Gadda's own peculiar and problematic brand of anti-fascism. My analysis of *Eros e Priapo* links this text to a central preoccupation of *La cognizione* – the insistence on exerting textual control over the new mechanisms of social mobility unleashed by fascism. Those mechanisms are, indeed, brought into stark relief in the pages of *Eros e Priapo*, where they become the target of Gadda's ferocious invective. With his unique blend of scorn and derision, he attacks the fascist regime's populist "allargamento delle basi" (expansion of the base), which he sees as a threat to the more regulated mechanisms of social mobility based on specialized, technical expertise.

I argue that Gadda does not object to the fascist displacement of class-based identity – on the contrary, his texts naturalize the fragmentation and incoherence of the labouring body: physical, mechanical labour should stay below; mental, organizational labour should stay above. The two realms reach their utmost efficiency when they specialize in their respective functions, that is, when they belong to different people. Gadda conflates organization from below with the following of priapesque instincts and loss of productive energy. He vehemently objects to the fact that fascism, while displacing and silencing the class-based identification of labourers, simultaneously provided a new cohesive principle of organization of those "fragmented" labourers in the exemplary, national, and indeed, collective figure of the Duce. It is this new mechanism of cohesion, not fascism as a political system, that Gadda's texts oppose with their focus on the "fragments below." The obsessive descriptions of lower parts in isolation, which effectively detaches them from the other parts, can be seen as Gadda's attempt to freeze them in their proper place, to discursively naturalize their separateness by focusing on their specialized function as parts.

Gadda's anti-populism and anti-socialism is not in itself remarkable or unique among writers of his generation. What I suggest is that his anti-populism and "anti-fascism" cannot be thought of apart from each other. To do so would play into Gadda's own postwar ideological re-visionist placement of himself, as the keeping apart of these two terms renders his detachment illegible and, hence, more unassailable.

If Gadda's discursive strategy is, ultimately, to protect the bourgeoi-sie by insulating it from the encroaching masses, Vittorini's strategy is to insulate the masses from the temptations of bourgeois values.

If Gadda's texts naturalize a fragmentary "below," Vittorini's texts naturalize an undifferentiated "below": a stable, homogeneous, essen-tial people not riven by internal differences. In chapter 4, "The Redemp-tion of Vittorini's *New Man*," I examine Vittorini's attempts to define the natural and essential qualities of the Italian people in his journalistic writings as well as in his novel *Uomini e no* (*Men and Not Men*) (1945). I trace an intertextual discourse in which Vittorini links the formative process of an emerging new man to the simple nature of "the people." Simplicity, I argue, is the term that allows Vittorini to literally replace the fascist new man – whose virtues he had extolled during the 1920s and 1930s – with the anti-fascist new man that he wants to personally embody and give life to in his postwar literary work.

During the 1920s and 1930s, Vittorini often advocated, along with other exponents of the regime, the sacrificial expulsion of bourgeois ele-ments from the fascist man. After the Second World War, however, and his concomitant disillusionment with fascism, he focused on another abject element that now needed to be expelled in order to elevate the people: Italy's fascist past. The simple nature of the young who "mis-takenly" believed in the fascist cause is presented as evidence of their ideological and political innocence in several articles he penned for the journal *Il Politecnico* (1945–47).

The novel *Uomini e no*, which portrays the struggles of the Resistance movement against the German occupation of Milan in 1944, enables a complex operation of recoding Vittorini's previous cultural policies. The textual and ideological perimeter of popular simplicity still in-cludes elements of a redemptive project but one that now attempts to shift the "real fascism" onto the Germans. Vittorini's narrative presents the final "simple" immolation of the novel's protagonist, a Resistance fighter, as the ultimate sacrificial act on the altar of national heroes. If the new man of the Resistance has to die in killing the German occupier, it is because the latter had ended up occupying much more than Italian soil: in Vittorini's novel, the occupier represents that old fascist self that has to be removed for the new man of anti-fascist Italy to claim a new beginning.

1 Discursive Ritual and Sacrificial Presentation: The Rhetoric of Crisis and Resolution in Fascist Italy

On 18 January 1925, the fascist Curzio (Suckert) Malaparte posed the following question: "il discorso del 3 Gennaio è stato un atto sincero di fede rivoluzionaria, o non piuttosto una mossa dell'abilissima tattica mussoliniana, una maschera rivoluzionaria gettata, per ingannare gli amici e gli avversari, sul viso della normalizzazione?" (Was the "discorso del 3 gennaio" a sincere act of revolutionary faith or, rather, a crafty move by Mussolini, a revolutionary mask thrown over the face of normalization to mislead friends and enemies?) In answering his own question, he depicted a sacrificial scene: fascism had been immolated on the altar of normalization.

> Si verifica oggi, cioè, quello che noi abbiamo avvertito da tempo: il Fascismo è il capro espiatorio della normalizzazione, la quale non può attuarsi che a sue spese attraverso un processo inevitabile di reazione del Governo non già contro l'Aventino, ma contro esso Fascismo.[1]

> We are seeing today what has concerned us for some time: That Fascism would be the scapegoat of normalization, which can only take place at its expense through an inevitable process of reaction by the government, not against the Aventine but against Fascism itself.

Historical accounts, as well as those of fascists less critical of their movement's institutional turn, of course, would disagree with Malaparte's choice of victim in relation to the speech of 3 January for the "normalization" that Mussolini promised – and inaugurated, in this famous speech – in fact, marked the end not of fascism but of Italian liberal democracy. Renzo De Felice has aptly described that day as the placing of a tombstone on other political forces.[2] Fascist and anti-fascist accounts, thus, seem to converge on this point: there was a political corpse and a political epitaph – the speech itself.

In this chapter, I propose a reading of this "epitaph" and a survey of the ideological and critical contours of the corpse that the speech produces. It was a national corpse, not only because it marked the death of Liberal Italy, but also because it was rhetorically installed by Mussolini as a specular double to his own body – the body that became the symbol of fascist national unity. In my analysis of the speech of 3 January, I will argue that Mussolini presents himself as a sacrificial victim by staging the substitution of his body with Giacomo Matteotti's body. This substitution allowed Mussolini to provide a sacrificial grounding to the formal inauguration of the fascist regime. The performative and ritual dimensions of the speech were crucial to this inauguration and, as I will argue, remained crucial to the fascist rhetorical articulation of crisis and resolution throughout the *ventennio*. Without an understanding of the rhetorical and performative logic underlying the contradictory images of Mussolini's public persona, we cannot adequately conceptualize the Duce's charismatic dimension or assess its relation to popular consensus.

In the past two decades, studies of Italian fascism have emphasized the role played by ritual practices in articulating and consolidating fascist ideology. Building on Emilio Gentile's analysis of the "sacralization of politics," which he defined as fascism's attempt to present itself as a political religion, the works of Mabel Berezin and Simonetta Falasca-Zamponi have explored the regime's deployment of ritualized political spectacles to elicit popular consensus.[3] Their efforts coincide with a resurgence in studies of nationalism and fascism and, more particularly, with renewed scholarly interest in the relationship between spectacle and ideology.[4] Walter Benjamin's famous characterization of fascism as the "aesthetization of politics" continues to resonate in studies that, like Berezin's and Falasca-Zamponi's, focus on the "formal" properties of fascist political communication in order to underscore the "non-rational" and "emotive" popular response that underpinned consensus. Departing from these categorizations, my analysis of ritual presentations directly links ritual practices to textual and linguistic categories, thereby enabling me to recognize patterns of meaning and rhetorical strategies employed in the service of regime consolidation.

Although thoroughly exploited by the fascist regime, rituals and spectacles cannot be defined as intrinsically fascist, for they are obviously present in a variety of cultures and political systems including present-day democratic societies. We cannot, therefore, merely assume that fascist ideology derived its persuasiveness from those practices' inherent ability to "tap" into the irrational and emotive side of people any more than we can assume that the mere staging of a modern political convention or festival will ensure the unproblematic reception and acceptance of its political message. To understand the relationship between culture and fascist ideology without falling into reductionist characterizations, we need to take seriously the textual implications of rituals, and that means that we have to assume that they can be read and not simply experienced.[5]

My analysis does not attempt to quantify the level of popular acceptance of fascist political performances; it seeks, however, to explore the textual mechanism that subtended Mussolini's charismatic self-fashioning. Specifically, I argue that Mussolini's charismatic dimension can be investigated by looking at the rhetorical mechanisms that constructed it as a text: a text that performed, rhetorically, its own logic of power presentation. Investigating such logic does not require assuming that the Duce's rhetorical performances were intrinsically powerful presentations, for that would be just a sanctioning of its intended effect. What is required is an investigation of the textual mechanisms that supported the construction of power *through its presentation*. Indeed, when we foreclose the possibility of reading such mechanisms, we validate (often unintentionally) Mussolini's self-ascribed demiurgic abilities. Furthermore, the performative dimension of fascist rhetoric becomes opaque (hence, retains its mystique) when the so-called various sides of Mussolini – the self-styled, often contradictory images that composed his public persona, are either lumped together under the rubric of a generic (and inscrutable) Mussolinian ambiguity, or are analysed in a way that discounts their interconnectedness and interdependence – what I call the "parcelling of the Duce" – the exclusive assignment of a particular ideological aspect, or Mussolinian "side" to a political or social constituency.

The perils of foregoing such legibility are particularly acute in studies where the experience of the ventennio is brought to bear on the political and cultural milieu of contemporary Italy. Questions of continuity or continued resonance of fascist culture and discourses are distorted, when not altogether precluded, by a resistance to grant legibility to fascist rhetoric, to Mussolini's ambivalence and, ultimately, to fascist consensus. I deliberately use the term "resistance" here to indicate the

danger of conflating the refusal to (read) fascist rhetoric and its ideological configurations with the historical experience of opposition to
fascism of the Italian *Resistenza*. The latter was undoubtedly justified,
indeed, necessary; nevertheless, in opposing the legitimacy of a repugnant regime, the resistance to grant legibility to fascist rhetoric continues to handicap our understanding of the historical experience and of
its significance for the culture and politics of modern Italy. Without
such legibility, ultimately, we curtail the possibility of recognizing and
effectively opposing neo-fascist movements as well as more embedded,
and less visible, remnants of the ventennio in contemporary cultural
practices.

A recent example of the exclusive assignment of a particular Mussolinian "aspect" to a specific social constituency is Sergio Luzzatto's otherwise intriguing study of the vicissitudes of Mussolini's cadaver after
1945, *The Body of Il Duce: Mussolini's Corpse and the Fortunes of Italy*.[6]
Before analysing the political and imaginary trajectory of the Duce's
corpse in postwar Italy, Luzzatto traced a "prehistory of the dead Duce's
body," that explores the ventennio and that ends with the following
observation: "It had taken the partisan firing squad mere seconds to
finish off Mussolini, but in fact he had begun to die two decades earlier,
when his henchmen plunged their knives into the body of Giacomo
Matteotti."[7]

This conclusion is striking as it is uncanny, for it is right despite itself, that is, despite what it means within the prehistory's narrative. It
is right, insofar as Luzzatto's book documents the extent to which the
specularity of the body of Matteotti with the body of Mussolini became
a national obsession during the ventennio and beyond.[8] More problematic, however, is his reading of this specularity within the ventennio. In
Luzzatto's narrative, the anti-fascist fantasy of the dead Duce fostering
the various assassination attempts becomes the historical nemesis, the
specular counterpart of the fascist fetishization of the body of the living Duce. "Le avventure del corpo del duce" (The vicissitudes of the
body of the Duce) come to occupy "la dimensione che è loro propria,
quella di una lotta pluridecennale combattuta all'insegna del più impi-
etoso fra gli adagi, *mors tua vita mea*" (their appropriate dimension – a
decades-long struggle fought in the name of the most merciless adage,
mors tua vita mea).[9]

The danger of a retroactive installation of an epic battle of two ir-
reducible forces is that, within this narrative, fascism can be read as
a Liberation in the making, hence, surreptitiously erasing itself. If the

Duce "began to die" the day Matteotti was killed, then fascism was, in a sense, dead on arrival – it was on its way out from the very beginning. The erasure of fascism might well have been the dream of the Resistance, as Luzzatto thoroughly documents, but it becomes a dead end for analytical explorations of the mechanisms of consensus.

Luzzatto correctly pointed to the duality, the close interplay of body/cadaver that governs the charismatic dimension of the Duce, but does not examine how this duality is articulated *within* a discourse that produces consensus – a discourse that, after all, runs counter to the narrative erasure of fascism as a Liberation in the making. Because his narration of the epic struggle between two forces has split the body/cadaver specularity into two separate "dreams," two inimical ways of envisioning Mussolini's body – the live body belonging to fascism and the dead body to anti-fascism – Luzzatto's account of popular consensus ends up reiterating, rather than analytically engaging, the commonplace view that the Duce's *live* monolithic body was the object of popular veneration during the ventennio.

If we essentialize each side of the opposition body/cadaver (life/death) as belonging to a particular historical entity – in this case, fascism or the Resistance – we cannot adequately read the way in which fascist rhetoric actually mobilized both sides of the equation and capitalized on this opposition's reversibility and instability. To say that Mussolini "began to die" the day Matteotti was killed is correct only insofar as we understand that through the rhetorical staging of a sacrificial ritual Mussolini was able to turn this "beginning to die" into his formal "beginning to live."

Sacrificial Substitution

The speech of 3 January was delivered in 1925 in response to the political crisis that followed the murder of the Socialist leader Giacomo Matteotti.[10] The speech constituted a pivotal moment in the passage from the liberal constitutional state to the fascist regime. It effectively put an end to what historian Stanley G. Payne has described as "the most serious crisis Mussolini would experience before World War II."[11] It was a time of political crisis not only for the parliamentary nation and its constitutional future, but also for Mussolini, who was faced with a most uncertain political future. It was, indeed, a time in which things for Italy could have gone differently and anti-fascist action had a chance to succeed.

The disappearance of Matteotti on 10 June 1924 had profound political repercussions. It was immediately assumed that Mussolini had personally ordered his assassination because the Socialist leader had openly denounced the illegality of the previous elections, in a parliamentary speech on 30 May 1924. It was later reported that, on that occasion, Mussolini had told a personal aide that Matteotti, after that speech, should not have been allowed to "circulate."[12] Despite a lack of conclusive evidence, all signs pointed to Mussolini's guilt. This situation prompted the Aventine Secession, a withdrawal from parliament of Liberal, Catholic, Socialist, Republican, and Communist deputies to protest and denounce the fascists' use of violence and illegal means of acquiring power. Hoping that the king might dismiss the government and that the general public would recognize opposition deputies as their only legitimate representatives, the political opposition remained essentially passive but confident that its moral outrage and legalistic stance would eventually prevail over fascist brutality.

Mussolini also faced opposition within his own party. Since the elections of April 1924, fascist hard-liners had feared that Mussolini would reach a compromise with other political forces, steering fascism towards conservative governance and away from their more extreme authoritarian aspirations. Another disaffected faction, the populist wing of the party, echoed Malaparte's sentiment that normalization was incompatible with fascist revolutionary ideals. Frustration was also mounting among local leaders and members of the fascist militia, who demanded that more decisive actions be taken against anti-fascist forces.

Pressure was mounting from all sides. By the end of the year, opposition had reached such an extent that Mussolini's position appeared untenable. On 3 January 1925, Mussolini delivered a speech that saved his political career, paralyzed the opposition, and dispelled any hopes that a return to liberal constitutional politics could occur. Thereafter, things turned quickly in Mussolini's favour, and he was able to carry on the "normalization" that had effectively begun in the speech. It is to the sacrificial aspect of this normalization that I now turn and to the performative dimension of language in the speech.

Contemporary scholarship has shown that the speech was more than "just words." It did things. In her ground-breaking textual analysis of the speech of 3 January as language event, Barbara Spackman has traced the rhetorical strategy that allowed the speech to construct its own conditions of self-validation and to "excuse" and redirect the violence towards women.[13] If the speech is a privileged locus for analysing the ways in which it "rhetorically performs an action," and "performed itself as an event,"[14] I ask to what extent can the speech also be thought of as a sacrificial ritual performance. In exploring this ritual dimension I rely on René Girard's conceptualization of sacrificial ritual as a mechanism employed by a community to stop a mimetic crisis: a representational crisis where the lack of distinction between bad violence and good violence threatens the social order. Unless properly differentiated and rechannelled onto the surrogate sacrificial victim, violence becomes mimetic and perpetuates itself through a cycle of vengeance and reprisals.[15] Girard's description of the role and characteristics of the sacrificial victim sheds new light on the rhetorical function of "troublemaking" in the speech: "The victim must appear not as a random instrument of a mimetic shift in the collective mood from conflict to peace but as a troublemaker and then a peacemaker, as an all-powerful manipulator of all human relations inside the community – in other words, a divinity."[16]

Mussolini's speech of 3 January 1925, indeed, begins with a mimetic crisis and with Mussolini posing as the troublemaker-in-chief. At stake is the very principle of substitutability, of the terms of exchange that define political representation as these are now tied to accusations of culpability, guilt, and violence. Who is to blame for misrepresenting the people and the circumstances of Matteotti's death? The question, as well as the answer, is foreshadowed in the first sentence that lays the ground for substituting a social contract with "social contact":

Signori!
Il discorso che sto per pronunziare dinanzi a voi forse non potrà essere, a rigor di termini, classificato come un discorso parlamentare. (DG 235)

Gentlemen!
The speech that I am about to give in your presence may not be classified, strictly speaking, as a parliamentary speech.

From the outset, the representational principle is discarded in favour of the presentational. As Mussolini makes clear, he is not looking for the traditional support of parliament:

Si sappia ad ogni modo che io non cerco questo voto politico. Non lo desidero: ne ho avuti troppi." (DG 235)

In any case, let it be known that I am not seeking this political vote. I don't wish to have it: I have had too many.

He will not represent, he will present himself as the accused ready to be sacrificed, daring the parliament to formally charge him:

L'articolo 47 dello Statuto dice: "La camera dei deputati ha il diritto di accusare i ministri del re e di tradurli dinanzi all'Alta corte di giustizia."
Domando formalmente se in questa Camera, o fuori di questa Camera, c'è qualcuno che si voglia valere dell'articolo 47. (DG 235)

Article 47 of the Statute states: "The House of Representatives has the right to accuse the king's ministries and to summon them in front of the High Court of Justice."
I formally ask if in this Chamber, or outside of it, there is someone who wants to invoke article 47.

Immediately thereafter, however, Mussolini promises a clarification of his presentation:

Il mio discorso sarà quindi chiarissimo e tale da determinare una chiarificazione assoluta. (DG 235)

My speech will be extremely clear and will therefore lead to an absolute clarification.

Here, as at the end of the speech, the principle of clarification signals a departure from the institutional process and a turn towards a fascist solution: it will not be parliament but Mussolini himself who will manage the resolution of the crisis. Throughout the speech, he will deny formal charges while at the same time presenting himself as the surrogate sacrificial victim that will end the mimetic disorder brought about by the original murder, the killing of Matteotti.[17]

To portray himself as the surrogate victim who will distinguish good violence from bad violence, Mussolini stages the rhetorical substitution of his body with Matteotti's body. Girard explains that the similarity between the two victims must be emphasized in order to provide meaning to the subsequent differentiation: "all victims, even the animal ones, bear a certain *resemblance* to the object they replace; otherwise the violent impulse would remain unsatisfied. But this resemblance must not be carried to the extreme of complete assimilation, or it would lead to disastrous confusion."[18]

For the circulation of Mussolini's body to be effective, Matteotti's body has to be taken out of circulation, and the traces of equivalence that make possible the substitution simultaneously affirmed and denied:

> Nessuno mi ha negato fino ad oggi queste tre qualità: una discreta intelligenza, molto coraggio e un sovrano disprezzo del vile denaro."
> (DG 236)

> To this day, nobody has denied that I possess these three qualities: a modicum of intelligence, much courage, and a supreme disdain for vile money.

Money, as the medium of equivalence and circulation par excellence, will not be the fetish of the new economy, but the traces of the (denied) substitution will remain as the shared properties of the two bodies: courage and intelligence. This is reiterated in the next page, where the parallel between Mussolini and Matteotti is explicit:

> come potevo pensare, senza essere colpito da morbosa follia, non dico solo di far commettere un delitto, ma nemmeno il più tenue, il più ridicolo sfregio a quell'avversario che io stimavo perché aveva una certa *crânerie*, un certo coraggio, che rassomigliavano qualche volta al mio coraggio e alla mia ostinatezza nel sostenere le tesi?" (DG 237)

> unless I had been seized by raging madness, how could I have entertained the thought, let alone of committing a crime, but of inflicting the most insignificant wound to that adversary whom I respected because he had a certain audacity, a certain courage, that at times resembled my courage and obstinacy in defending a point of view?

To perform the disavowed substitution, Mussolini's violence has to be portrayed as "intelligent," the property he shares with his opponent, in a match between equals, which is why the violence also has to be "*cavalleresca*" (chivalric):

> Quando due elementi sono in lotta e sono irriducibili, la soluzione è la forza. (DG 240)

> When two elements are locked in a struggle and are irreconcilable, the solution is force.

All common properties must, of course, just as readily be denied, as they are in the speech, and in the constant portraying of anti-fascist violence as essentially "stupid."[19]

But how would the portrayal of Mussolini as sacrificial victim function in ideological terms, that is, how are the Italian people called – ideologically interpellated – receptively "turning" towards authority and recognizing themselves in that voice? After all, thinking of Mussolini as a self-portraying victim is counterintuitive. Thinking of Mussolini's self-proclaimed guilt is also counterintuitive, insofar as the purpose of the speech seemed to be the excusing of an injurious act of violence – hence, to exonerate Mussolini. Yet, it is precisely the ideological implications of a counterintuitive logic that bear consideration here, a logic similar to the one that Paul de Man has identified in relation to Rousseau's autobiographical texts. "Excuses," de Man writes, "generate the very guilt they exonerate, though always in excess or by default."[20] The purpose (and, indeed, force) of Mussolini's failed confession is not so much to excuse violence as it is to stage violence as an excuse for the generation of guilt. As de Man points out in Rousseau's case, "The excuse is a ruse which permits exposure in the name of hiding, not unlike Being, in the later Heidegger, reveals itself by hiding. Or, put differently, shame used as excuse permits repression to function as revelation and thus to make pleasure and guilt interchangeable."[21]

But what is the function of "revelation" in the case of the "Discorso"? This is where we may recall Girard's characterization of the sacrificial victim as one who "must appear as a troublemaker and then a peacemaker," for the trouble of the mimetic crisis (who is guilty of political misrepresentation?) was, from the beginning, inextricably linked to a factual misrepresentation, or the obscuring of the identity of Matteotti's murderer. While appearing to excuse himself – "Dove? Quando? In qual modo? Nessuno potrebbe dirlo!" [(Where? When? How? No one can say!) – Mussolini is actually exposing/presenting himself as guilty:

Sono io, o signori, che levo in quest' Aula l'accusa contro me stesso" (DG 235) [. . .] Se tutte le violenze sono state il risultato di un determinato clima storico, politico e morale, ebbene a me la responsabilità di questo, perché questo clima storico, politico e morale io l'ho creato con una propaganda che va dall'intervento ad oggi." (DG 239)

It is I, gentlemen, who raise in this Chamber the accusation against myself!
[. . .]   If all violence has been the result of a particular historical, political,

and moral climate, then the responsibility is mine because I created it with constant propaganda from the time of intervention until the present.

As Girard writes, "The victim must be transfigured 'for the worse' because of its alleged responsibility in the mimetic disorders and 'for the better' because of the reconciliation brought about by its death, a reconciliation that will be imputed to that victim's omnipotence, beyond a certain level of scapegoat delusion."[22] Mussolini's rhetorical exchange of his properties/his body with those of Matteotti enables him to claim responsibility for the disorders, and for the very same reason (his "identity" with Matteotti) to claim the ability to bring about the reconciliation (promise of peace) that will be imputed to his omnipotence. This is why Mussolini can present himself as truly guilty of a misrepresentation before the Italian people, and stage by such a presentation a reverse interpellation. According to Girard, "These episodes of victimage are not reproduced and remembered such as they really happened but such as they must be (mis)understood by the community they reunified."[23] In other words, Mussolini presents himself as "called" by the Italian people to misrepresent himself for their own good, and their own good (peace and reconciliation) will be possible only if they willingly misunderstand what he stands for.

This wilful misunderstanding is the common element, the hinge, if you will, that binds the sacrificial rhetoric to the fetishization of the Duce: his much noted, and little analysed, charismatic appeal. It is important not to confuse wilful misunderstanding with the various characterizations of "the duping of the people" on the part of Mussolini and fascist rhetoric in general.[24] I conceptualize this "wilfulness" as applying both to Mussolini's intentional presentation of this ideological mechanism as well as to the possible acceptance of it by the public: an active, not a passive acceptance. By "misunderstanding," I refer not to an involuntary perceptual error but, on the contrary, to the voluntary error implied by the logic of fetishistic undecidability that, I think, underlies this ideological construct.

Mussolini's ability to stage the formal inauguration of his regime was based on the rhetorical production of a sacrificial double transfiguration which, in turn, structured a reverse interpellation that transformed his speech into an answering of the people's call: he had been summoned to misrepresent himself for their own good. This process is not a magic trick that immobilized people's rational faculties and that owed its effectiveness to Mussolini's natural charisma, but the other way around: charisma was produced by the successful articulation of a rhetorical confusion of the positive and negative valence of guilt, responsibility, and violence, which were tied to Mussolini's dual identity. It is the articulation of this misunderstanding that established the fundamental undecidability – in fact, a double undecidability – of the status and properties of Mussolini. His status became conflated with his properties (he is what he does and what he promises to do), and his status-properties acquired an irreducibly ambivalent character (what he does can kill you or save you).

The speech of 3 January 1925, thus, can be said to have performed what Jacques Derrida has described as the ritual of the *pharmakos* – the "expulsion from the city walls" of evil personified, the poisoner who is also a wizard and a magician (as Derrida points out in his discussion of Plato's Pharmacy, the word *pharmakos* is synonymous with *pharmakeus*: magician, sorcerer).[25] This enactment allowed Mussolini to allocate onto himself the properties of the *pharmakon* – the "substance" that is at once dangerous, lethal, crisis provoking, and its exact opposite: beneficial, therapeutic, pacificatory – the poison/medicine. In other words, Mussolini was able to portray himself as the living incarnation of the medium.

In discussing the ambiguity of the pharmakon, Derrida points out that as a medium, the pharmakon "does not have the punctual simplicity of a *coincidentia oppositorum*" and that it constitutes, rather, "the movement, the locus, the play: (the production of) difference."[26] Similarly, I would argue that Mussolini's pharmakonian self-portrayal was not just one of the many and often noted uses of ambiguity that characterized the rhetoric of the ventennio. The mechanism that subtended it did not merely bind pre-existing opposites, although it undoubtedly did that, too.[27] This mechanism had a more ambitious goal, for it presented itself, at the same time and because of its inherent instability, as the generative source of new oppositions, as the medium that would make new oppositions possible, indeed, make a new fascist language possible.

Revolution and Resolution

Scholars have frequently noted the extensive use of organic metaphors in fascist rhetoric. The nation was often represented in terms of its bodily properties – health, chief among them: it needed to be protected from parasites, cured from diseases, and, when necessary to resolve a health crisis, undergo surgery.[28] The connection between crises and violence, which Mussolini so often exploited with his posturing as "surgeon of the nation," was reinforced by the equally extensive use of sacrificial language. To understand how this reinforcement was possible, we should consider that the rhetorical field of a sacrificial crisis and its resolution is structured along the articulation of a strict analogy between linguistic categories, organic processes, and violence. This, of course, does not mean that, by itself, this rhetorical field (or any linguistic structure, for that matter) is intrinsically fascist. We can certainly imagine cases in which sacrificial language is used within the context of democratic politics or cases in which scapegoating only leads to job loss by a person who "takes the fall," thereby preventing the spread of blame to her or his associates or to the organization as a whole. What the firing of a CEO and the expulsions of Jews from a country have in common is clearly not fascism, but a rhetorical mechanism that is particularly suited for the channelling of blame and violence onto the victim and for naturalizing the outcome as protection (and production) of the social body. The transfer of properties from the body onto the social naturalizes the arbitrariness of the social act of expulsion. If naturalization is integral to this rhetorical mechanism, it need not be part of an analytical investigation of how this mechanism was applied to fascist rhetoric. Analysing the ideological implications of fascist sacrifice does not mean assigning a specific ideological content to sacrifice. It means, rather, to ask *how* sacrifice was put in relation to, and in support of, other discursive elements that comprised fascist ideology.[29]

The mimetic crisis, as conceptualized by Girard, is a crisis of violence threatening to perpetuate itself through revenge: the symmetry, or specularity of the two entities has to be blocked by an exchange that will break the cycle and channel violence away from the mimetic pair onto a victim that will not be avenged because it is similar to the original, yet different. Although violence is clearly not an organic process – it seems to possess the capacity for self-propagation in that it calls for retaliation either in kind or in some sort of equivalent punishment. Because of this mimetic appearance, violence can acquire, by metaphorical exchange, distinctly organic properties. We say that violence is like a disease, not because it is organic but because it spreads like one. When we talk of outbreaks of violence we indicate its "natural" propensity to become contagious and unstoppable.

The propagation of violence is, ultimately, not a natural process, but a cognitive one – the act of retaliation involves the assumption that perfect symmetry will somehow cancel out the original act of aggression. That violence's mimetic threat is stopped through a cognitive misrecognition (a substitution) of victims also indicates that what is stopped is a cognitive and not a natural process. Yet, precisely because this substitution, in order to be successful, has to appear natural (as well as arbitrary), it is an exchange that covers its tracks by facilitating the metaphorical exchanges of properties with natural processes. The violence of the expulsion that brought about the "miraculous" peace (the end of the mimetic crisis) is, therefore, differentiated in natural terms as pure and beneficial – from the undifferentiated, polluting, and dangerous violence of the crisis. Within this economy, violence is, at the same time, what needs to be differentiated and the differentiating principle itself – it defines both the crisis and its resolution.

The double role of violence is what permits different entry points into this rhetorical structure – the possibility of reversing the order of cause and effect. The crisis need not always be underway for the resolution to be brought about, for the crisis can be defined in terms of the benefits that its future resolution will bring about, hence, installed in advance, as necessary and beneficial insofar as it is already a part of the differentiating process that it, literally, anticipates. A beneficial crisis, within these terms, is a crisis that short-circuits itself by anticipating the resolution. The anticipatory gesture is also a gesture that repolarizes its own relation to desire: it "puts" desire in the place of a threat. The anticipation of the resolution, in a way, blots out the negative threat of the crisis and superimposes onto it a positive desire for the crisis. The desire for the resolution can be rhetorically exchanged, and redefined as the desire for the crisis, just as the desire for the purifying resolution can be cast in terms of the desire for the purifying crisis.

The articulation of an anticipatory crisis was clearly prevalent in the early days of Mussolini's political career. The need for differentiating violence is a refrain that dates back to his days of First World War interventionist propaganda: "What about Garibaldi? Was he also a warmonger? We need to distinguish between war and war, as one distinguishes between crime and crime, between blood and blood."[30] While the international crisis was depicted as inevitably drawing Italy into the conflict, a more specific national crisis was also at hand. Paradoxically, the threat to be averted above all was, for Mussolini, the possibility of Italian neutrality in the war: a state of general "indifference-iation" and passivity that needed to be "repolarized" if Italy was to regain its true national character and re-enter its proper historical trajectory as a dominating power of world events:

> Bisogna agire, muoversi, combattere e, se occorre, morire. I neutrali non hanno mai dominato gli avvenimenti. Li hanno sempre subiti. È il sangue che dà il movimento alla ruota sonante della storia![31]

> We must act, mobilize, fight, and, if necessary, die. The uncommitted have never dominated events. They have always endured the consequences. It is blood that moves the wheel of history!

If anticipating the fulfilment of a national destiny required a palingenetic moment when a dormant national identity would be rediscovered, the end of the war did not mark, for Mussolini, the end of the discovery or the end of the national historical trajectory. The "wheel of history" would "loop" the national trajectory into a circular logic of anticipation and fulfilment.

During the fascist rise to power, the palingenetic moment of national renewal was redefined as a constitutive moment of the fascist revolution: "War and revolution are two terms that are always paired: It is either the war that brings about revolution or it is the revolution that leads to war."[32] If the beginning of fascism coincided with the ending of neutrality and the entry into war, the beginning of fascism could be said to have produced the anticipatory crisis and, at the same time, to have been produced by it, for the war also brought about the beginning of the fascist revolution. And as a further twist to the loopy logic: insofar as an anticipatory crisis anticipates a resolution, the fascist revolution was depicted as a resolution – as the end of the crisis. A sudden break, and yet, a moment that would extend itself through time, that would generate and guarantee its own continuity in time: the fascist era would be one of normalization and peace, where violence would be differentiated, hence, would be "moral" and "controlled":

> Quando la nostra violenza è risolutiva di una situazione cancrenosa, è moralissima, sacrosanta e necessaria. Ma, o amici fascisti, e parlo ai fascisti d'Italia, bisogna che la nostra violenza abbia dei caratteri specifici, fascisti. La violenza di dieci contro uno è da ripudiare e da condannare. La violenza che non si spiega deve essere ripudiata . . . C'è una violenza che libera e una violenza che incatena; c'è una violenza che è morale ed una violenza che è stupida e immorale.[33]

Therefore, when our violence remedies a cancerous situation, it is highly moral, sacrosanct, and necessary. But, my fascist friends – and I address Italian fascists here – our violence must have specific fascist characteristics. The violence of ten against one must be repudiated and condemned. Unjustified violence must be repudiated. There is a violence that liberates and a violence that subjugates; there is a moral violence and a stupid and immoral violence.

To normalize the social body as fascist, violence would have to be defined as specifically fascist. It would have to be directed against the anti-fascist forces that threatened to bring that body back into a situation of crisis – to the socialist violence of the *biennio rosso* (two red years) or to the decaying state of liberal democracy. As a normalizing process, the fascist revolution would march forward and crush those attempting to roll it back, as Mussolini frequently warned with one of his favourite refrains: "Indietro non si torna!" (There is no turning back!)

The rhetorical forward thrust of fascist normalization displaced the crisis by localizing it spatially, as an organic disease that might reinfect the nation. A relapse into the time of crisis would be foreclosed by the violent ejection of the "cancer" of anti-fascism. Once displaced outside the temporal trajectory of the fascist revolution, however, the crisis had to be reinstituted inside that very trajectory. To be an extension through time of the moment of resolution, the fascist revolution would need to "go back" to the moment of crisis again and again to reinstitute the resolution. This going back to the moment of crisis was dramatized by the Mussolinian "personification" of the pharmakon in its "transfiguration for the worse" and by the construction of a rhetorical symmetry (a mimetic relationship) of his body with the body of Matteotti, or of the fascist nation with the forces of anti-fascism.

In the speech of 3 January, intelligence – the ability to make distinctions – is the term that establishes Mussolini's similarity with Matteotti as well as the means for distinguishing the two, for resolving the symmetry: "To be an agent of resolution, violence has to be surgical, intelligent, and chivalrous." The symmetry, of course, would never be resolved since, for violence to maintain its differentiating role, the symmetry had to be reinstated as soon as it was resolved. Fascist normalization or "peace" did not consist in a stable resolution (too much peace would lead to mummification) but in the possibility of rhetorically reiterating the cycle of normalization, of recharging violence so that normalization could be brought about over and over again. For the resolution to *continue to be* a resolution – that is, to retain the rhetorically charged positionality as "the end of the crisis" – the moment of crisis had to be reintroduced and simultaneously displaced. The permanent revolution could not afford a permanent resolution, only one that would be constantly in the making and, yet, already accomplished.

In a speech delivered about a month after the "Discorso del 3 gennaio," Mussolini said that the speech had "resolved" the crisis and that fascism had truly carried out a revolution. Yet, he quickly added, fascism had won a great battle but not the war: the opposition has lost, yet it continued to manoeuvre, consensus had already been achieved, and yet it required work to become definite. In other words, the crisis had been solved, and yet it was not over.[34] For Mussolini, "mission accomplished" was always a work in progress. And it would continue to be in progress, for the simultaneous displacement and reintroduction of the crisis continued to characterize fascist rhetoric (albeit with various inflections and shifting definitions of what constituted the crisis), until the end of the regime.

The rhetorical reiteration of the cycle of normalization allowed Mussolini to continue to present himself as a normalizing force and a "saviour of the peace" while preventing, at the same time, the routinization of charisma that would have resulted from actual prolonged normalcy. Perpetual peace would constitute such normalcy: hence, Mussolini considered it depressing and stifling.[35] As Pier Giorgio Zunino has observed, peace, from the fascist point of view, did not constitute an absolute and positive goal. Peace was a concept that acquired meaning in relation to other factors. War could also be subject to an inversion of values, or, as Zunino put it: "dalla guerra per necessità si approdava prima alla necessità della guerra e poi alla bontà della guerra" (from a war of necessity the shift was made first to a necessary war, then to the righteousness of war).[36] While Mussolini often said that Italy wanted peace, he just as often qualified "peace" in ways that would destabilize its original meaning as, for example, in the notion of "armed peace":

Le direttive della nostra politica sono chiare: noi vogliamo la pace, la pace con tutti. E vi posso dire che la Germania nazionalsocialista non desidera meno ardentemente di noi la pace europea. Ma la pace, per essere sicura, deve essere armata.[37]

Our political directives are clear: We want peace, peace with everyone. And I can tell you that National Socialist Germany desires, with an ardour equal to our own, peace for Europe. But for peace to be secure, it needs to be armed.

Since an inevitable war might, at any point, destabilize Italy's "peaceful" intentions, the country should think of peace not as the opposite of war but as preparation for war.

Crisis and Commemoration

Even during the years of fascism's full institutionalization, fascist rhetoric continued to foreclose ideological and charismatic routinization: "noi non siamo gli imbalsamatori di un passato, siamo gli anticipatori di un avvenire" (we are not embalmers of a past, we are harbingers of a future).[38] One way to prevent the embalming of the past was to commemorate fascism's origins as a time of crisis. Recalling the past was not simply a way of sacralizing retrospectively the beginning of the fascist revolution by remembering the supreme sacrifice of its "martyrs." Commemorative occasions often served literally as a recall: bringing the crisis to the present as a way of going back to the crisis and re-enacting its resolution. As Spackman has noted, the fascist regime attempted to exploit the "necessary iterability of martyrdom" – an event at once unique and repeatable – by commemorating in order to perpetuate. It was, as she puts it, "always in preparation for the 'war' that awaits in the future."[39]

The commemorative reintroduction of a past moment of crisis frequently served an additional purpose: to displace an actual and present crisis. Once "joined" to the old crisis, the cycle of normalization could be rhetorically reiterated and serve to guarantee a future resolution. In 1932, ten years after the March on Rome, Mussolini commemorated the event with a speech.

The year 1932 was in the middle of one of the most pacified periods of the fascist regime, at about the midpoint of an era that the historian Renzo De Felice has described as the years of consensus. This was a time of regime consolidation, characterized by increasing growth and bureaucratization of the Fascist Party and the development of corporatist economic structures. During this period, the regime appeared to be without substantial opposition and in no danger of imminent threats to its stability. So secure was the regime that it would pardon many who had been convicted of political crimes. By this gesture, the regime could both demonstrate its generosity and show how little it feared any anti-fascist threat.[40]

In retrospect, 1932 would be seen as the pinnacle of fascist consensus, with its upcoming decline not evident at that moment. Nonetheless, there were some storm clouds on the horizon. The year 1932 was also a time of economic difficulties for Italy, still in the midst of the Great Depression that had affected economies worldwide since 1929. Rising unemployment, salary reductions, declining industrial production, and failing industries resulted in numerous instances of social unrest, local agitation of unemployed agricultural workers, and a general feeling of demoralization among the Italian population.[41] As De Felice has observed, the commemorative celebrations of the *decennale* (tenth anniversary) also marked the beginning of the regime's "electoral campaign" for the *plebiscito* (plebiscite) that was to be held in March 1934.[42] It was a time that the regime would use to carry out a massive propaganda campaign emphasizing fascist accomplishments and goals.

Against this backdrop, Mussolini's use of a commemorative occasion to strengthen popular support for his regime is not surprising. Of interest, however, is how his speech of 16 October 1932 links a past crisis to the "resolution" of the present one.

> Camerati!
>
> Esattamente dieci anni fa, il 16 ottobre 1922, in una riunione da me convocata e tenutasi a Milano in via San Marco 46, fu decisa l'insurrezione.[43]

> Comrades!
>
> Exactly ten years ago, on 16 October 1922, in a meeting that I arranged and that took place in Milan in via San Marco 46, the insurrection was decided upon.

[Read: I called the meeting, I am responsible for the insurrection.]

> Tutti coloro che parteciparono a quella storica riunione sono presenti. Uno solo è assente: Michele Bianchi, che ricordiamo sempre con profondo rimpianto (*Applausi. Si grida: "Presente!"*). (PD 135)

> All those who participated in that historic meeting are present. Only one is absent: Michele Bianchi, whom we remember always with profound regret (*Applause. Shouts: "Present!"*).

[Read: Again, it was not about representation, it was about sacrifice and self-presentation.]

> [. . .] Se noi rileggiamo taluni discorsi politici del tempo, possiamo oggi essere *sorpresi* davanti all'apparente discrezione dei nostri obiettivi. Ma un esercito quando si mette in marcia deve partire nelle migliori condizioni possibili., suscitare il minore numero possibile di inquietudini e di disagi.
>
> Recenti esperienze politiche in taluni paesi di Europa ci dicono che allora, come sempre, la nostra forza fu accompagnata dalla saggezza. (PD 135)[44]

> [. . .] If we reread certain political speeches of the time, we can be *surprised* by the apparent modesty of our objectives. But when an army begins to march, it has to start under the best conditions and create the least possible apprehension and hardship.
>
> Recent political experience in some European countries demonstrates that our forcefulness, then as now, has been accompanied by wisdom.

The term "surprised" here marks the instability of Mussolini's pharmakonian "properties": was it about order or disorder? You think it was one thing but it was actually another. Read: "When we look back today we are surprised by how modest our objectives were. There was force, but as always, it was accompanied by wisdom and restraint (that is, it was intelligent violence). It was an insurrection but it was actually about order":

> [. . .] È tempo di dire una cosa che forse *sorprenderà* voi stessi, e che cioè, fra tutte le insurrezioni dei tempi moderni, quella più sanguinosa è stata la nostra. (PD 135)[45]

> [. . .] It is time to say something that perhaps will *surprise* you, that is, of all the insurrections of modern times, ours has been the bloodiest.

Here we have the by now familiar Mussolinian transfiguration for the worse. Read: "Correction! It is time to say something that will really surprise you – since it is, after all, the opposite of what I just said: Our insurrection was not moderate at all. In fact, it was the bloodiest in modern times":

> Poche decine di morti richiedette l'espugnazione della Bastiglia, nella quale di prigionieri politici non c'era più nessuno. Le migliaia, le decine di

migliaia di morti vennero dopo, ma furono volute dal terrore. Quanto poi alle rivoluzioni contemporanee, quella russa non ha costato che poche decine di vittime. La nostra, durante tre anni, ha richiesto vasto sacrificio di giovane sangue, e questo spiega e giustifica il nostro proposito di assoluta intransigenza politica e morale.

Siamo alla fine del primo decennio. Voi non vi aspetterete da me il consuntivo. Io amo piuttosto di pensare a quello che faremo nel decennio prossimo. (*Applausi*). Del resto basta guardarsi attorno, per convincersi che il nostro consuntivo è semplicemente immenso.

Ma avviandoci al secondo decennio occorrono delle direttive di marcia. Comincerò da quella che personalmente mi riguarda. Io sono il vostro capo (*Applausi vivissimi; grida di: "Viva il Duce!"*), e sono, come sempre, pronto ad assumermi tutte le responsabilità! (*Applausi*). Bisogna essere inflessibili con noi stessi, fedeli al nostro credo, alla nostra dottrina, al nostro giuramento e non fare concessioni di sorta, né alle nostalgie del passato, né alle catastrofiche anticipazioni dell'avvenire. (PD 135)

> The storming of the Bastille required the loss of a few dozen, among which no political prisoners remained. Losses in the thousands, tens of thousands, came afterwards, but they were part of the strategy of terror.
>
> As for contemporary revolutions, the Russian one only had a few dozen victims. Ours, in the course of three years, required great sacrifice of the blood of our youth, and this explains and justifies our stance of absolute political and moral intransigence.
>
> We are at the end of the first decade. You would not expect from me a balance sheet. I prefer, rather, to think about what we will do in the next decade. (*Applause*.) And besides, one only needs to look around to be convinced of our immense achievements. But as we turn towards the second decade, marching orders are needed. I will begin with one that touches me personally. I am your leader. (*Sustained applause; shouts of "Long live the Duce!"*) and, as always, I am ready to assume all responsibility! (*Applause*.) We need to be inflexible with ourselves, faithful to our belief, to our doctrine, to our vow of no compromise of any sort, be it in the name of nostalgia towards the past, or of catastrophic expectations for the future.

In a strategy similar to that of the speech of 3 January 1925, while appearing to be excusing fascist violence ("and this explains and justifies our stance of absolute political and moral intransigence"), Mussolini is actually staging violence as an excuse for the generation of guilt: "I am your leader and, as always, I am ready to assume all responsibility!"

The recall of the old crisis allows him to dramatize, once again, his own self-expulsion, thereby re-enacting the cycle of resolution and normalization. And it is at this point that the two crises are joined – or rather, the two resolutions. Precisely after the self-ascription of guilt, the present crisis is for the first time introduced and simultaneously displaced. The "looking back" to the old crisis is suddenly foreclosed by the injunction against concessions to "nostalgia towards the past" and its moment of resolution grafted onto the present crisis by the parallel injunction against concessions to the "catastrophic expectations for the future." The disavowal of the present crisis takes the form of a rhetorical freeze-frame that juxtaposes the two moments of resolution. If the commemorative "going back" served to re-enact the cycle of crisis and resolution, the sudden occlusion of crises past and future blocks the cycle and dramatizes the present moment as a moment of resolution frozen in time. As Mussolini makes clear in the next paragraph, fascist time is always the time of resolution even in the midst of a crisis. It might not be overcome immediately, but it will certainly be overcome eventually.

Displacement does not occur in Mussolinian rhetoric without a simultaneous reintroduction, and so the certainty of a future resolution comes to rest precisely on the fact that the crisis is cyclical:[46]

> Tutti coloro che credono di risolvere le crisi con rimedi miracolistici sono fuori di strada. O questa è una crisi ciclica "nel" sistema e sarà risolta; o è una crisi "del" sistema, ed allora siamo davanti a un trapasso da un'epoca di civiltà ad un'altra. (PD 136)

> All those who believe in resolving the crisis with miracle remedies are misguided. This is either a cyclical crisis "within" the system and, hence, it will be resolved; or it is a crisis "of" the system, in which case we are witnessing a transition from one epoch of civilization to another.

The crises of liberal democracies are systemic ("of" the system) because they are symptomatic of their inevitable decline and collapse, but the crises of the fascist nation are systemic in a very different way – they are cyclical occurrences natural to the system and, as such, they will always be localized ("within" the system) and solved from within. A further naturalization of this cycle occurs in the next paragraph, where Mussolini suddenly turns to the "problem of youth" to ward off the spectre of routinization:

Si è posto anche il problema dei giovani. Il problema dei giovani si pone da sé. Lo pone la vita, la quale ha le sue stagioni, come la natura. Ora, nel secondo decennio bisogna fare largo ai giovani. Nessuno è più vecchio di colui che ha la gelosia della giovinezza. Noi vogliamo che i giovani raccolgano la nostra fiaccola, si infiammino della nostra fede e siano pronti e decisi a continuare la nostra fatica. Occorre fascistizzare ancora più quelli che io chiamo gli angoli morti della vita nazionale, non farsi troppo assorbire dalla ordinaria amministrazione fino al punto di rinunziare a quella che è la gioia e l'ebrezza del rischio, essere pronti a tutto quello che può costituire il compito più severo di domani. (PD 136)

We also face the problem of youth. The problem of youth arises by itself. Life poses it, since it has its seasons, like nature. Now, in the second decade, we need to give way to the young. No one is older than he who is jealous of youth. We want our youth to carry our torch, to burn with our faith and be ready and willing to continue our work. We need to fascistize even more what I call the dead corners of national life, avoiding excessive involvement in ordinary administration which leads to giving up the joy and thrill of risk, to be ready for all that may be required to face tomorrow's more demanding tasks.

The systemic and cyclical nature of the crisis is emphasized by the introduction of the life cycle. Life itself poses a problem: like the changing of the seasons it inevitably leads into old age. But the fascist nation cannot afford to grow old and to settle into ordinary administration, for that would be, in fascist terms, a "crisis *of* the system." For the cycle to bring about a new springtime ("the joy and thrill of risk"), the "dead corners of national life" will have to be made more thoroughly fascist by the new generations. But what does it mean to fascistize the dead corners of society and why should that be the antidote to routinization? After all, if we follow Mussolini's analogy of the fascist national life to the natural life cycle, we would think that he is describing the danger of a fast-approaching national middle-age crisis. Left unattended, once the fascist nation has achieved its full potential, it would be headed for sedentary decline.

But if reaching the nation's full potential coincides with full fascistization of national life, why would further fascistization of those dead corners invert the process of routinization and energize the young, making them ready for "tomorrow's more rigorous tasks"? The logic seems to run counter to itself since more fascistization would, inevitably, lead to more routinization. Unless, of course, there is something in those dead corners that is not quite dead and not quite fascist, either. Could the fascistization of the dead corners, then, be a code word for violence to be directed, once again, against the forces of anti-fascism? The overall rhetorical configuration of the speech – which includes a citational recall of the speech of 3 January – supports this speculation, indeed, I would say, leads to this speculation. Once "localized," the crisis could then be "solved" internally and the solution become the occasion for fascist socialization: it would make fascists more fascist and, at the same time, less "sedentary." Furthermore, Mussolini's own rhetorical self-expulsion ("I am your leader and, as always, I am ready to assume all responsibility!") would then be underscored by the recall (and renewed murder) of his original mimetic double, the anti-fascist Matteotti.

If we discount the rhetorical and performative logic of the tenth-anniversary speech, we would be tempted to say that those corners are not occupied by anti-fascists, since the 1932 celebrations of the decennale were also the occasion when Mussolini granted the amnesty to the *fuorusciti* (exiles), as a benevolent gesture, or more likely, as De Felice has suggested, to show that "the few fanatics" were by now totally innocuous.[47] But if Mussolini sought to appear benevolent and peaceful, why deliver a speech that does not name, but that nevertheless conjures with its rhetorical structure a scene of violence against the very people he has just pardoned? My view, of course, is that the two moments of violence and peace are not fully separable in Mussolini's rhetoric and that it is precisely their simultaneous presence that allows Mussolini to inscribe them within a ritual performative logic of crisis and resolution. This is not merely to say, as many scholars have already noted, that fascist rhetoric fully exploited ambiguities, contradictions, and dualities. My point is, rather, that the two sides of Mussolini's demiurgic stance were held together by the performative rhetorical enactment or, in other cases, the citational reiteration of a sacrificial ritual. This performative "holding together" was more than a simple summation of opposites: it was not a static portrayal of a Janus Mussolini – the embodiment of "this" *and* "that" – it also, and most importantly, presented a Mussolini who was "this" *as* "that," where the *as* collapses the narrative sequence of the sacrificial ritual and preserves its iterability. The agent of peace insofar *as* he was the guilty troublemaker. Without the performative *as* we end up with a static duality that, as I will shortly illustrate, can be problematic for studies of fascism.

Mimetic Opposition

Returning to the question of the dead corners, I have pointed out that if one discounts the performative and reiterative logic of the speech one would be tempted to see those corners as not occupied by anti-fascists. For what was the need for violence if the exiles were so insignificant and powerless that they had even been pardoned? Mussolini provided an answer to this question in 1939 when he spelled out the content of those corners, which, apparently, seven years later, were far from dead and still in need of fascistization. The following is an excerpt of his "Discorso alla 'Decima Legio,'" also known as the "Discorso del 23 settembre" (Speech of 23 September):

> Ci incontriamo in questo momento tempestoso, che rimette in giuoco non solo la carta d'Europa, ma, forse, quella dei continenti.
>
> Niente di più naturale che questi eventi grandiosi e le loro ripercussioni in Italia, abbiano provocato una emozione anche fra noi. Ma di questo speciale, comprensibile stato d'animo ha approfittato la minima, ma ciò nondimeno miserabile zavorra umana, che si era ridotta a vivere negli angiporti, nei ripostigli e negli angoli oscuri. Si deve a questa zavorra la diffusione delle "voci" che hanno circolato, molte delle quali – e più ridicole – mi riguardavano personalmente.
>
> Il fenomeno era destinato ad esaurirsi, altrimenti, con mia somma mortificatione avrei dovuto dubitare di una cosa nella quale ho sempre fermamente creduto, e cioé che il popolo italiano è uno dei più intelligenti della terra.
>
> Senza drammatizzare le cose, perché non ne vale assolutamente la pena, la conclusione che se ne deve fare si riassume in queste parole: *ripulire gli angolini dove – talora mimetizzandosi – si sono rifugiati rottami massonici, ebraici, esterofili dell'antifascismo.* Non permetteremo mai, né a loro né ad altri, di portare nocumento alla salute fisica e morale del popolo italiano.[48]

We meet at this tempestuous time when in play is not only the map of Europe but, perhaps, even that of all the continents.

Naturally, these momentous events and their repercussions in Italy have provoked an emotional response among us as well. But this special, understandable sentiment has been exploited by that insignificant, but no less miserable, human flotsam, who had been living in alleys, closets, and dark corners. We owe to this flotsam the spreading of "rumours" that were going around, many of which, including the most ridiculous, concerned me personally.

This phenomenon was destined to disappear, otherwise I would have had to doubt, with profound mortification, what I have always firmly believed, namely, that Italians are one of the most intelligent people on earth.

Without attributing too much importance to this incident, which it does not deserve, the conclusion that we must reach can be summarized in these words: *clean out the corners, where, sometimes camouflaged [mimetiz-zandosi], the anti-fascist junkyard of masons, Jews, and lovers of all things foreign has taken refuge.* We will never allow them or anyone else to harm the physical and moral health of the Italian people.

The forces of anti-fascism that "lurk" in the corners are said to have mimetic qualities – they could sometimes be taken for fascists (in Italian that would be *scambiati* – literally, exchanged) and, hence, could spread undetected onto the body politic of the fascist nation. Their circulation would be doubly dangerous, for they are accused by Mussolini, in the speech, of spreading the rumour ("'voci' che hanno circolato") that he was dead or otherwise incapacitated: a literally deadly disease – or rather, deadly precisely because it would literalize a death that needed to remain symbolic in order to function within the rhetorical logic of sacrificial self-presentation and self-expulsion. If the rumour had continued, Mussolini says, it would have led him to put into question Italians' intelligence (read: their fascist credentials) and, hence, experience a "profound mortification." The thought of Italians believing that Mussolini was literally dead, despite proof to the contrary, would really kill him, for it would spell the end of his symbolic circulation – a crisis of gigantic proportions. It was crucial that the rumour be stopped, especially because, as Mussolini knew very well, the rumour did not come from anti-fascists but was a widespread phenomenon among the Italian population during the summer of 1939.

Localization of the rumour into the "corners" of anti-fascism, especially if carried out with "intelligent" violence is, I would argue, an invitation to kill the rumour (and a few "infected" anti-fascists in the process) and to re-establish the difference and boundary between Mussolini's real and symbolic death. The rhetorical strategy of localizing the rumour also served an additional and no less important purpose. It served to underscore, by analogy, Mussolini's ability to localize another potentially infectious crisis – the European conflict:

La nostra politica è stata fissata nella dichiarazione del 1° settembre e non v'è motivo di cambiarla. Essa risponde ai nostri accordi e patti politici ed al desiderio di tutti i popoli, compreso il germanico, che è quello di almeno localizzare il conflitto. (DL 312–13)

Our policy was set in the 1 September declaration and there is no reason to change it. It reflects our national interests, our political agreements and pacts, and the desire of all peoples, including the German one, to at least localize the conflict.

If Italians were confused as to where they would stand in relation to a European war, it was an unsurprising outcome of Italy's ambiguous foreign policy during the ventennio which has often been characterized as incoherent and as being driven more by domestic political concerns than by an evolving calculus of national interest.[49]

Italian foreign policy was concerned with two spheres of interest – a European one, where the primary question regarded where Italy stood with the great powers (England, France, and Germany), and a North African one, where the primary issue was one of colonial expansion. Indeed, it was in North Africa where Italy could stake out its most autonomous set of policies, and it did so by both brutally repressing a colonial rebellion in Libya between 1928 and 1932 and conquering Ethiopia in 1935–36.

The Ethiopian War, which avenged an earlier defeat in 1896, was the most critical engagement. Originally planned in 1932, the war was the major autonomous Italian foreign policy initiative, with wide-ranging effects on the economy and both domestic and international politics.[50] The industrial build-up for the war in Ethiopia was sufficient to bring Italy out of the Great Depression by 1935. In these campaigns, there were aspirations of building a neo-Roman empire with its dreams of imperial (colonial) expansion.[51] While popular in Italy, the Italo-Ethiopian War was a diplomatic setback in Europe. Great Britain and France sharply criticized the invasion, and the League of Nations enforced sanctions against Italy.

In the European theatre, Mussolini would eventually align with Hitler, but not before trying to improve Italy's standing in Europe by brokering better relations with France and Britain. In 1935, Italy called for a Four Power Pact with France, Britain, and Germany that would serve to both accept the German arms build-up and provide a forum for dealing with both European and colonial issues. This initiative, which was largely intended to cement Italy's standing as a major power in Europe, was ratified, but only after its scope and potential impact were radically diminished. This reputation for playing a mediating role would continue through Italy's efforts to promote the Munich Conference in 1938 as a way to avoid a European war.

The tendency to keep a discrete distance from Germany can also be seen in Italo-American relations. Indeed, when both Roosevelt and Hitler came to power in 1932, it was the American leader who Mussolini sought out. Italy would maintain friendly relations with the United States until 1937. In the 1920s, Mussolini was more concerned with consolidating his regime than with foreign affairs. Italy's cooperation with the League of Nations through the early 1930s led many Western powers, and the United States, in particular, to consider Italy a respectable member of the international community.[52]

Italy's relations with Hitler were much more equivocal during the early years of the 1930s. There was a recognition of mutual interest and, to a lesser degree, of ideological proximity. Hitler saw Italy as a potential ally and sought a political and diplomatic alliance. Italy originally saw the rise of fascism in Germany as drawing on and being a boon to Italian fascism. There was always an element of personal tension as Mussolini sought to maintain Italy's role as the "senior movement." The more repugnant aspects of German race policy were criticized both by Mussolini himself and by the house organs of the regime.[53]

Until the mid-1930s, there was little effort to develop a strategic alliance. Their bi-national relations would only improve with Italy's and Germany's participation in the Spanish Civil War on the side of Franco. This joint intervention would lead to the announcement of a Rome-Berlin Axis which would coordinate policy concerning both the civil war and relations with the League of Nations.

During this period, Mussolini concluded that Germany was the rising power in Europe and that Italy's national interests would be best served by strengthening its alliance with Hitler. In 1937, Italy would sign the Anti-Comintern Pact, joining with Germany and Japan in an agreement to resist Soviet expansion. Shortly thereafter, Italy would follow Germany's withdrawal from the League of Nations.

This alliance did not confer on Italy the equal partnership that Mussolini sought. Germany would annex Austria and invade Czechoslovakia in 1938–39 without consulting Italy. Germany's invasion of Austria was particularly exasperating, if only because Italy saw Austria as a buffer state between itself and Germany. Italy's initial response was to invade Albania, which was already an Italian protectorate, in order to demonstrate its capacity for autonomous action. In the end, Italy would opt for a formal military alliance with Germany. It signed the "Pact of Steel" in May 1939, which formalized the Rome-Berlin Axis agreement and, for all practical purposes, committed Italy to declare war when Germany did. As Stanley Payne argues, this was a much greater commitment than Hitler had requested, and it is unsurprising that the Italian populace would be perplexed as to where Italy stood in the fall of 1939.[54]

In a speech intended to clarify to the Italian nation what the 1 September declaration of non-belligerence meant (does it mean Italy will not enter the war?) Mussolini defined Italy's peaceful goals (non-belligerence = to localize the conflict) in terms of "localizing": a strategy that in the first part of the speech he has charged with violence. In other words, the analogy between the two forms of localization (they will both solve a crisis) serves to carry, perfomatively, the terms of the first localization (violence) into the terms of the second localization (non-belligerence/ peace). It allows Mussolini to reassure the nation of Italy's peaceful intentions while rhetorically charging that peace with the willingness and readiness for war. Not surprisingly, in the unofficial version of the same speech, a version that according to historians was deliberately circulated among the population, Mussolini takes great pains to distinguish neutrality from the violently charged "non-belligerence":

Noi abbiamo detto che non prenderemo iniziative militari. La nostra posizione è quella di un non intervento nell'intendimento di localizzare il conflitto, essa non è neutralità. Neutralità è una parola che non mi piace [. . .] Il nostro non intervento, in questo momento, giova anzitutto ai nostri interessi, poi a quelli del popolo germanico, e forse anche a quelli dei franco inglesi. Ma non si creda che noi si possa passare attraverso il fuoco come la salamandra, che i competenti dicono sia un animale invulnerabile dalle fiamme.[55]

We have said that we will not pursue military initiatives. Our position is one of non-intervention with the aim of localizing the conflict, it is not one of neutrality. I do not like the word neutrality [. . .] Our non-intervention, at this time, is first and foremost beneficial to our interests, then to those of the German people, and perhaps even to those of the Franco-English. But do not think that we can go through fire like the salamander, an animal that experts say is invulnerable to flames.

Non-intervention (localization) today does not mean that Italy will not catch fire tomorrow.

The Two Sides of the Duce

Historians have disagreed over the purpose of Mussolini's seemingly odd choice of targeting "i rottami dell'antifascismo" (the anti-fascist junkyard) in a speech meant to address the more worrisome international situation. Although some have noted that Mussolini might have made those comments to reawaken the bellicose spirit of the population in preparation for war, others have minimized their importance and have seen them as stemming from his irritation at the rumours.[56] The phenomenon of the rumours to which he was responding has also been the object of conflicting interpretations. Nicola Gallerano has written that the rumours indicated the desire on the part of Italians to suppress the Duce and, with him, the possibility of entry into war:

> Attaccare viceversa il corpo del duce significava distruggere simbolica- mente il potere che esso – è la parola – incarnava [. . .] Non è difficile in- terpretare il coro di queste voci come un'evidente proiezione del desiderio di scongiurare l'ingresso in guerra dell'Italia, colpendo simbolicamente la figura del duce e la sua suprema funzione di arbitro delle decisioni a riguardo.[57]

> To attack the Duce's body meant symbolically destroying the power that it – literally – embodied [. . .] It is not difficult to interpret the chorus of rumours as an obvious projection of the desire to forestall Italy's entry to war, symbolically attacking the image of the Duce and his main function as arbiter of the decisions regarding it.

On the other hand, Angelo Michele Imbriani offers the opposite interpretation and argues that the rumours were caused by fear of losing the saviour of the peace who had "miraculously" averted the international conflict a year before with his role as mediator at the Munich Conference (29–30 September 1938):

> Bisogna pensare che esse [voci], accompagnate come sono da una fidu- cia ancora radicata nella volontà di pace di Mussolini e nella sua abilità politica, esprimano più che un desiderio – come ha sostenuto Gallerano – una paura: la paura che possa venire a meno, proprio in un frangente così drammatico, la guida, ritenuta saggia e sicura del Duce.[58]

We should think that they [the rumours], linked as they are to an enduring trust in Mussolini's peaceful intentions and political skill, express not so much a desire – as Gallerano maintained – but a fear: fear that the Duce's leadership, seen as wise and safe, could be lost, particularly during such a dramatic event.

Although I will not attempt to settle the historians' dispute regarding the cause of the rumours, I do think it is significant that their interpretations of this particular phenomenon should produce diametrically opposed assessments of the relationship between Mussolini and the masses on the eve of Italy's entry into the war. Their views are clearly contradictory, but what concerns me here is not so much the unavailability of an accurate historical assessment, but rather, the ways in which the assumptions made regarding Mussolini's duality condition such assessment.

Neither interpretation considers that the two sides of the Duce that formed his public persona were performatively interwoven so that each element partook of the defining of the other. They were not merely added as two self-contained elements of a patchwork but, as I argue, they were rhetorically integrated into one another. For this reason, any attempt to neatly separate them, or eliminate one, while establishing categories of public reception becomes problematic.

In the case of Gallerano and Imbriani, the two sides of Mussolini are literally separated along the critical divide. Gallerano's account offers the image of a belligerent Mussolini that Italians unconsciously desired to destroy for fear that he might plunge them into war. Imbriani's offers the image of Mussolini as saviour of the peace that Italians loved and were afraid of losing, convinced that he would miraculously save them from war.

The only common factor between the two accounts seems to be that Italians in September 1939 wanted peace and not war. Although it is easy to understand why the spectre of impending war might not be welcomed by any given population at any particular moment, in the Italian case, one would also have to ask, what happened to the twenty years of ideological idealization of violence. Could this be seen as a monumental failure at ideological persuasion on the part of the regime? Imbriani thinks that it was, and he points out that while the regime succeeded in propagating the "myth of the Duce," it nevertheless failed to render popular the alliance with Germany and the heroic and militaristic lifestyle proper to the new fascist man.[59] This particular ideological aspect was never absorbed, according to Imbriani, by the majority of the population but was confined to the more militant and activist segments:

> Dopo la marcia su Roma si erano andati infatti diffondendo due diversi miti di Mussolini, il mito moderato dei fiancheggiatori e degli afascisti e il mito intransigente della base squadrista. Questi miti avevano un corrispettivo nelle due distinte figure in cui si articolava l'immagine di Mussolini diffusa e accreditata dalla propaganda: il "Presidente degli Italiani" e il "Duce dei Fascisti."[60]

> After the March on Rome, two different myths of Mussolini emerged, the moderate one of supporters and *afascisti*, and the intransigent one of the militant base. These myths, circulated and legitimized by the propaganda, corresponded to the two distinct figures comprising Mussolini's image: "President of the Italians" and "Duce of the Fascists."

Imbriani acknowledges the duality/ambivalence of Mussolini's public image but he argues that such duality was not perceived by the moderate majority: they, instead, received only a partial, one-sided image of the Duce:

> Già prima che inizino le ostilità, il salvatore, garante e patrono della pace si tramuta, spesso e volentieri, in un "signore della guerra" – nelle pose e negli atteggiamenti pubblici – lo Statista cauto e responsabile si produce in fieri e minacciosi proclami e si lancia in appassionate celebrazioni dei "valori" militari. Queste ambiguità, del resto, sono volute e ricercate deliberatamente dalla propaganda di regime e dal Duce stesso, che possono così rivolgersi con efficacia a destinatari diversi, fuori e dentro il Paese [. . .] L'azione della propaganda qui interessa solo nella misura in cui giunge ad influenzare e a condizionare l'opinione pubblica interna. È quindi interessante notare come la gente sorvoli sulla bipolarità e sull'immagine ufficiale di Mussolini, per recepire, invece, un'immagine ben più lineare e coerente. Si è già visto come nell'opinione pubblica moderata sia diffuso e trovi credito il mito dello Statista saggio e responsabile, salvatore e garante della pace, buon padre degli italiani, e come invece abbia poca incidenza il mito del Duce-Condottiero, benché esso sia presente nella propaganda di regime.[61]

> Even before the beginning of hostilities, the saviour, guarantor, and patron of the peace often and readily transformed himself into a "warlord" – in public posturing and demeanour – the cautious and responsible

statesman utters fiery and menacing declarations and sings the praises of military "values." These ambiguities, in fact, are deliberately cultivated by the regime's propaganda and by the Duce himself, thereby reaching with efficacy different audiences, inside and outside the country [. . .] We are interested in the impact of propaganda here only insofar as it succeeds in influencing and swaying domestic public opinion. Therefore, it is interesting to note how people disregarded the duality and the Duce's official image and perceived, instead, a much more linear and coherent image. We have already seen how moderate public opinion gave currency and credence to the myth of the responsible and wise statesman, saviour and guarantor of peace, good father to the Italians, and how, instead, the myth of the Duce-Condottiere was not very influential even though it was present in the regime's propaganda.

While Imbriani describes as failure the regime's inability to create a bellicose new fascist man, it would appear from the previous passage that the regime's bellicose message was never addressed to the group that would produce such a new man in the first place – the masses. If fascist ambiguity was not meant to be read – as ambiguous – by the collectivity but was, instead, as Imbriani suggests, a deliberately multivocal message directed to different audiences – peace for the masses, war for the *squadristi* (militant base) – one would have to conclude that the propaganda had succeeded rather than failed, since, in Imbriani's account, the moderate masses received the correct, that is, peaceful, part of the message. But this is not Imbriani's conclusion. He later describes the public's selective reception of the regime's ambiguous propaganda (the moderate majority only perceived the peaceful Mussolini) as demonstrating the fact that ideological propaganda does not necessarily succeed. What the majority of Italians did not select (the bellicose Mussolini) had failed to condition them:

> L'azione della propaganda viene dunque recepita selettivamente dall'opinione pubblica nelle sue varie componenti, e ciò dimostra che, se questa azione è importante, essa non è di per sé decisiva e non è sempre e automaticamente condizionante. Perché la propaganda risulti efficace, occorre che sia conforme ad esigenze ed aspirazioni collettive e che risponda a valori e modelli etici particolarmente sentiti nelle condizioni del tempo, o, ancora, che valga a esorcizzare paure e angosce.[62]

Propaganda is, therefore, selectively received by the public in its various components, which means that while its impact is important, it is, in and of itself, neither decisive nor always and automatically effective. For propaganda to be efficacious, it needs to conform to collective needs and aspirations and to reflect values and ethical models that are particularly resonant with the conditions of the time, or that it be capable of exorcizing fears and anxieties.

According to Imbriani, aside from the desire to exorcise the spectre of war, the moderate public's unilateral perception of Mussolini was also a result of the fact that the image of Mussolini as peaceful and just protector of his people could be more easily associated with, and hence, could draw on, a reservoir of embedded ethical values and pre-fascist cultural traditions such as Catholicism and Socialism. But again, one would have to ask, how is it that the public's selective reception is, on the one hand, an indication of propaganda's failure (they did not "buy" the bellicose Mussolini), and on the other, it would seem, a measure of its success. If the propaganda's efficacy depended on how well it conformed to the traditional cultural milieu, and people selected the side that most conformed with these traditions, then their selection would be – at least to a certain extent – an indicator of propaganda's success, not failure.

In keeping with his overall argument that the moderate majority sidestepped Mussolini's two images and perceived a more linear and coherent one, Imbriani describes the public's reception of the speech of 23 September as an interpretation 'in chiave decisamente "pacifista"' (that decidedly favoured the "peaceful' elements"), adding that "l'opinione pubblica tende a leggere nelle parole e negli atti di Mussolini ciò che più le è gradito e che più la tranquillizza" (public opinion tends to read in the words and actions of Mussolini what it wants to hear and what is reassuring).[63] In other words, since Italians wanted peace, they read peaceful intentions into Mussolini's ambiguous statements. Indeed, in Imbriani's account, their reading of the speech of 23 September 1939 seems to be almost indistinguishable from their reading of the "myth of the Duce" during the ventennio.

In my textual analysis of that speech, I have already pointed out that Mussolini's claims of peaceful intentions are simultaneously undercut by a rhetorical strategy of localization that charges that very peace with violence and belligerence. Furthermore, the inseparability of these two terms and their performative inscription into a ritual logic of crisis and resolution is not confined to this particular speech but is, as we have seen, a ubiquitous and fundamental component of Mussolinian rhetoric. The following question can then be posed: are we to assume that the inherent instability of these two terms within fascist rhetoric was, in fact, ignored by the "moderate majority" and that the popularity of the "myth of the Duce" rested on the condition that one side remain hidden? Or to rephrase the question more bluntly: was peace as defined by Mussolini ideologically different from the peace that Italians are said to have yearned for on the eve of the Second World War?

If it was, one is then left wondering how the same ideological aspects that Italians had continued to refuse in September 1939 (the very refusal upon which the popularity of the "myth of the Duce" was supposedly resting) suddenly "kicked in" the following spring, when, as Imbriani notes, "Al momento dell'intervento, la popolarità e il prestigio del Duce sono sempre altissimi, anche perché le motivazioni della guerra sono generalmente condivise e si ritiene che questa sarà facile e breve" (At the time of [military] intervention, the Duce's popularity and prestige are still very high, because the reasons for war are generally accepted and the expectation is that the war will be quick and easy).[64] A few pages later, one is struck by noting just how deeply Mussolini's motivations were, indeed, shared. In typical Mussolinian fashion, war was characterized by Italians in terms of peace and vice versa:

"Pace," "rivalsa," "giustizia," "benessere": sono queste le note fondamentali dell'interventismo popolare della primavera e dell'estate del 1940. E sono motivi che spesso troviamo associati, nei vagheggiamenti della gente: "da questa grande vittoria," scrive un informatore il 17 giugno, "attendono il *benessere* per l'avvenire e un lungo periodo di anni di *pace*." "Il popolo," scrive un altro informatore prima ancora dell'intervento, "sente moltissimo il fascino, il peso, la persuasione della vittoria. Esso, per i suoi molteplici bisogni di vita, non vede ora che la conquista e che Germania e Italia stanno per stroncare due popoli ricchi; e per i torti ingiustamente inflitti alla Nazione dal Trattato di Versaglia esso non aspetta che la vendetta di Dio."[65]

"Peace," "redress," "justice," "well-being": these are the basic themes of popular support for intervention in spring and summer 1940. And these are themes that we often find together in the musings of the people: "from this great victory," writes an informant on 17 June, "they expect future *well-being* and a long period of *peace*." "The people," writes another informer even before the intervention, "is very attracted by the import, the consequences, the allure of victory. Because of its many basic needs, it [the

Italian people] cannot wait for the conquest and for Germany and Italy to defeat two rich peoples; and as to the injustices inflicted to the Nation by the Treaty of Versailles, it only hopes for God's punishment.

If it was peace that Italians wanted, it was a strange peace, indeed. Somehow the bellicose side of Mussolini that Italians are said to have resisted for years, resurfaces in their desire for the peace that victory – hence, war – would bring about. Furthermore, if many Italians, as Imbriani says, "considerano questa guerra un passaggio obbligato per ottenere una pace stabile e sicura" (consider this war a necessary passageway to a secure and stable peace),[66] one cannot, in my view, discount the fact that this "necessary passageway" towards peace and well-being involved, in fact, a "passage" through Africa and other dis-puted territories. Some of the letters that Imbriani cites to illustrate the popular, if sudden, conviction of the necessity for war, as well as those collected by other scholars, leave no doubt that imagining a peaceful and prosperous future meant, for many, imagining a colonial future.[67]

2 Sacrificial Turns and Their Rhetorical Echoes

Qui in questi dialoghi l'intimo contatto tra oratore e popolo trova la sua più completa espressione; qui si palesa il legame e la solidarietà tra il condottiero e i suoi seguaci, allorché il popolo fa echeggiare la parola dell'oratore. E quando lo stato di comunione è stato raggiunto, Mussolini si muove su questo ondeggiare di sentimenti cha va e viene dal Duce al popolo e dal popolo al Duce, e che ha soltanto un unico motore, un unico punto di partenza e di arrivo, la persona di Mussolini.[1]

In these dialogues, the intimate contact between speaker and people finds its most complete expression; the tie and solidarity between the condottiere and his followers becomes apparent when the people echo the words of the speaker. When the state of communion has been reached, Mussolini is carried by this wave of sentiment that comes and goes from the Duce to the people, from the people to the Duce, and that has only a single engine, a single point of departure and arrival, the person of Mussolini.

In my analysis of the speech of 3 January 1925, I argued that the speech enacted the formal inauguration of the fascist regime as a sacrificial presentation. Mussolini's rhetorical self-immolation constituted a ritual event that dramatized his status and properties while inscribing them within a performative logic of undecidability. This logic was reiterated throughout the *ventennio* and was crucial to the regime's ideological articulation of crisis and resolution. In the preceding chapter, I have analysed the rhetorical strategies that allowed Mussolini to present himself as the agent of peace insofar as he was a guilty troublemaker, thereby charging the very notion of peace with violence.

I argued that Mussolini's self-ascribed dualities should not be read as static oppositions, but rather within their performative and, more specifically, sacrificial dimension. This dimension was often articulated in fascist rhetoric with the dramatization of Mussolini's "unstable" properties and inscribed within the two ritual moments of transfiguration that Girard had named "for the better" and "for the worse." Although I maintained that the two moments should not be neatly separated, my focus has been on the transfiguration for the worse: Mussolini's self-ascription of guilt/responsibility and the rhetorical construction of a mimetic relationship with the forces of anti-fascism that allowed a constant redeployment and recharging of the moment of violence.

In this chapter, I focus on Mussolini's "transfiguration for the better." Specifically, I examine how Mussolini's discursive style was rhetorically presented as a form of social contact that exemplified his communion with the Italian people. I will argue that these rhetorical presentations had a distinct sacrificial component that was crucial in maintaining their performative dimension. One of the *parole d'ordine* (slogans) the Duce never tired of repeating was *andare al popolo* (going to the masses). I am asking what this "going to the masses" looks like in discursive and sacrificial terms: Was it a going to, or rather, a going and coming from the masses? How is a social contact performed discursively?

In speeches and fascist accounts of Mussolinian linguistic style, I trace how the belabouring of the commonplace fascist refrain that the Duce's words are pure affirmations – synthetic utterances always already beyond speech that effect, rather than affect reality – is tied to a parallel Mussolinian self-limiting, self-cancelling turn, a temporary hollowing out/voiding of his position as speaker. The delineation of this void creates, rhetorically, a "proper place" to be occupied by the fascist *popolo* (masses) in its social contact with the Duce, and models, discursively, a sacrificial turn-against-oneself that the fascist subject will have to emulate in accepting a fascist identity.

Social contact was idealized as the absence of mediation between Mussolini and the people. A state of communion would render words superfluous and would, instead, be characterized by a direct propagation of the Duce's ideas into the hearts and minds of the people – what I call "fascist vibes" as means of communication. Denial of mediation, of course, meant denying that language occupied a privileged place in Mussolini's relationship with the masses: a stance reflected in the rhetoric of anti-rhetoric that permeated so many speeches during fascism. While the rhetoric of anti-rhetoric is usually viewed as part and parcel of the general anti-intellectual bent of the regime, it assumes a much more significant role when viewed in conjunction with the rhetorical field of sacrificial presentations.[2] Only by analysing their interrelation and mutual reinforcement can we properly assess the performative and interpellative functions of a discursive style that the regime considered essential for forging a new national identity.

Speaking as the Duce

In an apologetic study of Mussolini "oratore e scrittore" (orator and writer), published in 1941, Hermann Ellwanger, a disciple of the German philologist Emil Winkler, summarizes the Duce's recipe for speech making: "I punti fondamentali di Mussolini sono dunque: limitare i discorsi al minimo, dire solamente le cose essenziali con parole essenziali e possibilmente poche, muovere guerra agli antichi e tradizionali discorsi, all'eloquenza, vecchio stile, in tutte le sue manifestazioni" (Mussolini's fundamental points are: limit speeches to a minimum, say only essential things with essential words, few if possible, declare war on traditional speeches of the past, on old-style eloquence in all its manifestations).[3] To make war against the prolixity and inconclusiveness that characterized the old style of parliamentary, democratic politics, Ellwanger explains, a new fascist style had to be forged, one capable of producing a "discorso autoritario" (authoritative discourse), that is, a discourse that would limit by being self-limiting, that would acquire force by its very synthetic nature. Lack of self-limitation, and consequently of force, figures prominently in Ellwanger's illustration of the casus belli against the parliamentary old style: "Per lui [Mussolini], specialmente il discorso politico aveva subito una completa svalutazione attraverso l'abuso parlamentare, la parola spesso era fine a se stessa e il discorso politico era diventato un gergo parlamentare, privo di forza, logoro" (For him [Mussolini], political discourse in particular had lost all value through its abuse in parliament, words were often used for their own sake and political dicourse had become parliamentary jargon, devoid of force, worn-out).[4] The excessive and self-indulgent use of words had devalued political discourse, and fostered a lack of measure and disorder in the lifestyle of Italians:

> Il parlamentarismo e la democrazia avevano privato il popolo italiano del suo "stile" di vita; il Fascismo sorse per ridonarglielo. In primo luogo si doveva inculcare nel popolo un nuovo senso della misura e una salda

coscienza dell'ordine. La disciplina, come principio dell'ordine, doveva essere posta sopra ogni cosa, perché si arrivasse a una nuova forma di vita, allo "stile fascista."[5]

Democracy and the parliamentary system had deprived the Italian people of its "style" of life; Fascism rose in order to give it back. First, it was necessary to inculcate in the people a new sense of measure and a firm belief in order. Discipline, as a principle of order, had to be placed above all things, so that a new form of life, a "fascist style" could be achieved.

The new sense of measure would give back by taking away, it would produce by elimination, it would affirm by denying. Ellwanger's text returns insistently to this strange logic, and it does so in a mechanical and almost compulsory fashion. It is a textual configuration obsessively reproduced but unacknowledged by the author – a textual blind spot, yet seemingly essential to his ideological narrative.

While belabouring the commonplace fascist refrain that the Duce's words are pure affirmations – utterances always already beyond speech that effect rather than affect reality – and dutifully citing the Duce to that "effect" – "Vedete che io non amo la forma dubitativa e convenzionale. Io affermo" (As you see, I do not like the conventional interrogative form. I affirm)[6] – his narrative inscribes these "pure affirmations" within the logic of a self-limiting, self-cancelling, turn. Hence, we learn that the inauguration of a fascist measure, that phantomatic entity that would bring back the lost style, coincides with the retrieval and redeployment of a minimal fundamental discursive unit, a magic term that had been forgotten:

> Da troppo tempo si era dimenticata la parola "no," dice Mussolini: quella parola che è il freno ad ogni disordine e dissolutezza. Perciò dovrà adoperare questo termine magico, tutte le volte che sarà necessario, perché "solo con l'astinenza si corregge un abuso." Al popolo però deve essere lasciato ciò che gli è essenziale e gli appartiene originariamente: ossia "il calore, la forza, il pittoresco, l'inaspettato, il mistico; insomma tutto quello che conta nell'animo delle moltitudini." Il governare tuttavia non può essere compito della massa, ma solo dell'uomo che assomma in sé, per cosí dire, i caratteri principali del popolo, e del popolo è la spontanea e immediata espressione, cioè la persona del Duce.[7]

For too long the word "no" had been forgotten, says Mussolini: the one word that puts the brakes on every form of disorder and dissoluteness.

Hence, he will need to use this magic term every time it is necessary, because "only with abstinence can one correct abuse." To the people must
be left only what in essence and origin belongs to it: "passion, force, the
pictoresque, the unexpected, the mystical; in other words, everything that
counts in the soul of the multitudes." But governance cannot be a task for
the masses, only for the man who embodies, as it were, the main characteristics of the people and is the spontaneous and immediate expression of
the people, that is, the person of the Duce.

Ellwanger's paraphrase of the Duce is indicative of the rebounding
logic that guides his narrative whenever he tries to describe the Duce's
ability to create by pure enunciation. Not only does the unit of measure
of Mussolini's pure affirmative style turn out to be a negation – the
magic term "no" – but this negation also seems to implode at the moment of enunciation, creating, if anything, a negative space in the place
of the subject of enunciation. Up until the word *necessario* (necessary),
we seem to inhabit the standard fascist portrayal of Mussolinian speech
as action and deeds, with Mussolini as the doer, using (*adoperare*) the
magic word "no" to curb disorder and impose order. The image is a
familiar one of Mussolini disciplining the dissolute masses corrupted
by the excesses of liberal democracy, the necessity for this action being,
of course, obvious to all, just as the necessity for future disciplining of
anti-fascists. But then, just as Ellwanger calls in the Duce's word, citing
him directly, perhaps as a way to summarize and authorize his indirect
rendition of a fascist blow, the blow takes a different turn. The magic
word that was brandished as a tool for the beating in the first part of
the sentence is inscribed in a reflexive trajectory at the end of the same
sentence: "Hence, he will need to use this magic term every time it is
necessary *because* 'only with abstinence can one correct abuse.'"[8] Suddenly, the image of discipline imposed by Mussolini becomes an image of self-imposed discipline: abstinence. In Ellwanger's narrative, the
Duce's "direct" speech, it seems, redirects the blow against himself, as
he is grammatically conflated, becoming (the impersonal) "one" with
his corrective tool: abstinence.

The impersonal "one" also invites a certain exchangeability of the
subject of the self-limiting turn. The Duce seems to occupy this position at first, as in a momentary transit that will pave the way for the
masses' subsequent occupation of his, then their, proper self-limiting
position in the next two sentences. For his word to work its magic, that
is, to go beyond speech and assert itself as deed, suppressing the old
and inaugurating the new, his word, it seems, must "replace" him as

well. It must temporarily empty-out his position as speaker, leaving only a contour of himself, to make room for the masses' collective occupation of this space in the last sentence: "But governance cannot be a task for the masses, only for the man who embodies, as it were, the main characteristics of the people and is the spontaneous and immediate expression of the people, that is, the person of the Duce." A certain exchangeability of speaking positions is set in motion here. To be the immediate expression of the people, the unifying composite sum total of their traits, he must temporarily "vacate" his position. The multitudes will not speak *as masses* but *as Duce*, literally through his person.[9] They will replace him and be replaced at the same time, for in "passing through the Duce," the voice of the masses will become the voice of the fascist *popolo*.

There is also another type of exchangeability at work here. Ellwanger's curious description of the Duce's magic word, "hence, he will need to use this magic term every time it is necessary, because 'only with abstinence can one correct abuse,'" produces an uncanny effect since it allows the reader to substitute, in the impersonal "one," Mussolini for an individual member of the masses. If we allow this exchangeability of positions, Mussolini's self-reflexive turn can also be read as a discursive mechanism of production of fascist consensus. Mussolini as the "one" functions here as a sort of pronominal rhetorical relay, not unlike the perspective/spatial relay described by Kenneth Dean and Brian Massumi and applied by Karen Pinkus to her analysis of the visual language of fascist advertising: "The body of the leader undergoes a process of infinitization, as if stricken by a compulsion to become co-extensive with quasi-corporeal space . . . It can see as 'one' would see it, occupying every pronoun position simultaneously. It can stand on every pedestal and don every flag. It is exemplary. It is fractured."[10]

As Pinkus correctly points out, "In the case of Mussolini, however, one must be careful to understand fragmentation as multiplication rather than as dismemberment or castration."[11] The logic of fragmentation as multiplication seems in this case to depend on figures of example and exchange of positions:

In his many poses, Mussolini provided a basis for the performative acts of an ideal fascist citizen. He also appropriated monarchical stances as part of his long-standing campaign to replace the king. In other words, the body of the Duce managed to slip between its position as the single figurehead of the state and as the every body of daily life under the fascist regime. Neither the "king" nor the "subject" represents a true body; both are simulacra, endlessly reproduced in a chain of ever-lessening fidelity to some "original" whose very status has been occluded in the process.[12]

Mussolinian physical poses, gestures, and images undoubtedly possessed semiotic content, and constituted a visual language that can be properly considered performative. I would, however, as I have already argued in my analysis of Mussolini's dualities, extend the realm of the performative to his verbal language, as well, and ask whether poses and gestures to be imitated and reproduced by the ideal fascist citizen were not also modelled discursively.

Ellwanger's narrative troping of his model suggests that they were. While bent on illustrating the Duce's magic, he ends up illustrating a decidedly less mystical mechanism, that is, the role of the self-effacing "turn" of the Duce in modelling discursively the internalization of the external prohibition, the self-limiting mechanism that sustains consensus. The scene to be rehearsed over and over in the production of the political passion play is the scene of the fascist subject turning against himself and towards Mussolini, purchasing a fascist identity, as it were, through an *Imitatio Ducis*, reperforming the scene of an imposition as a voluntary (l)imitation. Indeed, no performance seems to have begun for Mussolini without a fight against himself: "Perciò Mussolini prova un intimo travaglio prima di tenere un discorso e deve combattere contro se stesso: 'La noia che io debbo superare tutte le volte che debbo pronunciare un discorso'" (Hence, Mussolini experiences inner turmoil prior to delivering a speech and is forced to fight against himself: "the boredom I must ovecome every time I have to make a speech").[13]

Lest this "intimo travaglio," this inner turmoil that coincides with the fight against oneself, be mistaken for a moment of reflection and organization of the words to be uttered, taken out from its dimension as performative example, Ellwanger adds that "egli non 'prepara' i discorsi se non nell'attimo in cui li pronuncia" (he only "prepares" the speeches in the instant in which he delivers them.[14] The Duce's speeches are not preformed: they are performed. They cannot be anticipated or explained – they can only be repeated. Indeed, Ellwanger's own illustration by example, with which he eagerly repeats the Mussolinian model, seems to validate the effectiveness of the Duce's exemplary performance, its formative, interpellative injunction to repetition:

Con quanta consapevolezza Mussolini si occupi della formazione di un nuovo stile oratorio e quanto gli stia a cuore tale problema appare chiaro dai suoi discorsi, allora che vi accenna incidentalmente. L'esempio che segue vale molto piú di una frase retorica; ci permette di spingere lo sguardo nell'officina dell'oratore, ci mostra il suo atteggiamento di fronte ai discorsi abituali e ci dà, nello stesso tempo, un piccolo programma di stile mus-soliniano: "Commilitoni! Quale discorso vi attendete da me? Mi accade talvolta di leggere le anticipazioni dei miei discorsi. È un esercizio del tutto singolare perché io penso i miei discorsi nell'attimo in cui li pronuncio."[15]

It is clear from his speeches, when he makes a passing reference to it, how much conscious effort he applies to the task of forging a new style of oratory and how deeply he cares about this problem. The example that follows is worth much more than a rhetorical sentence; it allows us to see up-close the workshop of the speechmaker, it shows us his stance towards common speeches and it gives us, at the same time, a little guide of Mus-solinian style: "Fellow soldiers! What kind of speech do you expect from me? Sometimes I happen to read the advance copies of my speeches. It is a very peculiar exercise because I only think out my speeches the instant in which I utter them."

The example, says Ellwanger, would enable us to glimpse into the "workshop of the speechmaker" the place where the "intimo travaglio" in its double valence of work and birth, takes place. Yet, this strange place of origin, this pre-discursive moment of speech formation, which we are led to observe, turns out to be voided, emptied out, as it were, precisely by the example: the Duce's speeches are never prepared be-forehand, they simply come into being (transforming themselves into deeds) at the moment of delivery. The moment we step into the "work-shop of the speechmaker," we encounter the speechmaker himself, who tells us that nobody's home.

We find this uncanny scene of the "disappearing Duce" also repro-duced in another fascist study of Mussolini's linguistic style. In his *La lingua di Mussolini* (*The Language of Mussolini*), Eugenio Adami, like Ell-wanger, feels compelled to describe the origins and originality of the Duce's words. Here, the place of origin coincides with his first written work, Mussolini's *Diario di Guerra* (*War Diary*). Hailed as no less than a "precursor to contemporary European literature," Mussolini's "*Bil-dungsroman*" is, according to Adami, a source of wonder for the reader because of the special language in which it is written:

Una lingua originalissima perchè ridotta alla ultima semplicità, scarnita al punto da sembrare fatta di briciole, pure nulla sacrificando alla chiarezza, anzi presentando le cose con pieno rilievo.[16]

A most original language because it is reduced to utter simplicity, skeletal to the point that it seems made of particles, without sacrificing clarity, on the contrary, presenting things in full relief.

For Adami the *Diario* is true poetry – poetry of the kind that can only be born from the experience of sacrifice and silence:

> Questi bagliori di poesia vera, nata così improvvisa mentre l'anima veglia sulla strage umana, mi ricordano ciò che ha scritto il Bertoni: "In ogni scrittore, che abbia da esprimere idee vissute e sofferte nel sacrificio e nel silenzio, la poesia non manca mai."[17]

> These glimpses of true poetry, born so suddenly when the soul is witnessing the human massacre, remind me of what Bertoni wrote: "Poetry is never absent in a writer whose ideas were lived and suffered in sacrifice and silence."

A deeply poetic work, and yet, thoroughly objective. In fact, so objective that the reader forgets Mussolini:

> Tanta obbiettività che il lettore dimentica lui, perché si osserva appena di scorcio e sembra più spettatore che attore, intento naturalmente a cogliere gli animi che passano e a fissarli. La sua persona c'è e non c'è. Frequente il "noi," rarissimo l'"io." L'uomo s'è fuso cogli uomini e con le cose, così come la lingua s'è condensata e assottigliata, spoglia d'ogni velame, d'ogni peso strutturale.[18]

> There is so much objectivity that the reader forgets him because he can barely be glimpsed and seems more spectator than actor, intent as he is, naturally, at capturing and holding the souls before him. His persona is there, and yet, is not there. The "we" is frequent, while the "I" is very rare. The man has bonded with men and things, in the same way that language has become streamlined and condensed, devoid of every veil, of all structural weight.

The condensation and streamlining of objective language has, it seems, reduced the Duce to such an extent that he is now fused with men and things. His persona is there, and yet, not there, like an intermittent apparition that we could define – borrowing Pinkus' definition of fascist bodily gestures – as quasi-semaphoric.[19] He has become "coextensive with a quasi-corporeal space" and "can see as one would see"

since he occupies the position of "spectator" more than that of "actor,"
the "we" rather than the "I," exchanging his position with the position
of the reader of his *Diario*.

The exchange of positions between the Duce and the fascist subject
grounds the rhetorical articulation of social contact: a primal fusion un-
mediated by language, where the Duce becomes the *popolo* and vice
versa. Consider the insistent use of pronominal relays in the following
display of fascist affection by Mario Appelius, in his essay "Vincere"
(To Victory):

> Vogliamogli bene.
> Stringiamoci tutti intorno a Lui.
> Ringraziamo Dio di averci dato al momento giusto il grande Condot-
> tiero del quale il popolo e la nazione avevano bisogno.
> [. . .] certissimo sempre della vittoria finale: sicurissimo del popolo ital-
> iano nel quale fermamente crede così come il popolo fermamente crede in
> Lui perché Noi siamo Lui e Lui è Noi.
> E Lui e Noi insieme, con l'emblema del Littorio e la Croce dei Savoia, il
> tutto illuminato dalla benedizione di Dio, siamo l'Italia [. . .] L'Italia nostra
> Madre, nostra Patria, nostra terra, nostra Gente, nostro immenso amore.[20]

> We should love him.
> We should embrace Him in unity.
> Let us thank God who has given us at the right time the great Condot-
> tiere that our people and nation needed.
> [. . .] always certain of the final victory: certain of the Italian people he
> firmly believes in, as the people firmly believe in Him, because We are He
> and He is Us.
> And He and Us together, with the emblem of the Littorio and the Savoy
> Cross, standing under God's light and blessing, we are Italy [. . .] Italy is
> our Mother, our Country, our land, our People, our infinite love.

Countless Mussolinian speeches begin with a curious discursive short-
circuit, a reference to direct contact and union of souls at the expense of
language: "Camerati! Come ben potete intendere, non sono venuto qui
per pronunciare un discorso. Sono venuto qui per prendere contatto con
voi, col vostro spirito e la vostra fede" (Comrades! As you can well understand, I have not come here to deliver a speech. I have come here to
make contact with you, with your spirit and your faith).[21] Social contact
eliminates the need for words, communion replaces communication, in

the bond between Mussolini and the Italian people. This seems to be the logic articulated by the rhetoric of anti-rhetoric that fascist writers never tired of belabouring in their analysis of fascist style and that characterizes so many "Mussolinian allocutions": "I miei non sono discorsi nel senso tradizionale della parola: sono allocuzioni, prese di contatto tra la mia anima e la vostra, tra il mio cuore e i vostri cuori" (Mine are not speeches in the traditional sense of the word: they are allocutions, points of contact between my soul and yours, between my heart and yours).[22]

Although we might be tempted to discount this logic as just part and parcel of the general anti-intellectual stance of the regime, or as just another cliché useful in attacking the old parliamentary style, we should refrain from dismissing it too easily. A crucial function of the rhetoric of anti-rhetoric, and of the fascist discursive style that it sanctions, is an interpellative one: a linguistic model aimed at calling into being the fascist subject. If in Ellwanger's "workshop of the speechmaker" the orator turned out to be voided while allegedly illustrating the origin of his words (the "intimo travaglio"), it is because the style that the Duce puts forth, models, as it were, as the example that the fascist subject will have to emulate is one of self-sacrifice, labour, and silence, or more precisely, labour in silence construed as sacrifice of one's voice, a renunciation/reduction of one's words, a self-effacing gesture:

> Tutte le volte che io sentivo qualcuno di voi rinunziare alla parola, tutte le volte che io dovevo sospingere qualcuno di voi alla tribuna, vi avrei abbracciato. L'ho sognata io la generazione italiana dei silenziosi operanti. L'ho voluta io, riducendo il mio stile e abolendo tutto ciò che era decorazione, fronzolo, superficialità. Annullando tutti i residui del seicentismo, tutta la ciarla vana.[23]

> Every time I heard one of you give up his words, every time I had to push one of you to the podium, I felt like embracing you. It is I who dreamed about the Italian generation of silent workers. It is I who wanted it, streamlining my style and ridding it of all decoration, embellishment, superficiality. Stripping all of the the seventeenth-century residue, all the vain babble.

Speaking as a Fascist

For the individual to be embraced by the Duce (to be ready to face the Duce) as a good fascist subject, he will need to acquire mastery of the fascist style, that is, learn to emulate the style of the master through silent (self-effacing) labour. But why should labour be part of a fascist discursive style? And why should learning how to speak like a fascist involve self-effacement? Judith Butler's discussion of Althusser's theory of interpellation sheds light on the relation between labour, mastery, and speaking properly.[24] Butler notes that, in a Lacanian vein, "Althusser links the emergence of a consciousness – and a conscience ("la conscience civique et professionelle") – with the problem of speaking properly (*bien parler*)."[25] The skills of labour, and the rules that govern the division of labour, appear inseparable, within the Althusserian scene, from the mastery of speaking skills: "The reproduction of the subject takes place through the reproduction of linguistic skills, constituting, as it were, the rules and attitudes observed 'by every agent in the division of labour.' In this sense, the rules of proper speech are also the rules by which *respect* is proffered or withheld. Workers are taught to *speak* properly and managers learn to speak to workers 'in the right way [*bien commander*].'"[26] Learning how to speak in a certain way appears crucial for the reproduction of distinct social roles within the dominant ideology, and yet, one learns how to properly occupy one's place in society – how to command or be commanded, as it were – through a learning process that is grounded, paradoxically, by a certain exchangeability of those very roles:

> The more a practice is mastered, the more fully subjection is achieved. Submission and mastery take place simultaneously, and this paradoxical simultaneity constitutes the ambivalence of subjection. Though one might expect submission to consist in yielding to an externally imposed dominant order and to be marked by a loss of control and mastery, paradoxically, it is itself marked by mastery. The binary frame of mastery/submission is forfeited by Althusser as he recasts submission precisely and paradoxically as a kind of mastery. In this view, neither submission nor mastery is *performed by a subject*; the lived simultaneity of submission as mastery, and mastery as submission, is the condition of possibility for the emergence of the subject.[27]

As one critic has astutely pointed out, "In browsing through Mussolini's texts, one cannot avoid the uncanny feeling that Mussolini had read Althusser!"[28] I would add Butler to Mussolini's phantasmagoric reading list for, indeed, the "lived simultaneity of submission as mastery and mastery as submission" appears to be the condition of possibility for the emergence of the *fascist* subject. Mussolini's discursive style models this simultaneity as an exchangeability of positions between himself and the *popolo*. The rhetoric of social contact undergirds this exchangeability by providing a performative model to be imitated: a sacrificial turn against oneself of the speaking subject – the silencing of one's speaking position as the condition of possibility for embracing a fascist voice and facing the law: "Sono certo che voi non vi attendete da me un discorso di lunghe proporzioni. Finalmente, mi è dato di guardarvi in faccia ed è dato a voi di guardare in faccia a me"[29] (I am certain that you are not expecting from me a speech of disproportionate length. Finally, I have the chance to look you in the face and you have the chance to look me in the face).

In facing the Duce, the fascist subject should not expect words but a discursive sacrificial performance that provides a formative model to be mastered in constant repetition – by subjecting oneself to mastery, as it were. Not surprisingly, Ellwanger lists spirit of sacrifice along with loyalty, in describing what is formed and revealed in the contact between Mussolini and the *popolo*:

Quello che importa al Duce nei suoi discorsi è ancora e sempre la presa di contatto attraverso la quale si formano e si manifestano la fedeltà e lo spirito di sacrificio del popolo: "Non so se la mia *parola* sia giunta a tutti voi. Ma il mio *cuore* sí!"[30]

Now as always, what is important to the Duce in his speeches, is the making of contact through which the people's loyalty and spirit of sacrifice are formed and revealed: "I do not know if my *word* has reached all of you. But my *heart* has!

But what kind of voice, we may ask, is the fascist subject left with as a result of mastering the Duce's discursive style? If silence and self-sacrifice appear to be the condition of possibility for acquiring a fascist identity, it is also quite evident that *actual silence* cannot be the end product of this learning process. Some kind of voice would have to emerge. It is equally obvious that despite his constant belittlement of words, and constant exemplary performances of self-limiting abnegation, Mussolini delivered thousands of speeches, most of which were punctuated by responses from the crowd. His favourite characterization of those speeches was that they represented a "dialogo con il popolo" (dialogue with the people), and eliciting answers from the crowd became a staple feature of his style: "Voi sapete che il dialogo tra me e la folla mi piace, che amo essere interrotto perché dal colloquio sorge il *grido rivelatore* dei vostri stati d'animo" (You know that I am fond of the dialogue between me and the crowd, that I like being interrupted because from this conversation comes forth the *revealing shout* of your inner spirit).[31]

There seems to be a contradiction, or at least a stylistic incoherence between injunction to discursive self-abnegation and solicitation of speech – a fissure that has become almost invisible, prone as we are to quickly dismiss these dialogues as artificial, vaguely ridiculous (albeit strangely disturbing) in their mechanical canned-answer format. It is a fissure that becomes legible, however, when we consider that these answers were not, in fact, elicited as voices but as disembodied echoes of the Duce's words, returning to him as confimation of the Duce's capacity to *comprehend* the people:

> Il palco dell'oratore non sta piú dunque in Parlamento, ma nella piazza, in mezzo alla folla ondeggiante. Qui, in questo vivace e drammatico ambiente, dove un vasto cielo si volge sopra i dialoghi animati del condottiero del popolo, qui si forma il comune credo politico. Il Duce diventa allora l'interprete del suo popolo che, con le interruzioni, annuendo ed acclamando, fa eco alla parola del Capo.[32]

> The speaker's platform is no longer in Parliament, but in the *piazza*, in the midst of the undulating crowd. Here, in this environment so lively and full of drama, where a vast sky frames the dialogues brought to life by the *condottiere* of the people, here the common political faith is formed. The Duce becomes at that point the interpreter of his people who, with the interruptions, nodding and cheering, echo the words of the Leader.

There are countless references to this strange echo or, more precisely, echo-ustic mirror in fascist writings, where the dialogue between the Duce and the crowd is idealized as contact through propagation of what I would call fascist vibes – *vibrazioni* (vibrations), *pulsazioni* (pulsations), *irradiazioni* (radiations), *scosse telluriche* (seismic tremors), *folgorazioni* (lightning), *fermenti* (ferment), *fremiti* (quivers), and *energie* (energies), – *onde* (waves) travelling with the Duce's voice, returned to him by the "pulsating," "vibrating," "undulating," echoing crowd: "Mi piace questa eco degli umili – *esclama l'on. Mussolini, il quale poi riprende il sonante dialogo con la folla*"[33] (I like this echo of the humble

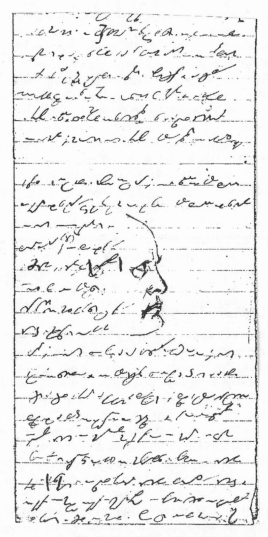

Figure 1. "Take my words to everybody. The speech can remain unpublished. [Addressing the stenographers.] Stenographers: I do not believe it necessary to give everything I say to the press. Spare yourself the effort, since I will shred your drafts." Benito Mussolini, original stenographic transcription stapled to archival copy of Mussolini's speech, "Riunione del Direttorio del Partito a Palazzo Venezia," 24 June 1943, ACS; MCP, Gabinetto, b.83, PNF, Direttorio Nazionale. Reprinted with permission n.1092/2013 Archivio Centrale dello Stato (Rome), Ministero per i Beni e le Attività Culturali.

populace – *exclaims the honourable Mussolini, who then returns to his resounding dialogue with the crowd*).

I refer to the staging of this scene as echo-ustic mirror, or echoing mirror, to suggest a parallel with what Kaja Silverman has referred to as an acoustic mirror in her incisive analysis of the female voice in psychoanalysis and cinema.[34] Silverman analyses the theoretical implications of an acoustic mirror stage of identity formation in the child occurring prior to the visual one famously described by Jacques Lacan.[35] Her hypothesis is that the maternal voice acts as the initial source of reference for the child's perception of self and other, as it organizes the world and activities that surround the infant.[36] Because the mother's voice dominates the first aural sphere that the child encounters, it is also a voice that the later cultural "paternal" sphere has a stake in controlling, displacing, or disavowing in order to assert its primacy. As Silverman puts it, "The theoretical and cinematic equation of the maternal voice with 'pure' sonorousness must therefore be understood not as an extension of its intrinsic nature, or of its acoustic function, but as part of a larger cultural disavowal of the mother's role both as an agent of discourse and as a model for linguistic (as well as visual) identification."[37]

Likewise, I would like to suggest that the strange echoing scene that fascist rhetoric stages, in describing the relation between the Duce and the masses, should not be understood in naturalistic terms. What fascist rhetoric truly propagates on a national level are not actual sound waves but the enactment of a scene of origins, of the process that enables the ideal fascist subject to be formed in language. What this particular depiction of origins disavows (by displacing it onto the echo circuit) is the voice of the fascist subject that is reduced to silence (or pure echo sound, if you will) at the same time as it is valorized ideologically for its specularity to the voice of the Duce. Although all ideological interpellations (within the Althusserian/Butlerian parameters) involve the mastery of certain speaking skills, and indeed, such mastery requires a degree of linguistic self-alienation in all subjects, the scene of fascist subjection, I believe, is distinct in its injunction – for it calls not just for the laborious reproduction of a certain speaking style but for the reproduction of a certain speaking style understood as labour *in silence*. The acquisition of a fascist identity, which gives the subject a national, collective voice, is purchased through the voluntary sacrifice of one's individual voice and through the constant echoing reiteration that this transaction has taken place.

Membership in the echoing circle would require verifiable proof of purchase and one that needed to be exhibited promptly and repeatedly in front of the interrogating authority. This logic is illustrated by the structure of the Duce's *discorsi-dialogo* (speech-dialogues). The answer from the crowd is an echoing return that presents a fundamental fissure, a dislocation of sorts in its eerily automatic character. On the one hand, it is a return construed (and elicited) as a reciprocation of feelings and ideas on the part of the fascist subject, a spontaneous response confirming the Duce's position as representative of the will of the people, the embodiment of an authority that comes from below, or as he preferred to call it, a manifestation of "ondate di consenso" (waves of consensus). In Mussolini's words: "E questo consenso io lo vedo profondo, spontaneo, sincero e non richiesto, perché, voi lo sapete, se c'è un uomo al mondo che non cerchi i facili successi della demagogia, quello sono io" (And I see this consensus as deep, spontaneous, sincere, and unexpected, because – you know this – if there is a man in the world who does not seek the easy success of demagoguery, it is I").[38] On the other hand, the same return is barred from any form of spontaneity other than spontaneous submission to absolute authority. It is a voice that cannot talk back, it can only go back to the eliciting source. As the following passage makes clear, with an interesting negative use of pronominal relay, stray voices would not be tolerated:

O la mia è la verità, o è la tua; o è la tua, e non è la mia. Se io penso che la mia è la verità e sono sicuro che sulla mia strada marcio verso grandi mète, non posso tollerare vociferazioni clandestine, il piccolo agguato di traverso, la calunnia codarda, la diffamazione infame. Tutto questo deve essere soppresso, travolto, sepolto. Lo volete voi? (*"Sì! Sì," rispondono centinaia di voci*).

Questo discorso – *conclude l'oratore* – voleva essere una presa di contatto, voleva essere un atto di fede, o, se vi piace, un atto di comunione. La comunione c'è stata. Viva il Fascismo![39]

The truth is either mine or it is yours; if it is yours, it is not mine. If I think that truth is mine and I am sure that my path leads to great goals, I cannot tolerate clandestine rumours, petty ambush, cowardly insult, vile defamation. All this must be suppressed, overturned, buried. Is this what you want? (*"Yes! Yes," reply hundreds of voices.*)

This speech – *concludes the speaker* – was meant to establish contact, was meant as an act of faith, or, if you prefer, an act of communion. Communion has taken place! Long live Fascism!

The "contacted" subject is a subject who denies, by the very act of responding, his own autonomous status as speaking subject. The "vibrating" shout-response might carry sound waves but it is still marked by silence for it points to the absence, not the presence of a speaking subject: it is a voice "without a body" that returns to the Duce as echo of his own voice, and as trace, remainder, and proof of the sacrifice that the individual subject has made.[40] Were the voice to originate from another source, say, a body other than the Duce's, it would become a "vociferazione clandestina" (clandestine rumour) that disrupts the echoing circuit on which the "atto di comunione" (act of communion) depends. Perhaps, in an effort to mark Mussolini's body as the one and only source of speech, his arms and fingers were depicted as instruments of sound – initiators of the sound-wave, as it were – that stroked the air searching for strings to vibrate and carry his words: "Nei rari momenti in cui questa raccolta figura d'oratore si apre e si libera, le due braccia roteano alte sulla testa: le dieci dita s'agitano come cercassero nell'aria corde da far vibrare; le parole precipitano a cateratta" (During the rare moments when the poised figure of the speaker opens up and frees himself, the two arms rotate high over his head: the ten fingers are agitated as if they are reaching for chords to vibrate in the air; words fall like cataracts).[41]

Not surprisingly, fascist writers intent on describing the stylistic virtues of Mussolini's *discorsi-dialogo* (speech-dialogues) invariably end up illustrating a dialogue that features, paradoxically, *one voice*. Ellwanger's attempt to describe the scene in dramatic terms, with an alternation of voices between the Duce and the *popolo*, quickly gives way to reinsertion of these voices into the *voce unica* (voice in unison) of the protagonist:

In certo qual modo il Duce provoca il dialogo per far partecipare il popolo e per metterlo in grado di dare sfogo alla sua indole vivace ed animata. Il protagonista di questa drammatica azione è però il Duce, e le voci che si alternano confluiscono sempre in un'unica voce, in cui si palesa la volontà di uno solo: quella del Duce che rispecchia le aspirazioni del popolo italiano.[42]

In a certain way, the Duce provokes the dialogue to make the people participate, so that it can release its lively and animated temperament. The protagonist of this dramatic action, however, is the Duce, and the voices that alternate always coalesce into a single voice, which expresses only the will of one: of the Duce who reflects the aspirations of the Italian people.

Giuseppe Ardau sees no such dramatic qualities. The only actors present in his rendition of the same scene are the Duce's ideas and his voice:

> La sua eloquenza non ha qualità drammatiche; egli non riesce a obbiettivare (come suol dirsi) le sue idee, a proiettarle fuori di sè e dar loro una personalità: s'immedesima in esse al punto che ne fa gli attori della sua azione. Di qui i discorsi-dialogo dei quali dirò più avanti, e che in verità hanno una voce sola, la sua: limpida prova di tale tendenza ad annullare il contrasto nel suo spirito.[43]

> His eloquence has no dramatic qualities; he cannot, as we say, objectify his ideas, project them beyond himself and give them a personality: he is so present in them that he makes them actors of his own performance. Here we see the speech-dialogues, to which I will return later, that actually have only one voice, his voice: clear proof of the tendency to annul any contrast within his spirit.

The very notion of a *discorso-dialogo*, that is, a speech in the form of a dialogue that features a single voice is puzzling, for such a situation could occur only if the protagonist assumes different roles, that is, exchanges speaking positions while actually maintaining one voice. It is a less puzzling concept if we consider that the rhetoric of social contact articulates, performatively, a fundamental exchangeability of the master/subject categories of identity formation.

The voice of the fascist subject is denied at the same time as it is being elicited, or, more precisely, it is elicited as a self-denying voice that mirrors – echoes – the master's voice. Within the parameters of this echoing mirror, the formation of a fascist identity depends on recognizing one's voice as the voice of the master – accepting submission to discursive self-abnegation as a condition for achieving a fascist consciousness and, indeed, for being a fascist in good conscience.

It is not by chance that Mussolini so often presented as evidence of his own good conscience his willingness to exchange roles: to be the laborious servant of the people, hence, offering the ultimate example of mastery as laborious submission:

> Vi prego, signor sindaco, di tediarmi tutte le volte che sarà necessario, *perché io, lo ripeto, sono il servo, non il padrone della nazione*, ed alla mia fatica, spesso aspra, spesso accompagnata da qualche amarezza, io non chiedo compensi di sorta. Mi basta il *responso della mia coscienza* e mi ritengo pago

il giorno in cui posso a tarda sera riposare un poco, constatando che in quel giorno ho fatto qualche cosa di utile per il popolo italiano.[44]

I ask that you, Mr. Mayor, call on me every time it is needed, *because, I repeat, I am the servant, not the master of the nation*, and for my toil, often harsh, often accompanied by some disappointment, I do not ask for any sort of compensation. The *voice of my conscience* is enough for me, and I consider myself fulfilled when I can rest a little, late in the evening, thinking that during that day I have done something useful for the Italian people.

Within this economy of role exchange, monetary speculation has to be foreclosed if a symbolic speculative economy is to take place: to echo the Duce's voice is to follow the voice of a fascist conscience, a voice that demands, paradoxically, that it be followed freely. Conscientious labour, in order to be repaid, has to be free, that is, freely given, and yet, the response of conscience appears to be precisely the compensation for the labour involved in submitting to its demands. In following the Duce's performative example, one obeys a fascist conscience and is repaid, so to speak, for the loss of voice that the submission entails by acquiring a clear conscience. Notice how, in the following passage, Mussolini uses the example of his own good conscience to present, with "dramatic elements," what he acknowledges to be a contradictory scene: the laborious submission involved in freely obeying the voice of conscience:

Il popolo italiano, il buono, il saggio, il forte, il laborioso popolo italiano, sente che non sono un tiranno, non sono un padrone, né sono tormentato da folli ambizioni. Ho l'orgoglio invece di essere il servo della nazione, ho la coscienza di fare tutto il possibile per rendere il popolo italiano grande, prospero, potente all'interno ed all'estero. (*Acclamazioni*).

Voi mi domandate come saneremo questa contraddizione. Poiché il contrasto voi lo afferrate nei suoi elementi drammatici. Si dice che noi siamo un esercito accampato nella nazione, che noi governiamo contro la volontà del popolo italiano. (*Dalla folla si grida: "Non è vero!"*)

Lo so anch'io, *risponde il Presidente. Poi continua:* Si dice che se il popolo potesse esprimere liberamente la sua voce, questa sarebbe di rampogna o di condanna. Ebbene noi lo abbiamo consultato questo popolo, siamo andati verso questo popolo, continuamente.

Perché siete qui? C'è forse qualcuno che vi ha costretti, che vi ha imposto di venire in questa piazza? (*"No!," urla a gran voce la folla*).

Siete venuti perché la vostra volontà ve lo da detto, perché avete obbed-
ito alla vostra coscienza.[45]

The Italian people, the good, wise, strong, laborious Italian people, feel
that I am neither a tyrant, nor a master, nor am I consumed by insane
ambition. Instead, I am proud to be the servant of the nation, I have the
conscience to do everything possible to make the Italian people great, ·
prosperous, powerful in the domestic and foreign arenas.(*Acclamations.*)

You are asking me how we will solve this contradiction, since you perceive contrast in its dramatic elements. Some say we are an occupying
army in the nation, that we govern against the will of the Italian people.
(*Shouts from the crowd: "It's not true!"*)

I know, I know, *replies the President. Then continues*: Some say that if the
people could freely have a voice it would be one of complaint or condem-
nation. Well, we have consulted the people, we have moved closer to the
people all the time.

Why are you here? Is there someone who demanded, who forced you to
come to this *piazza*? (*"No!," the crowd shouts loudly.*)

You are here because your will told you so, because you have obeyed
your conscience!

The Duce's voice presents itself as the voice of conscience – indeed,
a *voce unica* (voice in unison) that surreptitiously responds to its own
demands: Why are you here? Because your conscience told you so! It is
a strange way to consult the people considering that, within the logic
of a Mussolinian *discorso-dialogo* (speech-dialogue) the "voice in unison" cannot be replied to but only echoed – sent back to its source. To
echo the Duce's voice is, thus, not only to follow the voice of a fascist
conscience but also, with each echoing return, to justify and reconfirm
the presence of the Duce: "Why are you here? Because your conscience
told you so!"

The Duce's Confessional Mode

What is, then, the discursive status of the Duce's conscience? The rhetoric of social contact with all its exemplary performances of laborious
and discursive self-abnegation seems to function within the logic and,
indeed, to provide the justifications for being in good conscience. The
"continuous consultation" with which Mussolini goes to the people reflects – echoes, if you will – the legitimacy of his position: No tyrant

here, just the humble servant of a people who confirm, at every occasion, the good faith of his conscientious dedication. And yet, as I have argued in the previous chapter, Mussolini's self-ascription of guilt/responsibility was a ubiquitous feature of his speeches throughout the ventennio and was crucial to the rhetorical articulation of his status as sacrificial victim. Mussolini's rhetorical self-immolation, of which the speech of 3 January provides the most vivid instance, was grounded in the performative dramatization of the two ritual moments of transfiguration "for the better" and "for the worse." The logic of undecidability that governs these two moments, holds together the so-called Mussolinian dualities not as a simple summation of opposites but as a discursive performative mechanism that draws its cohesiveness by its very instability. Was the Duce's discursive conscience, then, also marked by this very instability? Was the voice of conscience a voice that belonged totally and always to his "good side," or was it also in some way implicated in the moment of guilt/responsibility that is an essential part of the Duce's sacrificial dimension? Certainly, the anti-rhetorical, discursive turn against oneself that the Duce models over and over as an example of fascist style is in line with his overall self-sacrificial image, but how does this turn relate to the problem of good conscience?

The answer to this question begins to emerge when we consider that the rhetoric of social contact articulates a fundamental exchangeability of the subject/master categories of identity formation and that the terms of this exchangeability are grounded in the social reproduction, and performative modelling, of speaking skills. Butler's analysis of the Althusserian theory of interpellation is once again very useful here – for she sheds light on the connection that exists between the mastery of skills and the status of one's conscience before the law: the centrality of the subject's precarious declaration of innocence within the process of identity and, indeed, ideological formation:

> For Althusser, to perform tasks "conscientiously" is to perform them, as it were, again and again, to reproduce those skills and, in reproducing them, to acquire mastery. Althusser places "conscientiously" in quotation marks ("pour s'acquitter 'consciencieusement' de leur tâche"), thus bringing into relief the way in which labor is moralized. The moral sense of s'acquitter is lost in its translation as "to perform": if the mastery of a set of skills is to be construed as an acquitting of oneself, then this mastery of savoir-faire

defends one against an accusation; quite literally, it is the accused declaration of innocence [. . .] To become a "subject" is thus to have been pre-
sumed guilty, then tried and declared innocent. Because this declaration is
not a single act but a status incessantly *reproduced*, to become a "subject"
is to be continuously in the process of acquitting oneself of the accusation
of guilt. It is to have become an emblem of lawfulness, a citizen in good
standing, but one for whom that status is tenuous, indeed, one who has
known – somehow, somewhere – what it is *not* to have that standing and,
hence, to have been cast out as guilty. Yet, because this guilt conditions the
subject, it constitutes the prehistory of the subjection to the law by which
the subject is produced.[46]

Mussolini seems to have known his guilty "prehistory" very well,
and he took great pains to make sure that the people did not forget that
his symbolic origin coincided with his sacrificial expulsion. While, on
the one hand, he was always in the process of acquitting himself by
"laboriously serving the people," he also never tired of reminding them
just how tenuous his innocence was and, hence, how important it was
that the status of his conscience be constantly examined and the argu-
ments belaboured (!) in a never ending deliberation. Evidence should
be presented and considered, but a *final* verdict should be delayed indefinitely. The single most damning piece of evidence that pointed towards his guilty conscience, and hence, to the necessity of providing
further proof of his innocence, was that Mussolini was, in fact, constantly betraying his principal injunction: that one should labour in
silence. The inescapable contradiction embedded in each presentation
of his own voice as the voice of conscience was precisely that his exemplary, performative modelling of discursive self-abnegation was, after
all, discursive. It is not coincidental that so many Mussolinian speeches
begin with a "confession" or "excuse" related to his failure to *fully* ad-
here to his own discursive proscription.

> Popolo di Vercelli! Camicie nere!
> Io avevo promesso di assistere alle cerimonie solenni di questa giornata
> senza pronunciare discorsi ed *ecco che io manco alla mia parola. ("Viva! Viva
> Mussolini!," rispondono molte voci dalla piazza).*
> Il vostro applauso così cordiale e fraterno – *continua il Presidente del Con-
> siglio – mi ha già assolto.* Del resto, *vi confesso* che sono io che desidero di
> parlare a voi.[47]

People of Vercelli! Blackshirts!

I had promised to partake of the solemn ceremonies today without making speeches, and *here I am reneging on my word*. (*"Long Live Mussolini!," reply many voices from the piazza*.)

Your warm and fraternal applause – *continues the Head of Goverment – has already acquitted me*. As a matter of fact, *I confess* that it is I who wish to speak with you.

We, of course, know from the previous chapter that Mussolinian confessions are invariably failed ones and that, likewise, his excuses are ruses meant to generate rather than defuse guilt. But what is worth noting in this particular case is the almost literalization of the function of guilt in grounding the never-ending process of acquittal necessary to maintain his exemplary status. His *mancanza* (which in Italian has a dual meaning of absence and fault) will stand as an originary void that the people will have both to occlude with their acquittal and acceptance and reproduce in their own daily sacrifices.[48] His confessional exposure and prompt absolution that he claims to have (always already!) received from the people of Vercelli in the next sentence are positioned as a surreptitious textual prehistory to the city's history of heroic offerings:

Voglio, dinanzi a tutta la nazione, mettere all'ordine del giorno la città di Vercelli (*"Bene! Bene!"*), non solo per le pagine stupende che essa ha scritto in ogni tempo nel libro della storia italiana, non solo per la mole imponente di eroismi che essa ha offerto alla guerra, non solo per le sue sedici mirabili medaglie d'oro, ma anche perché *quando il Governo ha chiesto qualche rinunzia, Vercelli ha accettato senza discutere*, con un altissimo senso di disciplina nazionale (*Bene! Bravo!*).[49]

As I stand in front of the nation, I want to place at the top of today's agenda the city of Vercelli (*"That's right!"*), not only for the marvellous pages of Italian history that she wrote in every epoch, not only for the impressive number of heroic deeds that she offered during the war, not only for its sixteen esteemed gold medals, but also because *when the Government has asked for some renunciation, Vercelli has accepted without discussion*, with a very high sense of national discipline. (*"That's right!"*).

Vercelli's history of renunciation in silence is grounded rhetorically by Mussolini's own prehistory of subjection – somehow, despite his best intentions, and somewhere in an indefinite discursive place, which in this case conveniently happens to be the preceding sentence, he was not in good standing before the law – in fact, he was literally standing guilty as sin before (spatially) the people, and before (temporally) the people absolved him.

That the Duce's absolution was never a final verdict but a provisional one that needed to be re-examined and reconfirmed over and over again is clear by the frequency with which his confessional mode appeared during his "consultations" with the people. This confessional propensity apparently so impressed one fascist writer that he described it in his *Mussolini immaginario (Imagining Mussolini)* as occurring at every occasion:

> *In ogni occasione il Duce chiama il popolo alla ribalta e gli si confessa* meglio che a tu per tu con i più intimi, meglio che a sè stesso, e gli narra le sue ansie e *spessissimo interroga*. Quello che apprende negli istanti di aperta *comunione* con la folla gli giova più di ogni altro consulto. Mille elezioni non arriverebbero a selezionare il pensiero del popolo come lo ha selezionato lui e come lo seleziona ogni giorno con sintesi portentosa nelle sue *prese di contatto*.[50]

> *On every occasion the Duce puts the people centre stage and confesses to them* more thoroughly than when he is face to face with his closest acquaintances, more thoroughly even than to himself, and often recounts his anxieties, and *very often interrogates them*. What he learns in the moments of open *communion* with the crowd is more useful to him than every other consultation. One thousand elections could not select the people's thoughts as he has selected them and as he selects them every day with portentous synthesis *while he makes contact*.

Social contracts lead to elections but the Duce obviously preferred the selective process of social contacts. The "portentous synthesis" that he models discursively in his "contacts" and that he naturally fails to fully achieve *at every turn*, succeeds nevertheless, in articulating its own rhetorical logic of ideological reproducibility. To successfully interrogate the fascist subject into being, through the reproduction of a fascist discursive style, the status of the Duce's conscience has to remain undecidable: only then can the Duce's presentations of his own voice as a "voice in unison" that *comprehends* the people truly function performatively as a rhetorical mirror of *mutual* summoning before the law – Why are you here? Because your conscience told you so!

The rhetoric of sacrifice sutured a fundamental fissure of fascist discourse. The function of a "voice in unison" that simultaneously suppressed and elicited speech was to provide not only an image of consensus and popular support of the Duce and the regime, but also a blueprint for the role of the individual in fascist society.

Ideal reproduction of fascist ideology occurred when fascist subjects shared a linguistic void that was not mere absence of speech but comprehension of the Duce in sacrificial silence, a productive, labour-intensive silence that required skill and discipline to be achieved and maintained. Within this logic, being a fascist was being a skilled worker who had mastered the task of self-abnegation and, hence, could reproduce it, model it for others, just like the Duce would, with exemplary conduct.

Sacrificial rhetoric articulated the image of a labouring body that acquired coherence – filled in, occluded the linguistic void – by disavowing its own autonomy of speech, hence, reproducing the image of an empty place-holder, a space of displacement and replacement where social contact would occur and the formation of the fascist subject could take place. This sacrificial matrix, or discursive blueprint, of ideological reproduction became ubiquitous during the ventennio and characterized countless speeches by Mussolini and other writers eager to imitate his style. It was, literally, a workable fiction for sanctioning a new proximity of individuals and social groups within the nation. However, the suture on which the articulation of a silent labouring body depended – the passage from displacement to replacement, the turn from alienation to embrace, from fragmentation to homogeneity – was not always entirely seamless. Tensions between populist and anti-populist strains did remain within fascist discourse and even in the rendition of its most zealous proponents, as we have seen with representations of the "disappearing" Duce by writers intent on reproducing his anti-rhetorical style, the portrayal of a linguistic void as a "proper place" to be occupied by the fascist man and masses often resulted in depictions of an eerie presence as absence: places and men that have been "vacated," emptied out.

It is to the rhetorical construction of this "proper place" as a sacrificial ideological landscape that established the "correct" proximity of groups within the nation that we now turn. As we will see in the next two chapters, it is a place where the incoherence of the labouring body is underscored with the portrayal of empty towns and fragmented workers in Gadda's case, and simplified men in Vittorini's.

The writings of the two authors provide a particularly fertile ground for tracing the contours of this discourse and not merely because sacrificial rhetoric occupied a prominent position in their literary as well as non-literary output. Their respective turns from fascism to anti-fascism allow us to probe the outer limits of this rhetorical field as it was folded in upon itself as a barrier against legibility of a former ideological allegiance, indeed, against legibility of a former self. In their anti-fascist writings, sacrificial rhetoric had an afterlife: it shaped a counter-discourse that remained, nevertheless, tethered to the terms and mechanisms it set out to oppose, hence, affording us the opportunity to look at them inside-out, more completely because also reversed.

The selected texts reflect this set of themes: the concern with sacrificial rhetoric and with the ways in which the authors' turn away from fascism is constructed and justified by its deployment. The proximity (or distance) that I seek to bring into view is, thus, not confined to the space between social groups within the nation but, equally as embedded in the narratives selected, one of personal "relocation" – between a past and present ideological position of the writers themselves – a discourse about *their own* proper place.

I also analyse non-literary texts of both authors that illustrate these issues from the perspective of detached and "objective" technical reporting or, at the other extreme, overt political advocacy. Read in conjunction with the literary works, these texts permit a broader understanding of the function of sacrificial rhetoric as well as of the malleability of the boundaries between different types of writing that facilitated the formation of an overarching ideological discourse of social mobility.

In Gadda's case, I focus on two literary works, *La cognizione del dolore* (*Acquainted with Grief*) (1938–41), which portrays sacrificial mothers (mothers whose sons died in war) as gatekeepers of social exchange (verbal and sexual) and *Eros e Priapo* (*Eros and Priapus*) (1967), which affords a further opportunity to clarify the relation between sacrificial figures and "lower parts" that governs the narrative of *La cognizione*, as well as providing an insight into Gadda's own peculiar and problematic brand of anti-fascism.

These texts enable me to revisit and further illustrate my analysis of Mussolini's speeches regarding the ways that the sacrificial moment of violence, of displacement, is linked to a moment of replacement, the acquiring of a fascist identity or entry into the fascist collectivity.

The intertextual project between novelistic and programmatic writings serves to clarify the extent to which Gadda's concerns about social mobility are underpinned by a long-standing extra-literary preoccupation with the creation and enforcement of physical distance among social groups. I examine Gadda's portrayal of social space in his description of development projects, urban and rural, which similarly construct the distance between social classes that are found in his literary writings.

I have adopted a similar intertextual strategy for the case of Vittorini. In the last chapter, I trace Vittorini's attempts to define the natural and essential qualities of the Italian people in the novel *Uomini e no* (*Men and Not Men*) (1945) as well as in journalistic writings that appeared in the critical political-cultural journals of the day. This choice of texts permits me to show how Vittorini's preoccupation with popular elevation contrasted with Gadda's and coincided with Mussolini's rhetoric regarding the regime's attempt to forge a more heroic and less bourgeois "new man."

I examine a series of articles in the journal *Il Politecnico*, which discussed politics and culture from an independent perspective of the left, with a particular focus on "Fascisti i giovani?" ("Are the young fascist?") in *Il Politecnico* no. 15 (5 January 1946). These articles, which sought to exculpate Italian youth from their fascist missteps, provide an appropriate counterpoint to the novel *Uomini e no*, as they deal with similar strategies of elision construed as simplification.

In *Uomini e no*, Vittorini's narrative deployed sacrificial expulsions and displacement of an old self as a way of producing a regenerative politics that, paradoxically, echoed Mussolini's efforts to keep the revolutionary zeal of the early fascist period in play as the regime aged.

3 Gadda's Sacrificial Topographies

During the 1930s and early 1940s, Gadda did not devote himself exclusively to literary matters. His background as an electrotechnical engineer, a profession he practised most intensively from 1925 to 1934, came into full display in several articles he penned for newspapers and journals, on a variety of technical and scientific subjects as diverse as, to name just a few, new construction projects in Vatican City, the utilization of mineral resources in Ethiopia, the military assets of combatant nations, and agrarian reform in Sicily.[1] While the geographical coordinates of the settings featured in his technical articles could not be more different, one particular landscape or ideological scene keeps emerging with insistence and little variation: places that have been cleared of the labouring masses.

In an article published in 1934 that praises the new landscaping, building, and renovation projects undertaken in Vatican City, following the Lateran Pacts of 1929 between the Catholic Church and the Italian fascist state, Gadda describes in glowing terms how new "structures of silence" (struttura di questo silenzio) have replaced the former "edilizia 'pittoresca'" ("picturesque" edifications).[2] To build the governor's palace and the train station, the "quartiere folkloristico" (folkloristic neighbourhood) that previously housed the "varia e povera folla d'umani" (sundried and poor human multitudes) had been almost entirely demolished.[3] Its former presence, however, framed as *memento mori* in the "before" photographs, was still lending significance to the completed clearing operation:

> Oltremodo significativi i documenti fotografici del mondo che fu, "*vestigia temporis acti.*" Ricordo delle stecconate, i cartelloni d'un circo, le *réclames*

d'un'acqua gazosa. Oggi l'ordine, il silenzio, ed i fiori. Davanti la garitta, in travertino, del Governatorato, il gendarme pontificio saluta le autorità, decorando la compiuta struttura di questo silenzio.[4]

Of great significance are the photographic documents of a bygone world, "*vestigia temporis acti.*" I remember the fences, the circus bill-boards, the advertisements for a mineral water. Today, order, silence, and flowers. In front of the travertine sentry box of the governor's pal-ace, the papal guard graces the completed structure of this silence as he hails the authorities.

The new orderly, silent space, graced by the guard hailing the passing authorities, had replaced the "folla di casupole e d'orticelli, d'urtiche e di siepi che ne intricavano e ne moltiplicavano la superficie" (a multi-tude of huts and vegetable patches, nettles, and hedges that crowded and expanded the surface).[5] The busy, loud pattern that seemed to be to multiplying in a disorderly and uncontrolled fashion had been muted by the elegance of travertine marble and flowers.

Gadda did not confine his penchant for depopulation schemes to ur-ban contexts. In 1941, he published two articles that lavished fulsome praise on the fascist law passed in 1940 to reform the Sicilian latifun-dia.[6] The creation of eight new *borghi* (villages), each dedicated to the memory of a soldier fallen in a past war or in the fascist revolution, was, it seems, noteworthy for its lack of rural labourers:

Il borgo deve esser visto come una cittadina sfollata: piccola capitale funzionalistica senza stento e senza gravezza di plebe. La plebe sana è nei campi, al lavoro. Ecco una idea chiara, delle più positivamente innovatrici.[7]

The *borgo* should be viewed as an evacuated town: a small functional capi-tal without hardship or the weight of plebs. Healthy plebs are in the fields, at work. Here is a clear idea, of the most positively innovative kind.

Here, again, we have the image of an empty or, more accurately, emp-tied town, suggesting a forceful process of relocation of the "plebs," rather than simple absence. The "clear idea" is made even clearer in the next sentence:

È assolutamente escluso che il "borgo rurale" della bonificazione sicula abbia a dar ricetto ai lavoratori della campagna: dal momento che questi lavoratori si vogliono strappare agli attuali villaggi, e si vogliono immettere e direi spargere nelle ricreate colonìe.[8]

It is absolutely out of the question that the "rural village" of the Sicilian reclamation could house the agricultural workers, since these workers are to be taken away from the current villages, reintroduced, and I would say, scattered in the recreated colonies.

Gadda reproduces the fascist rhetoric of silencing the labouring body. The violent connotation of the verbs *strappare/immettere/spargere* suggests a certain zeal in reproducing the image of workers' displacement that is, not surprisingly, counterbalanced by the compensatory logic of sacrifice. The workers sent to the new rural villages are chosen from a long list of families who have voluntarily applied for the special relocation project. The honour is accorded to those who have distinguished themselves not in agricultural tasks but in the magnitude of sacrifice in blood spilled on the battlefield:

Le famiglie mandate ne' poderi sono le piú numerose e capaci: quelle altresí che hanno conosciuto nel sangue de' loro uómini la disciplina della battaglia.[9]

The families sent to the farms are the largest and most able: those who have known through the blood of their men the discipline of battle.

The compensatory aspect of sacrifice is not new to us. As we have seen in the previous chapters, in fascist rhetoric the sacrificial moment of violence, of displacement, is inevitably linked to a moment of replacement, the acquiring of a fascist identity or entry into the fascist collectivity. To Gadda, however, the second part of the equation must have been deeply troubling. As I will show, he attempted to take it back or, rather, to "write it back" by structuring what is arguably his main literary creation, and certainly one of Italy's greatest novels, *La cognizione del dolore* (*Acquainted with Grief*), in opposition to it.[10] What is of interest here is not that Gadda engaged in the sort of rhetoric that we would consider fascist but that it is precisely on the question of sacrifice that his fascism textually unravels and is reversed into anti-fascism. The sacrificial suture that he dutifully reproduces in journal articles devoted to technical and scientific topics bursts at the seams in Gadda's creative narrative and in so doing allows us to see the binding mechanisms up close and provides a measure of their centrality in fascist discourse.

Acquainted with Grief

The problematic status of forewords, which Jacques Derrida often reminded us of, certainly applies to the preface of the 1963 edition of *La cognizione*. Referring to the novel's belated publishing date and lack of ending, the publisher (who is actually Gadda himself posing as the publisher) seems to be delivering an "absolution" of sorts to the author (hence, to himself). He tells us that the text was interrupted not by the author's lack of willingness, work plan, or moral responsibility, but by external factors that were internalized: the spectre and then the onset of war had "a un tal segno sconturbato l'animo dello scrivente da ostacolargli (fino al 1940) indi a rendergli a poco a poco inattuabile ogni sorta di prosa" (perturbed the soul of the writer to such an extent as to make it increasingly difficult (until 1940), and eventually impossible, to generate any kind of prose).[11]

Yet, the lack of an ending was not the only fragmentation in the output of this work. As the fictitious publisher quickly points out, *La cognizione* had previously appeared in instalments, between 1938 and 1941, in the journal *Letteratura*. The external/internal vicissitudes that surrounded this work, formed, it seems, the traumatic context that still "reverberated" out of the 1963 text: As Gadda put it,

> Il testo pervenuto alla stampa riverbera per altro le tragiche, livide luci o le insorgenze tenebrose d'anni precedenti e lontani; di fatti, di mutazioni che sono e saranno forse di sempre, interni ed esterni ai cuori, alle menti mortali.[12]

> The published text reverberates from the tragic, livid lights or dark contours of the preceding years now far away, of facts, events that are, and perhaps always will be, internal and external to hearts and minds.

Ironically, the publisher's efforts to provide a contextual frame in the preface, perhaps in an effort to contain the "livid" reverberations still being emitted from *La cognizione*, are undermined by his summoning of the author. After a conversational exchange between "the two," Gadda (the author) is given the last word of the preface: clearly a tactical mistake if textual containment was the goal. We are presented, instead, with a scene of intense acoustic reverberation: the sound of bells that had caused so much pain and aversion to the protagonist, Gonzalo, throughout the novel:

Vive angustiato del comune destino, della comune sofferenza. L'idea patria è chiara, ben circostritta, ben ferma, in lui: risponde a un fatto: a un sistema di fatti accertati. Le campane e i loro batocchi in tempesta aumentano il sovraccarico di tensione nervosa mentr'egli si raccoglie perché vuole, perché deve "tecnicamente" raccogliersi ne' suoi studi filosofici o algebrici.[13]

He lives anguished by the common destiny, by the common affliction. The idea of the homeland is clear, well defined, firmly grounded in his being: It responds to a fact, to a system of proven facts. The bells and their storming clappers increase the overload of nervous tension while he gathers himself because he wants, because he must, "technically" collect himself in his philosophical and algebraic studies.

As if to provide even less closure and more textual reverberation, Gadda attaches to the last sentence a lengthy fragment in the guise of a footnote that describes a strange "battaglia dei battagli" – a battle between the clappers (*battagli*) of the town bells and the eardrums of the inhabitants who are subjected to the relentless acoustic assaults. The bells are described in physical as well as mechanical terms: they have ears that resemble wheels on the sides of cannons, and a gaping mouth (*bocca preposturale*) that shapes and directs the slow waves as it swings laboriously from side to side. The wind carries back and forth their roaring vibration, dispersing it over fields and houses. The battle of the clappers and eardrums is not confined to the introductory footnote, and it immediately spills over into the novel's main text.

The acoustic vibrations from the bell-tower that echo through the hills of the surrounding countryside are, indeed, a central preoccupation of Gonzalo Pirobutirro d'Eltino, the protagonist of *La cognizione*. They create a disturbance in his psyche so overbearing that the reader at first suspects the presence of a pathological condition or perhaps of a traumatic event that in some way resurfaces upon hearing the bells.

The clues pointing to past trauma in the life of the protagonist are, in fact, not hard to find. Having come back from the war years earlier, he lives in self-imposed isolation in the family villa with his old and frail mother, whom he frequently terrorizes with outbursts of uncontrollable anger. Episodes of rage directed at his mother are interspersed throughout the novel, and they have given critics ample material for a reading of the story in psychoanalytical terms.[14] The famous scene of Gonzalo stepping over the portrait of his father seems an obvious indication of an oedipal conflict. Gonzalo's recriminations about his mother's stinginess in demonstrating affection during his childhood, and his jealousy for the attention that in her old age she lavishes on the servants' children, are all elements that support such a reading.

Less obvious and more deeply embedded in the fabric of *La cognizione* is the articulation of an economy of failed martyrdom that by its very nature cannot be brought to proper closure or integration within the novel's ideological landscape. As if to underscore such impossibility, lack of closure stands, in the novel, as a symptomatized figure for the pain and discomfort of unrecognized sacrifice, of a loss that cannot accrue ideological value, that cannot find a proper resting place in the home or the nation. If the veterans in Gadda's article on the Sicilian latifundia had been rewarded upon return from the war, compensated for blood spilled in battle by being selected for occupation of the new rural *borghi*, the theme of *un*compensated sacrifice is central to *La cognizione* and, indeed, it is set up in its very first pages:

Negli anni seguenti al 1924 vi erano perciò, tanto nel Maradagàl quanto nel Parapagàl, dei reduci di guerra, alcuni dei quali appartenevano e appartengono tutt'ora alla benemerente categoria dei mutilati: e zoppicavano, e avevano sul volto cicatrici, o un arto irrigidito, o erano privi di un piede, o di un occhio. Non è infrequente, nei piú ciaccolosi caffè del Maradagàl o del Parapagàl, venir fissati da un occhio di vetro. Di taluni reduci si sapeva che erano stati feriti, per quanto non apparisse; le cicatrici, nascoste dai panni, venivano cosí defraudate della quota di ammirazione a cui avevano diritto. Vi erano poi anche dei sordi di guerra.[15]

In the years after 1924, therefore, both in Maradagàl and in Parapagàl, there were war veterans, some of whom belonged and still belong to the worthy category of the disabled: and they limped, or had scars on their faces, or a stiffened limb, or they lacked a foot or an eye. It is not unusual, in the more squalid cafés of Maradagàl or Parapagàl, to be stared at by a glass eye. Of the veterans, it was known they had been wounded, though this wasn't evident; the scars, hidden by clothing, were thus cheated of the meed of admiration to which they were entitled. There were also some deaf from the war.

The fictional landscape of *La cognizione* is not an ideologically neutral place. It is marked, at least in the eyes of the protagonist, by blackness: "'Ma via, signor Gonzalo!' fece il medico. 'Lei vede nero anche il sole!'" ("'Come, come, Señor Gonzalo!' the doctor said. 'Everything looks black to you, even the sun!'").[16] We find countless references to this colour throughout the novel and one in particular that dispels any doubt as to what country is similarly colour-coded. The landscape of the Maradàgal looks a lot like the ideological landscape of fascist Italy: a portrait in "livid" colours of bold towers, black peaks, and crowds:[17]

> Dietro *nere cime* il sole improvvisamente risfolgora: i suoi raggi si frangono sulla scheggiatura del crinale e se ne diffondono al di qua verso il Prado, scesi a dorare le brume della terra, di cui emergono colline, tra i velati laghi. *Qualcosa di simile, per il nome e piú per l'aspetto, al manzoniano Resegone.* Ivi alcuna piú *ardita torre, (con mattutine campane), lacera il velo dorato delle nebbie;* il vapore, un bioccolío bianco, dilunga in un filo; si smarrisce; sibila per lontani rimandi tra le colline, e rigiri: porta la stipata, *nera folla* degli uomini poveri, che ne traboccano verso gli opifici e le fabbriche o, sul poco fiume, il maglio.[18]

> Beyond *black peaks* the sun suddenly shines: its rays break against the ragged line of the mountain and are spread beyond toward Prado, descending to gild the earth's mists, from which hills emerge among the shrouded lakes. *Something similar, in name and even more in appearance, to Manzoni's Resegone.* There, *some bolder tower (with matutinal bells) rips the gilded veil of the fogs;* the mist, a white tufting, stretches out in a thread, is lost, whistles through distant echoes among the hills, and twists: it bears the crammed, *black crowd* of poor men, who spill from it toward the factories and the plants or, on the scant river, the smith's drop hammer.

Not only is black the predominant colour that envelops the poor workers of a region of lakes and mountains bearing a striking resemblance to the one famously described by Alessandro Manzoni, but this blackness is placed within clear chronological coordinates in the very first sentence of the novel, telling us that the story about to unravel takes place "in those years, between 1925 and 1933."[19] Furthermore, the local association in charge of patrolling the neighbourhoods at night (*Nistitúos provinciales de vigilancia para la noche*) describes its services with words that seem taken out of a Mussolinian speech with the familiar refrain of "going to the people": "all'attività della nostra casa che vuole andare incontro ai bisogni del popolo" (the activity of our firm whose sole aim is to satisfy people's needs).[20]

Mother is very much a part of this black landscape. She looks like the tower that contains the infamous bells, and like the tower, her ominous presence haunts Gonzalo: "Un sogno . . . strisciatomi verso il cuore . . . come insidia di serpe. Nero. [. . .] là . . . nera, muta, altissima: come rivenuta dal cimitero. (A dream . . . wriggling toward my heart . . . like the treachery of a serpent. Black. [. . .] There . . . black, silent, very tall: as if she had come back from the cemetery).[21]

As if to underscore her full objectification as part of the ideological landscape, Mother herself comes to doubt her personhood as she takes stock of the tragic fate of her two sons. The youngest has died years before in the war against Parapagàl, and Gonzalo, the first-born who came back from the war, appears completely alienated from his surroundings. Mother's face is petrified by angst as she looks back at her maternal experience, recoiling with dread every time the bells mark the hour, when they release their strokes into the void as a "memento innecessario, crudele" (an unnecessary, cruel reminder).[22] The bells from the tower seem cruel to Mother because they are a constant reminder of what she can no longer do: reproduce. They are replacing her as "matrix" of sacrificial material, as producer of future martyrs – a role that had shaped her self-image to such an extent that "non poteva piú pensare a una madre se non come a un groppo di disumano dolore superstite ai sacrificati" (she could no longer conceive of a mother except as a lump of inhuman grief surviving the victims).[23]

The genital/reproductive function of the bells could not be more clearly stated. The pride of the community, they issue their "joyous invitation" through the air with an obscene oscillating motion as they turn "their inside out": "tripudio di arrovesciate, pazze, propagandanti Fede, campane: dalla torre [. . .] Il batacchio-clitoride era la gloria, enorme, del paese festante" (jubilation of upturned, mad Faith-propagating church bells: from the tower [. . .] The clitoris-clapper was the glory, enormous, of the rejoicing village).[24]

Her reproductive days now over, Mother finds comfort, however, in the bittersweet realization that it is now other people's turn to continue the sacrificial offerings: "Si considerava alla fine della sua vicenda. Il sacrificio era stato consumato" (She considered herself at the end of her vicissitude. The sacrifice had been consummated).[25] She had fulfilled her role by giving her beloved young son to the state, stoically placing "her flesh and blood" at its disposal. At the end of her sacrificial journey, she is overcome by grief of that most painful transaction, and yet, almost relieved of having paid in full her dues to society.

Failed Martyrdom

If the sound of the bell-tower is cruel to the mother, it is utterly un-
bearable to her son Gonzalo. The reason for this seemingly inexplicable
aversion can be found, I would argue, by examining the sacrificial configurations articulated in the novel. The protagonist Gonzalo is, first
and foremost, a failed martyr. Unlike his younger brother, he came back
from the war, and he came back without visible signs of combat. No
scars, no loss of limb, nothing to show for his efforts. His father had
at least lost an eye and an ear in war but Gonzalo seemed unscathed.
Even his mother could not quite process the fact that one day he simply
came back home, and her reaction upon seeing him reappear had been
more of disbelief than joy: "Oh! il 'suo' Gonzalo! Era troppo evidente
che l'arsenale della gloria aveva rifiutato di prenderlo in carico" (Oh!
"her" Gonzalo! It was too obvious that the arsenal of glory had refused
to place him on its roster).[26] Her disappointment at the sight of her son,
in fact, can be traced back to his infancy, when looking at his little body
she saw a "fallito sperimento delle viscere" (failed experiment of her
womb).[27] His return from the war had similarly failed to produce a
positive recognition from the community.

The/her "arsenal of glory" had somehow failed her son: what came
out of it was unworthy of recognition. This sense of failure is not lost
on Gonzalo who hates the bell-tower, I would argue, precisely because
it keeps on producing subjects worthy of recognition – that is, able to
enter into a sacrificial economy of exchange. Their loss is "repaid" by
recognition and often by more tangible rewards as well: a disability
pension, a monetary translation, as it were, of that recognition. Gonzalo, on the other hand, feels constantly pressured to compensate others and has come to despise all the people (servants, in particular) who,
"like parasites," seem intent on draining his household financially.
They continually "invade" the confines of the family villa with what he
perceives to be unreasonable demands:

> Pirobutirro è pagare, è offrire, è dare, è dar via . . . Via, via, via! Tutto quello
> che si può dar via, dare agli altri . . . ai cari altri . . . E se il nipotino crepa,
> dopo una indigestione di fichi e di cioccolatini, sono io ad averne la colpa.
> E dovrò pagare, come sempre.

> Pirobutirro means paying, donating, giving, giving away . . . away,
> away, away! Everything that can be given away, given to others . . . to

the beloved others. And if the grandson dies, of indigestion after the figs and the chocolates, I'm the one to be blamed. And I'll have to pay, as always.[28]

Outside the walls of the villa, a physical and psychological line of demarcation that separates his possessions, is an imaginary world of parasitical beings bent on trespassing and encroaching on Gonzalo's fragile inner equilibrium. The outside world does not leave him in peace: it voraciously demands that he give what is his, and he feels besieged by those imperatives. Like boundaries in general or lack thereof, personal pronouns are problematic to Gonzalo. On one occasion, he launches into a lengthy, and rather hallucinatory, tirade against them, accusing them to be "pidocchi del pensiero" (lice of thought.) They somehow contaminate the thought process because they can easily "coagulate" and affect the "I" – the most problematic pronoun of all.[29]

The denunciation of pronouns that in the novel goes on uninterrupted for four pages seems at first bizarre and just another way to emphasize the fragility of Gonzalo's psychological state. It appears decidedly less incidental when we recall the discursive function of pronominal exchanges in fascist rhetoric that I have described in the previous chapter. For Mussolini to rhetorically function as the "one" he has to function as a pronominal rhetorical relay that allows him to slide into all pronominal positions, or as Pinkus put it, to undergo a "process of infinitization" in which fragmentation is understood as multiplication.[30]

For the Duce's discursive self-sacrificial stance to be reproduced by the fascist subject – a subject whose voice has to echo the Duce's voice – a fundamental exchangeability of discursive and, indeed, pronominal, roles has to obtain. The subject-master category has to function as an empty place-holder that the Duce and the masses can alternatively occupy.

Gonzalo's hallucinated indictment of pronouns is, in fact, an indictment of the failure of this process to fully include him in its compensatory mechanisms of exchange. He has been unable to master the terms of his own subjection to authority, and he is constantly reminded of his imperfect status by the activity of the bell-tower, the ideological matrix that, unlike his frail, old mother, keeps on reproducing perfect subjects, indeed, *the* subject of *every* pro-*position*:

"Il solo fatto che noi seguitiamo a proclamare . . . io, tu . . . con le nostre bocche screanzate . . . con la nostra avarizia di stitici predestinati alla putrescenza . . . io, tu . . . questo solo fatto . . . io, tu . . . denuncia la bassezza della comune dialettica . . . e ne certifica della nostra impotenza a predicar nulla di nulla, . . . dacché ignoriamo . . . il soggetto di ogni proposizione possibile . . . ."

". . . Quale sarebbe? . . . ."

". . . È inutile ch'io lo nomini invano . . . *Quello che ha appena finito di venir fuori di là . . . ,"* col volto significò la torre, *"dalla matrice* di quelle mènadi scaravoltate a pancia all'aria . . . col batacchio per aria . . . Bestie pazze! per cui ho patito la fame da bimbo, la fame!

Cinquecento pesos! cinquecento: di munificenza pirobutirrica: cinquecento pesos! [. . .] perché il caro batacchio venisse buono . . . buono agli inni e alla gloria . . . il batacchio . . . a intronare la cara villa, con le care patate, nel caro Lukones . . . a romperci i timpani per quarant'anni![31]

"The mere fact that we go on proclaiming 'I, you' with our uncouth mouths . . . with our avarice of the constipated, predestined to putrescence, I, you – this very fact, I, you – reveals the baseness of common dialectics . . . and guarantees our impotence in preaching anything about anything . . . since we are ignorant of . . . of the subject of every possible proposition –"

"Which would be?"

"It's useless for me to take its name in vain. *What just finished coming out of there" – with his face he indicated the tower –"from the matrix of those maenads hurled bellyfirst into the air* . . . with clapper hanging out. Mad beasts! And I went hungry because of them, as a child, hungry!

Five hundred pesos! Five hundred: Pirobutirro munificence: five hundred pesos! [. . .] so that the dear clapper would turn out well . . . good for anthems and glory . . . the clapper . . . to deafen the dear villa, with the dear potatoes, in dear Lukones . . . to break our eardrums for forty years!"

What comes out of the tower-matrix is an exemplary subject that can occupy every discursive position – even the position of its own generative source: mouth and vagina have lost their fixed bodily position as the upper and lower properties of the mother-tower-matrix and are seemingly interchangeable. Out of this rearranged and vocalized genital opening comes an entity that reproduces itself acoustically: an intermittent and fragmentary sound-matrix that emits strokes, vibrations, and waves and that is able to proliferate through the air precisely because its parts can be unhinged from their fixed location and redistributed to form new configurations. Fragmentation and unhinging do not, however, imply castration in this case. On the contrary, they are a figure of multiplication through the reassignment of Mother's parts *onto a phallus*. This is not, technically speaking, a phallic mother, but rather a "towering" phallus that has incorporated Mother's genitals.[32] Notice how, in the famous passage that follows, the sound-matrix is transformed into a phallic Enormous Bronze despite the fact that the bells on its top are feminine androgynous bacchantes who proffer their "entrails" to every grey-haired offerer:

Intanto, dopo dodici enormi *tocchi*, le campane del mezzogiorno avevano messo nei colli, di là dai tègoli e dal fumare dei camini, il pieno frastuono della gloria. Dodici *gocce*, come di bronzo immane, celeste, eran seguitate a cadere una via l'altra, indeprecabili, sul lustro fogliame del banzavóis: anche se inavvertite al groviglio dell'aspide, molle, terrore maculato di tabacco. Vincendo robinie e cicale, e carpini, e tutto, *le matrici del suono si buttarono alla propaganda di sé*, tutt'a un tratto: che dirompeva nella cecità infinita della luce. Lo stridere delle bestie di luce venne sommerso in una *propagazione di onde di bronzo*: irraggiàrono la campagna del sole, il disperato andare delle strade, le grandi, verdi foglie, laboratori infiniti di clorofilla: *cinquecento lire di onde! cinquecento, cinquecento!* basta basta, signor Francisco, ma questo qui non fa male . . . . *di onde, di onde! dalla torre*: dal campanile color calza, artefice di quel baccano tridentino. Furibonda sicínnide, offerivano il viscerame o poi lo rivoltavano contro monte, a onde, tumulto del Signore materiato, baccanti androgíne alla lubido municipalistica d'ogni incanutito offerente.

  Arrovesciate nella stoltezza e nella impudicizia, esibivano alternatamente i batocchi, come pistilli pazzi, pesi, o per la fame del povero la inanitá incaparbita della cervice: e la ruota a fianco ogniduna, intricava il disegno: ed erano i convovoli del *Bronzo Enorme*, cui arrovesciasse bufera di demenza. *Ebbre di suono altalenarono un pezzo a evacuare la gloria; gloria! gloria! di cui eran satolle: a spandere in ogni campo quella annunciazione clamorosa*, d'un po' di puchero. E di chiquoréa tritata, condita con l'olio di linosa.[33]

Meanwhile, after twelve enormous *strokes*, the bells of noon had sent into the hills, beyond the tiles and the smoking of the chimneys, the full uproar of glory. Twelve *drops*, as if of monstrous bronze, celestial, had gone on falling, one after the other, inexorable, on the shiny leaves of the banzavóis – even if unperceived in the tangle of the asp, soft, tobacco-speckled terror. Overcoming locusts and cicadas, and hornbeams, and everything, *the matrices of sound were flung into self-propaganda*, all of a sudden: which burst forth in the infinite blindness of the light. The chirping of the animals of light was submerged in a *propagation of bronze waves*: they irradiated the sun's country, the desperate progress of the roads, the great green foliage, infinite laboratories of chlorophyll: *five hundred lire of waves, of waves! Five hundred, five hundred!* Enough, enough Señor Francisco, but this can't do any harm – *of waves, waves! From the tower*: from the stocking-colored spire, artificer of that Trentine din. Furious Sicinnis, they proffered their entrails and then turned them back against the mountain, in waves, tumult of the Lord made matter, androgynous bacchantes at the municipal lubido of every gray-haired offerer. Upturned in folly and shamelessness, they displayed alternately their clappers, like mad heavy pistils, or to the poor man's hunger, the obstinate inanity of the cervix; and the wheel, at each one's side, made the pattern more complex; and they were the morning glories of the *Enormous Bronze*, upset by stormy gusts of madness. *Drunk with sound they swung for quite a while in evacuating their glory! glory ! glory! with which they were glutted: to spread in every field that clamorous annunciation*, of a bit of puchero and of chopped chiquoréa, seasoned with linseed oil.

Marking "high noon" are the tower's twelve strong *tocchi* (a term of multiple valence in Italian: touches, strokes, beats, or tolls), followed by emissions that land on the lush vegetation of the surrounding hills. So far the phallic depiction is clear. But complicating the otherwise crisp rendition of what we might call Gadda's narrative "money shot," is the number of close-ups of female genitals edited into the panoramic "long shot": they momentarily unsettle the clear male designation of the organ that dominates the landscape. The Enormous Bronze, it seems, has female genitals on top that are exposed in the furious, undulating motion of the skirtlike bells. The androgynous bacchantes go into such an exhibitionist frenzy that their cervix is displayed as a lure to the municipal male bystanders, who become the listeners/spectators, and potential (grey-haired) offerers in the acoustic transaction (five hundred lire of waves). The bacchantes – drunk with sound and swinging – are depicted as the source, not the receivers of "glorious evacuation" throughout the countryside. But the fact that this sound-matrix is incorporated into, or more exactly, *onto* the male organ, has the effect of underscoring the ultimate male dominance of this particularly rich scene.

Robert S. Dombroski has correctly linked the phallic function of this image in *La cognizione* to another famous Gaddian depiction: In *Eros e Priapo* (*Eros and Priapus*), a scathing pamphlet against fascism published in 1967, wherein the Duce's rhetorical outpourings are described as ejaculations on the heads of his adoring listeners.[34] The similarities between the two passages are, indeed, remarkable and, I believe, worthy of renewed attention – for in both cases the acoustic reproduction of sacrifice is the central feature of the landscape depicted:

Eretto ne lo spasmo su zoccoli tripli . . . il somaro dalle gambe a ìcchese aveva gittato a Pennino ed ad Alpe il suo raglio. Ed Alpe e Pennino *echeggiarlo, hì-hà, hì-hà, riecheggiarlo infinitamente hè-jà, hè-jà,* per infinito cammino de le valli . . . a ciò che tutti, tutti!, i quarantaquattro millioni della malòrsega, *lo s'infilassero ognuno nella camera timpanica dell'orecchio suo,* satisfatto e pagato in ogni sua prurigo, edulcorato, inlinito, imburrato, imbesciamellato, e beato.[35]

Erect in its spasm upon triple-high hoofs . . . the knock-kneed donkey had flung its braying to the Apennines and to the Alps. And Alps and Apennines *to echo, hee-haw, hee-haw, and re-echo it endlessly, hee-haw, hee-haw,* through the endless windings of their valley . . . so that everyone, every single one! The forty-four million participants in this disgrace, *might each stick it into the tympanic chamber of his ear,* and have every itch and desire satisfied and fulfilled, sweetened, smeared with ointment, buttered all over, covered in béchamel and beatified.

Standing erect on triple hooves, the Duce – whom Gadda calls a knock-kneed donkey – launches his "bray" through the Alps and Apennines, reaching every hill and especially the valleys.[36] The forty-four million inhabitants of Italy facilitate the reception of his "slick" message into their own physical valleys, their tympanic chambers, and promptly echo the bray. The echo continues to bounce back and forth and, in the repetition of this exchange, the donkeyish *hì-hà, hì-hà* becomes the fascist salutation *eja, eja, alalà* (*hè-jà, he-jà*).[37] The cast of characters also includes priests who are thanking the Omnipotent for his gifts and housewives who, that evening, feel "very hopeful" while fortifying the sauce with celery.

Indeed, the metaphoric of verbal and sexual climax operates in both passages, as Dombroski puts it, "nel transferimento del potere spermatico e seminale degli organi genitali alla retorica virulenta di

Mussolini che eiacula sulle teste dei suoi adoratori" (in the transfer of the seminal and spermatic power of the genital organs to the virulent rhetoric of Mussolini who ejaculates on the heads of his worshippers).[38] But there is also another link between the two passages that points to the central role of sacrifice as an organizing principle in the narrative economy of La cognizione. In both cases, reproduction occurs acoustically: in and through the ear of the listener, or as the second passage makes clear, echo-ustically, by reproducing the sound and sending it back to the eliciting source.

Gadda here provides us with a colourful, albeit thoroughly misogynist, rendition of the fascist rhetorical configuration that I have analysed in the previous chapter. The echoing mirror-circuit between Mussolini and the people depends on the acceptance of a self-effacing, "silent," and laborious role on the part of the fascist subject: "I migliori fascisti ... obbediscono in silenzio e lavorano con disciplina" (The best fascists ... obey in silence and work with discipline).[39]

A conscientious imitatio-Ducis is an integral part of this process for it provides a performative blueprint of sacrificial acceptance and reproduction: "Vi ricordo che in pace e in guerra una cosa sola supremamente vale, decisiva spesso, trascinatrice sempre: l'esempio" (Let me remind you that in peace as in war only one thing has supreme value, is often decisive, and always compelling: the example).[40]

But the temptation to turn the people's ideological acceptance into an image of female sexual receptivity must have been too strong for Gadda to resist.[41] The text of Eros e Priapo clearly acknowledges the centrality of sacrificial rhetoric in the production, and indeed, reproduction, of the exemplary Duce: Gadda calls him Modellone (All-purpose model).[42] But while Gadda mocks and debunks sacrificial reproduction in it, he also simultaneously joins the misogynist conception of a female universe divided into mothers and whores. Gadda's ferocious invective against sacrificial rhetoric is at the expense of women since in his iconoclastic fervour of reversals he ends up conflating mothers with whores. Not exactly the turn that one would wish political parody to take, even if we consider that it allows Gadda to deliver the ultimate Italian "male" insult to the Duce: to call his mother a whore for her role as sacrificial matrix-in-chief.

Egli si autopromosse e si antepose ad epònimo della patria e del popolo che soli il sacrifizio de' sacrificati aveva e il travaglio de' travagliati arebbe, per quanto fortunosamente, portata a salvezza. E questo per esser venuto a luce, secondo il poeta D'Annunzio, con testa di ciuco e codonzolo di verro. Per aver "sofferto" cioè imbroccato al malcantone la nottivaga da du' lire che gli versò nel cervello i destini imperiali della patria.

He self-promoted and estabished himself as eponym of the fatherland and of the people that would only be saved, albeit fortuitously, with the sacrifice of the sacrificed and the labor of the laboring. And this because he came into this world, according to the poet D'Annunzio, with the head of an ass and the tail of a boar. Because he "suffered" when he took the wrong way with that tawdry woman of the night who flooded his mind with the imperial destiny of the fatherland.[43]

Having established the "primordial exchange" that produced the *Modellone*, Gadda continues his invective against mothers and the sacrificial transactions that they engage in. The raging Bacchantes of *La cognizione* resurface here with another name used to identify Dionysus' companions: *Mimallones*, which a clever play on the Italian word for big female breasts, *mammellone*, turns into *mammillone*. Gadda links the drunken ease with which they make their "offerings" to narrow-minded protection of their relative economic position. What is exchanged here is "movement" for stability: their frenzied "sacrificial activity" safeguards the constant interest of the household.

Un disinteresse economico quasi assoluto contraddistingue i loro nitriti di mammillone malgré-elles, ove non si voglia portare in conto l'interesse "statico" del saper rispettate dalla possidente le posizioni economiche di sua casata. Che questo o altro modo dell'interesse, comunque, sussista almeno in alcune, lo dimostra la facilità ebbra e quasi la voluttà con cui elle offerirono il loro sangue alla bella guerra, "orgogliose" di barattare il cadavere del figlio (del marito, del fratello) con un cenno di assenso del tumescente Giove Ottimo Massimo che le chiamava madri spartane, madri romane, e simili baggianate. Guiderdone alla pena antica de' lor visceri, schermo alla tenebra repentina che aveva avviluppato il vivente sorriso d'un figlio era un "presente!" ugolato da un federalastro in orbace, era un diploma di morte con ghirigori, un dischetto di metallo appuntato loro sul seno, debitamente nero, dal Generale Fessetti.[44]

An almost absolute economic disinterest characterizes their neighs of *mammillone malgré-elles*, unless we consider their "constant" interest, as proprietors, in knowing that the economic position of the household is respected. That one or the other type of interest is present in at least some of them, is demonstrated by the drunken ease, bordering on voluptuosness, with which they offered their blood to the beautiful war, "proud" to barter the corpse of their son (husband, brother) for a slight aknowledgment of the tumescent Zeus Optimum Maximum that called them Spartan mothers, Roman mothers, and similar idiocies. Indemnity for the ancient tribulations of their wombs, screen to the sudden darkeness that had enveloped the lively smile of a son, was a sound of "present!" intoned by a black-clad officer, was an ornate death diploma, a small metal disk placed on their bosom, appropriately black, by General Foolish.

If in *Eros e Priapo*, Gadda insists on, and indulges in, sarcastically debunking the regime's sacrificial rhetoric, a rhetoric that he had, in fact, faithfully reproduced in his technical journal articles, it is because, I would argue, in *La cognizione* the sacrificial accounts had not been settled: they had, in fact, remained painfully open to the protagonist Gonzalo. The narrative of *La cognizione* betrays an almost obsessive preoccupation with sacrificial figures and the motility of their body parts, with sites open to exchange, movement, and proliferation. Not coincidentally, the bells "drunk with sound" that discharge their glory through the countryside, are engaged in a "clamorous annunciation": a not so subtle and irreverent Gaddian reference to the Annunciation delivered by the archangel Gabriel to the Virgin Mary, heralding the arrival of the ultimate sacrificial figure, Jesus.

The text of *La cognizione* affords us a glimpse into the Gaddian logic of targeting mothers as sacrificial propagators. The suspicion that there must be something else operating in conjunction with misogynist sentiment is confirmed by the pivotal role of Gonzalo's mother in the novel's economy. She is, literally, the gatekeeper of the Pirobutirro household, determining the movement of people and things in and out of it.[45] Gonzalo resents her readiness to compensate, monetarily and with affection, the various labourers and lowly peons (as Gadda calls the Pirobutirros' servants) that gravitate around the house. But what really enrages him the most is their constant physical presence in the house – the willingness with which Mother lets them in. Every entry they make he perceives as a violation of the family's space and privacy, an intrusion into his property and into his most prized possession – his brain – that causes economic and psychic *downfall*. His upper organ, the site of rationality and introspection, is delivered a sensory attack from below, by the sight of the peons' feet, the sound that their multiplying *zoccoli* (in Italian both hoofs and clogs) make in entering his house, and the sound/smell of the belch that announces their arrival.

> La turpe invasione della folla . . . Gli zoccoli, i piedi: nella casa che avrebbe dovuto essere sua . . . I calcagni color fianta, i diti, divisibili per 10, con le unghie . . . e la piscia del cane vile, pulcioso, con occhio destro pieno di marmellata, dentro cui sguazzavano cicík e ciciàk le piante quadrupedanti di quegli zoccoli. Un rutto enorme, inutilità gli parvero gli anni, dopo le scempiaggini di cui s'erano infarciti i suoi maggiori.[46]

> The indecent invasion of the crowd . . . The clogs, the feet, in the house that should have been his . . . The horse-shit-coloured heels, the toes, divisible by ten, with the nails . . . And the piss of the cowardly dog, flea-ridden, its right eye full of jam, where splat splot the quadruped soles of those clogs slopped. An enormous belch, futility, the years seemed to him, after the idiocies with which his elders had stuffed themselves.

Below are the animal parts, the divisible and multiplying feet of peasants that in the clamouring of their clogs assume the animalesque semblance of hoofs. "Splat splot . . . enormous belch": the proliferation of feet that is so often described in *La cognizione* is yet another rearrangement of parts into a "vocalized below," just as the maternal genitals had been vocalized by their placement on top of the phallic bell tower.[47] It is not a stretch at this point to surmise that the reason why Mother is transformed into a whore with her belly in the air is because, in Gadda's narrative, she stands for fascism's populist appeal. She invites the multitudes in, just like Gonzalo's mother invites the clogging peons into the house. The animalesque consortium that they engage in is, needless to say, akin to an echoing chamber, with the multitudes belching back their response to the call from the upturned bell-tower matrix. Just like the sound of the tower is assigned a provenance from "below," the sound that comes out of the mouths of the peons originates from a lower body part – their stomach:

> Il consorzio: come lo amavano mamma e papà, dentro casa, con zoccoli dei cari peoni e peonesse; gutturavano le loro variazioni, rutti indoeuropei al 100/100 dopo tripudio di arrovesciate, pazze, propagandanti Fede, campane: dalla torre.[48]

The congregation: as Papà and Mama loved it, in the house, clogs of the dear peons, male and female; they gutturalized their variations, a hundred per cent Indo-European belches after jubilation of upturned, mad Faith-propagating church bells: from the tower.

We have already encountered a similarly animalesque consortium in the passage that I quoted earlier from *Eros e Priapo*, where the Duce was standing on his triple hoofs issuing his asinine bray to the echoing public. It is to this strange consortium of bodily parts and their sounds that we now turn.

Sacrificial Exposures

Troping Gadda's fictional publisher, we could say that the presence of these bodily fragments extends beyond *La cognizione* for their livid re-verberations still pulsate in *Eros e Priapo*, transformed into dark, low, impulses. What is of interest to us here, however, is not a simple inter-textual tracing of a particular thematic element, but rather, the strategic deployment of those fragments to form a particular narrative configu-ration. Their textual position in relation to "voice" sheds light on the crucial role of sacrifice in the *discursive* organization of the fascist body as well as providing us with clues as to why sacrificial figures appear to be the main target of Gadda's anti-fascist invective.

In *Eros e Priapo*, Gadda openly condemns fascism on the grounds that it represented the victory of libidinal instincts over the rational Logos, and he conveniently illustrates this high and low divide by placing women's genitals – centre stage, as it were – in a lewd scene turned tragic. The Bacchantic women resurface, yet again, with another one of their names, *Bassarides*, that plays with the Italian word for low, *basso/a*. For twenty years, lustful *Bassaride* and her "needs" had dominated na-tional events by casting aside the sublimations and gentle overtures of Logos:

> Eros nelle sue forme inconscie e animalesche, ne' suoi aspetti infimi, e non
> ne' sublimati e ingentiliti, ha dominato la tragica scena. Vent'anni. Logos
> è stato buttato via di scena dalla Bassaride perché inetto a colmare la di lei
> pruriginosa necessità.[49]

Eros, in its unconscious and animalesque forms, in its lowest manifes-tations, not even sublimated and ennobled, dominated the tragic scene.

Twenty years. Logos was cast aside by Bassaride because it was inept at satisfying her prurient needs.

Gadda's strategic relegation of women, and sacrificial mothers, in particular, to the low end of the moral resistance spectrum, masks, I believe, a preoccupation with another kind of degraded national scene, one that he sees occurring during the *ventennio*, and that is also centred on exchanges between high and low, or more precisely, between those who are above and those who are below in the social hierarchy: fascism's claim to represent the voice of the people, and the people's acceptance of this claim.

The exchangeability of speaking (subject/master) positions that, as we have seen in the previous chapter, is articulated by positing an echoing circuit between Duce and masses, is represented by Gadda as a form of inferior communication that corrupts the Logos by bringing it down to the level of incoherent, animal-like, sound. We could agree with him on the fact that the "silencing" of the masses that was articulated by the fascist echoing scene was a form of inferior communication, but once we take a closer look at the technical specifications that Gadda-the-Electrotechnical-Engineer attaches to the fall of the logos, the agreement begins to be qualified.

In *Eros e Priapo*, Gadda informs us that the spiritual tension or work energy of the collectivity can be dissipated through short-circuiting, that is, it can suddenly fall to the ground – as it did during fascism, when the young and unskilled (that is, those who should be below in the social hierarchy) were allowed to advance socially and economically based on their ideological merits and not their professional expertise – or what he calls "la corsa al più nero" (the race to be the blackest):[50]

> Socialmente provenivano, senza professione specifica e quindi senza disciplina ideale tecnica, da una povertà "infantile": erano in fase di ascensione cortocircuitante, verso lo stipendiucolo.[51]

> Socially, they emerged, without a specific profession and thus without an ideal technical discipline, from an "infantile" poverty: they were in a phase of short-circuiting ascension, launched towards a pittance of a stipend.

Their social climbing leads to national downfall as the energy of the community is wasted in comedy-style mimicry and pointless babble:

La "tensione spirituale" della collettività subisce in codesti corti-circuiti una repentina caduta. L'"energia attuale" (cioè il lavoro) della collettività subisce in essi una ingente dissipazione: talora una dissipazione verso terra, cioè verso il nulla. La tensione morale della collettività si annienta per tal modo in un verbiloquio vero e proprio, l'energia "storica" della collettività si spappola in un mimo inane da commedianti.[52]

The "spiritual tension" of the collectivity suffers in these short-circuits a sudden fall. The "actual energy" (namely, work) of the collectivity, suffers a sizable dissipation: at times it is a dissipation towards the ground, that is, towards a void. The moral tension of the collectivity reduces itself in this way to a veritable babble, the "historic" energy of the nation implodes in the inane mimicry of comedians.

Armed with a dictionary to shore up my lack of technical knowledge, I find the following definition of an electrical short-circuit: "Abnormal connection of low resistance between two points of a circuit that usually causes a high, potentially damaging current to flow." In other words, low resistance between fascism and the masses caused the nation's historic energy to be transformed into the dangerous high energy of mimicking and incoherent speech (*hee-haw, hee-haw*). Dunces who had skipped (short-circuited) grades for the wrong reasons were allowed to "graduate with honours" for their excellent performance in "verbiloquente-basedowoide agitazione viscerale" (verbose-basedowoid visceral agitation.)[53] Their infantile "poverty," their lack of a specific professional discipline and technical know-how, caused the nation to regress into a pubescent, impulse-driven, narcissistic state:

Oltre al narcisismo tipico e al tipico appetito della fase narcissica attraversata (onto e socia), c'è da portare in calcolo il fatto che le reclute puberi e minorili della fantasmagoria non conoscevano ancora la disciplina di un mestiere, di una professione: che questa disciplina non è soltanto abilità tecnica (e mentale-manuale) ma complessa dedizione della psiche ai compiti gravi del lavoro.[54]

Beyond the typical narcissism and the typical appetites of the narcissistic phase experienced (*onto e socia*), one has to bear in mind that the pubescent draftees of the phantasmagoria did not yet know the discipline of a craft or a profession: and that a discipline is not only a technical ability (and mental-physical) but also a complex dedication of the psyche to the serious task of work.

If we were to read *Eros e Priapo* without having read *La cognizione* or Gadda's article on the Sicilian latifundia reform, discussed earlier, we could perhaps assume that Gadda's background as electrotechnical engineer led his critique of fascism to focus on the detrimental effects of placing political power into non-specialized hands. But his techno-cratic stance becomes more problematic when we consider the issues of labour specialization and discipline in each of Gadda's "popular" groups: the peons of *La cognizione*, the fascist social climbers of *Eros e Priapo*, and the "relocated" Sicilian plebs.

Unlike the rural workers who had been selected to colonize the new *borghi* for their knowledge of sacrificial discipline or, as he put it, fami-lies who "have known through the blood of their men the discipline of battle," the labouring peons of *La cognizione* are undisciplined – they constantly enter a space where they do not belong. The emptied spaces that Gadda so insistently focused on, and we might say rhetorically patrolled, in his technical articles, are encroached upon in *La cognizione* where the breach is painfully registered as an uncontrollable open space. In the novel, loss of (crowd) control is not (at least not fully) countered by the exercise of authorial control over narrative space but is, instead, amplified by it, redoubled as lack of containment, spill-over, and textual refusal to be "enclosed" by an ending. The scene of encroachment is even further amplified in the pages of *Eros e Priapo*, where parody functions as stylistic ally to unbound discourse and the logic of border trespassing.

In *La cognizione*, the peons' bodies, not just their countenance, are un-disciplined for their upper and lower body parts constantly exchange properties: their "vocalized belows" are a conflation of Logos and Eros that reproduces incoherent sound. In other words, the peons embody lack of labour specialization: they are a collection of undisciplined body parts that have lost their fixed position and, hence, the ability to coalesce into a socially acceptable body, a body that can speak properly and that, in turn, can be part of a larger, productive, social organism. Like their fascist counterparts in *Eros e Priapo*, the peons' energetic movements and emissions amount to useless work:

Quelle emissioni di voce e quei gesti, secondo il teorema base della fisica moderna, equivalevano a cospicue cariche energetiche liberate in lavoro (inutile): col qual vistoso gioco di tutti i muscoli, la facies e gli omeri maradagalesi credono di poter supplire alla inesistenza di una sostanza linguistica.[55]

Those vocal emissions and those gestures, according to the basic theorem of modern physics, were the equivalent of considerable electric energy released in (useless) labour: with that showy play of all the muscles, the Maradagalese facies and shoulder blades believe they can compensate for the non-existence of a linguistic substance.

Gadda's anti-fascism, if we can call it that, is (d)riven by a deep and peculiarly technocratic, anti-populist streak.[56] If labouring bodies and their parts are so central to his critique of the regime, it is perhaps because in one fundamental respect he finds it hard to distance himself from the fascist conception of the labouring body. In Gadda's narrative *and* in fascist rhetoric, the labouring body is represented as marked by an infantile linguistic and organizational incoherence. The body parts that comprise it do not add up to an autonomous organism capable of exercising linguistic control over the environment. It is what we could define as a "pre-mirror stage" fragmented body that does not yet perceive its own unity and that needs something external to organize it and give it coherence: an exemplary Duce, or in Gadda's case, a cadre of experts – managers or professional figures who, to use Butler's term, have acquired the skill of *bien commander*, and hence, can speak properly.[57] Unsupervised labour, like a child full of undisciplined energy, falls to the ground.[58]

When coherence is attempted from within, that is, when the "fragmented" body attempts to speak as an autonomous organism without external guidance, only a noisy disturbance is produced. In other words, Gadda's narrative sides with fascism against the independent formation of labour organizations: no collective body of labourers should acquire linguistic coherence, no whole should speak for the part. Labourers should not have a unified, collective body that can give voice to their manual skills, and possibly direct their feet into areas where they do not belong. Their hands must remain labouring hands, their feet walking feet – their parts should remain disembodied silent parts and not be organized into a body that can speak for them and advance their cause.[59] But while Gadda's narrative, like fascist rhetoric, forecloses the possibility that labour may be an autonomous social actor, the modalities of this foreclosure could not be further apart, and it is from this divergence that Gadda's opposition to the regime acquires its distinctive anti-sacrificial bent.

For both Gadda and fascism, the labouring body should be silent. But the regime's articulation of a silent labouring body, while effectively foreclosing any class-based identification of workers, is also the fundamental discursive pre-positioning for the reaggregation of that fragmented, "incoherent body" in the image of the self-effacing Duce. Through silent submission, one acquires a fascist voice that echoes the sacrificial master and gains entry into the fascist community: "la Patria si serve sopratutto in silenzio, in umiltà e in disciplina, senza grandi frasi ma col lavoro assiduo e quotidiano" (One serves one's country above all in silence, in humility and discipline, not with grand phrasemaking, but with assiduous, daily work).[60] Exchangeability, rather than specialization characterizes the ideal discipline in the relationship Duce-*popolo*, or as Mussolini puts it:

> io non sono tanto favorevole all'eccessiva specializzazione. Non vorrei che a furia di guardare l'albero, si dimenticasse la foresta: non vorrei che, a guardare un lato, un elemento, un frammento del corpo umano si dimenticasse il complesso del corpo umano, il quale, o signori, è unitario e totalitario come il Regime Fascista.[61]

> I don't favour excessive specialization. I worry that in the rush to see the tree, one might forget the forest. I worry that by looking at only one side, one element, one fragment of the human body, one might forget the wholeness of the human body, which, gentlemen, is as unified and totalitarian as the fascist regime.

Mussolini is, of course, both the tree and the forest: "Quando sento la massa nelle mie mani, quando avverto la sua fede, o quando io mi mescolo con essa, che quasi mi schiaccia, allora mi sento un pezzo di questa massa"[62] (When the masses are like wax in my hands, when I stir their faith, or when I mingle with them and am almost crushed by them, I feel myself to be part of them).[63] In fascist rhetoric, self-sacrifice becomes the skill to be learned and modelled, the ultimate performative discipline against which individuals are measured: "Ho l'orgoglio di essere quello che sono, cioè un uomo che prima di imporre dei sacrifici agli altri li impone a se stesso, e prima di chiamare la disciplina per gli altri a questa disciplina si sottopone" (I pride myself in being what I am, that is, a man who imposes sacrifices upon himself before imposing them on others, who imposes discipline upon himself before imposing it on others).[64]

Fascist rhetoric constantly pointed to sacrificial identification as the privileged process of individual and collective aggregation: what is inchoate and fragmentary (that is, non-fascist or pre-fascist) achieves unity, identity, and coherence through a sacrificial submission to the state. In the Duce's view: "il patriottismo non è che un sentimento. Diventa una virtù solo mediante il sacrificio. Questa virtù aumenta secondo la natura del sacrificio"[65] (patriotism is no more than a feeling. Sacrifice makes it a virtue. The virtue is greater in proportion to the magnitude of the sacrifice).[66] Through the proper spirit of self-abnegation (and displacement of class identification), the individual can coalesce with and enter, literally, into the state: "Il popolo è il corpo dello Stato e lo Stato è lo spirito del popolo. Nel concetto fascista il popolo è Stato e lo Stato è popolo" (The people is the body of the State and the State is the spirit of the people. For the fascist ideal the people are the State and the State is the people). What was previously "scattered" and unaware of itself is now reconciled in the nation-state:

Oggi, quando vedete i reduci marciare a tre o a quattro, quando vedete questa magnifica disciplina nel popolo italiano, che marcia per le strade non più a torme di gregge, come una volta, ma in battaglioni serrati, vi rendete conto che una profonda trasformazione si è operata nel popolo italiano, vi rendete conto che il popolo italiano sta per entrare o è entrato nello Stato [. . .] Le masse, riconciliate con la nazione, entrano, per la grande porta spalancata della rivoluzione fascista, nello Stato. E lo Stato, con la monarchia in alto, ha allargato smisuratamente le basi. Non vi sono più soltanto sudditi, ma cittadini; non vi è più soltanto una nazione, ma un popolo cosciente dei suoi destini.[67]

Today, when you see the veterans march in threes and fours, when you see the magnificent discipline of the Italian people, that march through the street no longer like hordes, as they once did, but in disciplined battalions, you become aware of the profound transformations that have taken place in the Italian people, you become aware that the Italian people are ready to enter into or have entered into the State [. . .] The masses, reconciled with the nation, enter through the doors, opened wide by the fascist revolution, into the State. And the State, with its monarchy at the top, has immeasurably increased its base. They are no longer mere subjects, but citizens, no longer a mere nation, but a people conscious of its destiny.

National (fascist) "reconciliation" has broadened social participation, has opened the door to the "servile" multitudes and given them a new conscience and mechanism of self-recognition in serving the nation. The(ir) new S/state has been extended to them, and the previously scattered individuals and groups ("torme di gregge" – herds/hordes walking presumably with hoofs) have become a unified organism with marching feet in military formations.[68]

The passage from animalesque aggregation to self-conscious human formation, which Mussolini sees occurring with the entry of the masses into the fascist state, is partly reversed in Gadda's mocking portrayal of the Duce "erect upon triple-high hoofs": hoofs never turn to feet in the process of "allargamento delle basi" (expanding the base), that is, with the entry of the masses – *they simply keep multiplying as hoofs* and devolve into a national animalesque consortium that brings work energy to the ground. The image of the grotesque multiplying feet, which Gadda seems to employ so frequently as an anti-fascist derisive parody, masks, in fact, and deflects Gadda's real bone of contention with the regime, and one that ultimately makes his brand of anti-fascism quite problematic: the regime's *mobilization* and *vocalization* of the "incoherent peons." Indeed, the "increasing of the base" seems to coincide for Gadda with a perverted mechanism of social inclusion that threatens the proper channels of social mobility based on specialized and *naturalized* labour functions: the "head" directs the "feet" and does not extend them its vocal properties. Ideological reaggregations based on such extensions produce "sub-human" collective formations.

In *Eros e Priapo*, Gadda's view of the masses is structured by what he describes as his a-narcissist belief. He "loves and respects" their popular language and salt-of-the-earth qualities as long as individual identities do not undergo a "narcissist extension to the collectivity." In other words, what is atomized and not conscious of its potential unity should stay that way.[69] The parody by Gadda, the social critic, masks the real preoccupation of Gadda, the engineer, whose role as planner of spaces, and hence, as privileged gatekeeper of the internal movement of people within those spaces, is threatened by the entry of a stampeding mob that might well decide to ignore Gadda's technical specifications and take the elevator to the upper floor. Mobility, especially of the vertical kind, seems to concern him greatly: "ho della folla grande non meno che d'ascensori e di macchine una fifa maledetta" (I am terrified by large crowds as well as by elevators and cars).[70] Stairways, elevators, and entrances are problematic sites because they are open to the potential intermingling and illicit consortium of different social classes, depicted here as the confusion of different types of "expertise":

La costruzione delle case popolari, specie delle "villette operaie," propone al progettista gli spinosi problemi del vicinato: fra questi il problema delle scale. Ne' villini a due piani (terreno e primo), di due appartamenti. Certe società hanno affrontato la notevole spesa della doppia entrata, e della scala separata per il primo piano, perché il figlio del capo-operaio X non incontrasse sulle scale la figlia o la moglie del capo-tecnico Z. L'incontro scaligero è un momento cruciale, come direbbe il Somaro, per la continenza del sesso forte: pare che la tenebra di certe scale di casamenti popolari o magari signorili, specie ne' paesi ove il sole e il sangue e' sono più vivi e corrono come foco a ogni vena, sia estremamente propizia a certi esibitivi madrigali. Bisognerebbe esser donna, e donna del Mezzogiorno, a poterlo accertare. Il madrileno e bonaerense piropo, ch'è di parole susurrate al passeggio, doventa piropo, tacitamente e pure metricamente parlante nella semi-oscurità della scala comune.

In constructing public housing, especially "working class houses," the planner faces the acute problems of adjacent spaces: among these, the problem of staircases in two-floor houses (ground and first) with two apartments. Some communities have shouldered the considerable expense of putting two entrances and a separate stairway on the first floor in order to prevent the son of head-worker X to run into the daughter or wife of head-technician Z. The stairway encounter is a crucial moment, as the Dunce would say, for the restraint of the dominant sex: it seems that the obscurity of certain staircases in public housing complexes, and even in upscale ones, especially in countries where sun and blood are hot and run like fire in every vein, is extremely propitious for certain madrigalian exhibitions. One need only be a woman, a Southern woman, to confirm this. The Madrilenian and provincial *piropo*[71] from words whispered while strolling becomes the *piropo*, spoken silently, and even metrically, in the semi-obscurity of the common staircase.[72]

Not surprisingly, lack of sexual restraint, and the transgression of social boundaries during the fatal stairway tryst is imputed to certain inviting "madrigalian" exposures. Once again, Mother's genitals stand as a figure of gatekeeping, for in the semi-obscurity of the common stairway, the civilized Logos of "words whispered while strolling" descends, literally, into the "silent" and "metric" verse of priapesque Eros. Although I want to refrain from sliding into the biographical realm, especially of the anecdotal kind, I cannot help but think that Gadda's alleged penchant for transvestitism finds a striking textual correspondence in the rivalry between gatekeepers: the engineer and the sacrificial tower matrix seem to compete for the same (authorial) right to De Madrigal's (Gadda's alter ego in *Eros e Priapo*) fictional "exposures" and final control over what is made public.

Ultimately, what the text of *La cognizione* makes public – and it is undoubtedly an exposure that was painful to Gadda – is the upper floor of the house. In the final scene, the peons have not only reached the upper floor of the family villa, but they are all surrounding the bed of the moribund mother who has mysteriously been bludgeoned to the head by intruders in the middle of the night.[73] The "belows" have finally gotten to the "top": there is nothing left for the engineer to do but to report the transgression with the detached description of a crime scene. That the murder is left unexplained owes more, I believe, to the nature of the crime than to the fact that Gadda did not finish this novel. The explanation is irrelevant, for the real *textual* motive of the crime is to stage the ultimate exposure of the tower matrix: her sacrificial corpse is now the central point of organization of the infantile peons, a potentially cohesive event that might lead to their maturity and possible unstoppable reproduction: Gadda's ultimate nightmare.

In the family villa (aptly referred to as *Villa-idea*) of *La cognizione*, the peons' reproductive potential (which I read as the spectre of their class uncontrolled multiplication) seems to be a constant sensorial threat to Gonzalo. Their multiplying hoofs are as offensive to him as the precarious status of their pants – always on the verge of dropping to the floor, the endangered trousers might at any point cause a disorderly exposure:

Intanto entrò, zoccolando, la miseria e il fetore d'un peone [. . .] Il peone annaspava con la testa dentro la bocca del camino, poi si levò: sembrò che da un momento all'altro gli dovessero cadere i pantaloni, tanto li aveva bassi anche in rapporto alla cintola [. . .] Lo hidalgo, pur nelle dilaganti ombre della nevrosi, non pretendeva speciali abluzioni dai villici del Serruchón: per essi, dopo la defunzione di Caracalla, il Santo Battesimo gli pareva lavacro sufficiente. Solo constatava il fatto odorifero con una tal quale costernazione e talora con ira. Nel caso in oggetto, poi, sapeva che il contadino avrebbe potuto tenersi un po' piú in ordine. Il delirio insorgente dalla còllera gli lasciò identificare in quello sconcio una premeditata ostentazione di miseria, una dimostrazione a carattere sindacale: rivendicativa d'una qualche ulteriore larghezza de' padroni in soccorso della miseria stessa.[74]

Meanwhile there came in, clogging, the poverty and fetor of a peon [. . .] [He] groped with his head inside the mouth of the fireplace; then he stood up: it seemed as if, at any moment, his trousers were to fall, they were so low over his hips with respect to his belt [. . .] The hidalgo, even in the spreading shadows of neurosis, did not demand special ablutions of the villeins of the Serruchón: for them, after the decease of Caracalla, Holy Baptism seemed to him sufficient cleansing. Only he perceived the odor-iferous fact with a certain consternation and at times with wrath. In the case in point, then, he knew that the peasant could have kept himself a bit more in order. The rising delirium of rage allowed him to identify in that indecency a premeditated ostentation of poverty, a demonstration of a trade-unionist nature: demanding some further *largesse* from the masters in aid of that same poverty.

The "trade-unionist demonstration" of the incoherent peons that causes Gonzalo's delirium can only be of the non-verbal kind, the only one that their pre-human condition would allow. And yet, it is precisely this verbal incoherence coupled with horrific sights that triumphs at the end of the novel as the gutturalizing of the cavemen replace the dying elegant whisper that is swept away by the unstoppable wind of change. Notice how in the passage that immediately precedes the description of the peons' entry into the bedroom of the moribund mother, Gadda naturalizes the ideological landscape of the change that is about to take place: In the garden of the "villa signorile" adjacent to Gonzalo's, the wind is still gently caressing (combing the hair of) the "head" of the trees as each passing breeze seems to deliver an ominous warning of the arrival of the unkempt and the uncombed:

E poi lazzi e meraviglie ironiche per la torcia, che cosa è successo e pro-teste e nuove egutturazioni dei cavernicoli, stanati per quell'allarme dagli antri illuni del sonno. Un va e vieni di voci, per lo piú monosillabiche, epigastriche, a urti, a urli, o tutt'al piú bisillabe, ma in tal caso ossitone, a spari, a scoppi . . . Una folla dalla gola ossitona latrava e ingigantiva nella notte, con pantaloni pericolanti, quadrupedanti zoccoli, sui ciottoli cro, cro, zoccoli . . . zoccoli, zòkur, triangoli di luce, fumo e smoccolature di lanterne e giornali al suolo, buttàtivi dall'irrompere di una ventata. Dal parco conchiuso del cav^r Trabatta, invece, si animavano a quando a quando i pini, i tigli all'unisono, del loro signorile susurro. A ogni passag-gio del vento aveva preluso il lontano stormire della notte: a ogni respiro del vento che i mandorli qui, presso casa, cercavano invano di carezzare, quasi ad attenuarne, a ravvivarne la stolida chioma, come pettini, con rada fronda.[75]

And then quips and ironic amazement at the torch, what's happened and protests and new gutturalizing from the cavemen, routed by that alarm from the moonless lairs of their sleep. A bustle of voices, mono-syllabic for the most part, epigastric, jolting, shouting, or at most bisyl-labic, but oxytone in that case, in spurts and shots . . . An oxytone-throated crowd barked and grew enormously in the night, with endangered trou-sers, quadruped clogs, crunch crunch, clogs . . . clogs, *zòkur*, triangles of light, smoke, the waxy drip of lanterns and newspapers on the ground, thrown there by the onrush of a gale. From the closest park of Captain Trabatta, instead, the pines, the lindens were animated from time to time, in unison, by their elegant whisper. To every passage of the wind the distant rustle of the night had been a prelude: to every breath of the wind that the almond trees here, by the house, tried in vain to caress, as if to attenuate, to rearrange their stolid tresses, with their rare fronds, like combs.

If Gadda's narrative in *La cognizione* ends with a blow to the head and the exposure of the foundational act of a society of "cavemen," in *Eros e Priapo* Gadda revisits, and we might say, tampers with, the scene of the crime. As he returns incessantly to that "blow to the head," he tries to recolour, in fact, literally redress the crime – this time by exposing the priapesque instability of the *black* pants. In the absence of the peons, who is there to blame but Mother herself? She had, after all, always left the door open and allowed a proper empty space to be filled by the bearers of a very improper "infantile poverty," a poverty that is not fully aware of its own limits and limitations and, hence, does not know its place in society.

The incoherence of the labouring body emerges and is thematized in Gadda's writings as a problem of knowledge. Fascism had allowed professional discipline, or mastery of specialized knowledge, to be sub-stituted by sacrificial discipline as a privileged mechanism for social advancement, thereby perverting the proper gatekeeping functions of cultural capital. Sacrificial rhetoric had short-circuited the correct social distance between classes, or the proper amount of empty space and silence that Gadda evidently thought should buffer those who possess knowledge, and hence, are in control, from those lacking it. If his dis-tancing efforts, which culminate with the exposure and attempt to put an end to the sacrificial matrix, failed and resulted in the triumph of encroachment, Gadda reclaimed mastery, at least partially, by refusing to grant unity to the "fragments below" or a textual closure that would perhaps make them intelligible in retrospection. The very lack of control that his portrayals of the labouring body as infantile is meant to underscore can only be open ended since it is the incoherence of labour as a class, its failure to coalesce into a mature self-aware body, that Gadda's texts attempt to capture in order to make it permanent. Infantilization serves to "fix" the representation of the labouring class as an abject part of the national whole, extending ad infinitum its subaltern, or dependent status.

Expelling an abject part and infantilizing the lower classes in order to establish the "correct" distance of social groups within the nation was not a textual strategy unique to Gadda. In the next chapter, we will trace these two rhetorical configurations in the writings of Elio Vittorini, who deployed them unsparingly, albeit for opposite ideological ends, in his portrayals of a "new man" grounded in sacrificial self-abnegation. The irritating babbling infants that Gadda had so insistently tried to shut out with his invocation of lower-class dispersal are adopted by Vittorini and given a proper home, a proper national space where they may coalesce into a respectable collective body. As we will see, this operation will require the deployment of a sacrificial discourse to ensure that their propriety is recognized along with the propriety of Vittorini's own ideological replacement as he moves from fascism to anti-fascism.

4 The Redemption of Vittorini's *New Man*

In this chapter, I will examine Elio Vittorini's attempts to define in sacrificial terms the natural and essential qualities of the Italian people (*popolo*). Such efforts at naturalizing the spirit of self-sacrifice of the *uomo nuovo* (new man) are present in many of his newspaper and journal articles and in one of his most famous novels, *Uomini e no* (*Men and Not Men*).[1] The trajectory that I follow is not strictly chronological for what I aim to illustrate is not Vittorini's intellectual trajectory which, despite persistent de-emphasis (and often outright elision) of his adherence to fascism during the *ventennio*, has been mapped in all its twists and turns.[2] I trace, instead, an intertextual discourse (often running parallel to and at times counter to, his more well-known trajectory) in which Vittorini links the formative process of an emerging new man to the simple nature of "the people." This operation is not confined to a specific ideological period of Vittorini's life, such as his initial fascist sympathies or later anti-fascist militancy, but represents, instead, a discursive mechanism that allows Vittorini to move from one end of the ideological spectrum to the other, while preserving a semblance of intellectual continuity and integrity.

Moving from right to left was not the only trajectory that had preoccupied Vittorini. The project of cultural elevation of the people, or recasting the low and high coordinates of the social class continuum remained a central concern throughout his career. Gadda too, as we have seen in the previous chapter, was intensely preoccupied with social mobility, albeit from a different perspective. If Gadda's discursive strategy is to defend the bourgeois by insulating it from the encroaching masses, Vittorini's strategy is to insulate the masses from the temptations of bourgeois values. The sacrificial expulsion of bourgeois parts from the Vittorinian *uomo* is a textual operation that we might read as the *trait d'union* between his fascist writings and the postwar anti-fascist stance of *Uomini e no*. How Vittorini attempted to naturalize the sacrifice of parts of his man and why this is important for his own repositioning in relation to fascism, are the central questions of this chapter.

The Illusion of Youth

> La giovinezza d'Italia segue Balbo, i pallidi adolescenti della Marcia su Roma rispondono in coro ai suoi appelli, felici di diventare avieri e assicurarsi un avvenire periglioso. Molti – lasciando gli studi, i parenti, la monotona sicurezza di una vita borghese – si buttano, con nuovo entusiasmo, alle scuole di volo. "Questo è il segno più confortante dello slancio con il quale la gioventù italiana segue gli sviluppi dell'aviazione" afferma con ragione Balbo. Darsi all'aviazione sta diventando oggi comune presso il popolo come un tempo darsi alla guerra errante, alla cavalleria. "È un esercito intero di volatori – aggiunge soddisfatto il Nostro – Infoltisce la schiera dei veterani e porta l'ardore di un entusiasmo e di una fede che può dirsi tipicamente fascista."[3]

> The youth of Italy follows Balbo, the pale adolescents of the March on Rome respond in unison to his appeal, happy to become airmen and to secure a perilous future for themselves. Many – leaving their studies, their relatives, the monotonous security of a bourgeois life – throw themselves, with renewed enthusiasm, into the flight schools. "This is the most reassuring sign of the impetus with which the Italian youth follows developments in aviation," rightly affirms Balbo. Today, dedication to aviation is becoming as common for the people as the roving warfare of the cavalry of yesteryear. "It is an entire army of airmen" – he adds with satisfaction – "that makes the ranks of veterans swell and exudes the ardour and enthusiasm of a faith that can be defined as typically fascist."

It is hard to associate Vittorini with the stultifying prose of passages such as the one above taken from the 1931 biography of Italo Balbo, one of the most prominent exponents of the fascist regime. Yet, Lorenzo Greco, in his *Censura e Scrittura* (*Writing and Censorship*), has convincingly attributed it to him. "Our" Vittorini, or the Vittorini we are more familiar with, is associated with the post–Second World War public intellectual who has enjoyed much popular and critical acclaim as militant anti-fascist, avid translator of American literature, *Il Politecnico* impresario, and author of works such as *Conversazione in Sicilia* (*In Sicily*) and *Uomini e no*.[4] "Our" Vittorini, it seems, bears no resemblance to what we find in articles, early novels, and ghost-written hagiographies where he extolled the virtues of fascism and the attraction it had for "pale adolescents" eager to take to the skies and embrace a dangerous future.[5]

Undoubtedly, much of the distance that we perceive between the fascist and post-fascist Vittorini is imputable to his progressive abandonment of the official ideological positions of the regime, or what he has portrayed as the disillusionment following "la scoperta dell' inganno fascista" (the discovery of the fascist deception). But some of the uneasiness that we experience in comparing the two has more to do with our disillusionment than with his: the Vittorini that we had read and admired in our formative high-school days could not possibly have been "formed" that way. Upon further reflection, one realizes that the discomfort comes not from discovering that Vittorini had been a fascist – for some literary biographies had, after all, mentioned it – it comes, rather, from realizing just how marginal that fact has appeared to be in such biographical accounts and, more importantly, in critical analyses of his later works.[6] Lest I be misunderstood here, I do not mean to say that works such as *Conversazione in Sicilia* should be read exclusively through the lenses of Vittorini's early fascism, for such an approach would be as reductive as are readings that assume unproblematic ideological transfers between personal (past or present) biographies and literary texts. But, in at least one instance, Vittorini himself "authorized" us to compare his fascist and post-fascist positions and to dissect concepts central to his intellectual and literary production. In a 1946 article, published in *Il Politecnico* as a response to "letters from young people who, today, seem still confused or desperate, or at least humiliated, to have been fascists," Vittorini offers sympathetic, if remarkably self-serving, comments:

Debbo dirlo a questi ragazzi che mi scrivono. Anch'io sono stato uno di loro. Sono stato "non acuto" e "non forte." Non-uomo? Sono stato "dei deboli" [. . .] Io sono sicuro che il *modo* continuò a essere per loro (i "deboli" dentro all'inganno, *semplici* militanti operai o *semplici* militanti studenti, *semplici* ragazzi in buona fede, pronti a pagare di persona, e non quelli che c'erano per far carriera) più o meno lo stesso ch' era stato per me fino al '36: un modo sciocco se vogliamo, ma non reazionario [. . .] Non dobbiamo dimenticare che *la propaganda fascista è stata tale da coltivare nei giovani l'illusione di essere rivoluzionari ad essere fascisti* [. . .] Io voglio dirlo loro. *Voi non siete mai stati fascisti.* Il vostro modo di esserlo, fino a qualunque data lo siate stati, è stato un modo "antifascista."[7]

I have to tell it to these young people who are writing to me. I too was one of them. I have been "not perceptive" and "not strong." Not a man? I have been one of the "weak" [. . .] I am certain that *the way* it was for them (the "weak" inside the deception, *simple* militant workers, or *simple* militant students, *simple* young people in good faith, ready to pay personally, and not those who were there to advance a career) was more or less the same as it had been for me until '36: a foolish manner, if you will, but not a re-actionary one [. . .] We should not forget that *fascist propaganda was geared towards giving youth the illusion that to be fascist was to be revolutionary* [. . .] I want to tell them this. *You have never been fascists.* The manner in which you were so, until whatever date you have been so, was an "anti-fascist" manner.

Here, Vittorini draws a line in the sand between the revolutionary "fascismo di sinistra" (fascism of the left) that he and other ordinary folks (students, workers, young people) strenuously supported and the reactionary fascism that "lurked behind it" and that eventually emerged as a great betrayal of their simple, "in good faith" militancy. The swindle was so complete, the logic goes, that they did not even realize that their brand of fascism was *really* anti-fascism. Because they had actually been anti-fascists from the beginning, they now (in 1946) have the same right to call themselves anti-fascists as other, well, less cryptic anti-fascists: "Voi [giovani ragazzi fascisti] avete lo stesso diritto dei più vecchi antifascisti ad essere, oggi, antifascisti. Avete diritto ad essere 'uomini'" (You [fascist youths] have, today, the same right of the oldest anti-fascists to be anti-fascists. You have the right to be "men").[8]

Vittorini's masterful retrospective is problematic on a number of fronts. The sheer richness of historical and semantic revisionism that it contains could warrant a full-fledged analysis that, although tempting, is beyond the scope of my present investigation of sacrificial economies. There is, however, one aspect of Vittorini's efforts to rehabilitate the "giovani fascisti" that is of particular interest for my inquiry and that begs for a comparison with Gadda's treatment of "incoherent" peons and young fascist climbers.[9] In assessing Vittorini's single-handed ex-pansion of the ranks of historic anti-fascism, the question that emerges is the following: Who exactly are these "*simple* militant workers," "*simple* militant students," "*simple* youths in good faith" that were ready to pay personally, yet were weak, fascist believers until the end ("until whatever date you have been so"), and yet always anti-fascists in their ways ("the manner in which you were so . . . was an 'anti-fascist' manner"), and why is *simple* the adjective that despite their obvious differences (and apparently complex profiles) encompasses them as a group? Who they are biographically is not the question I am after or that I think is relevant here, but rather, who they are fictionally within the context of Vittorini's intellectual and literary production.

In citing Vittorini's reply to the young fascists, Anna Panicali has suggested that since it is presented as a collective response – "a tutti insieme" (to all of them together) – the article itself might be a "finzione letteraria" (literary fiction).[10] The implication of Panicali's suggestion is that Vittorini's answer was never elicited in the first place and that the use of a collective address masks the lack of an actual addressee while providing the occasion for public self-exposure and justification. Although agreeing with Panicali, I believe that Vittorini's gesture to collectivize the young fascists is part of a more complex discursive operation that bears further scrutiny: the literary fiction is not simply a formal device that enables the confessional moment, it also provides a textual moment of semantic reorganization of Vittorini's populist stance in relation to fascism. It is not coincidental that the fiction begins with a figure of unstoppable multiplication that takes place on Vittorini's editorial desk as if to indicate that it is the multitudes and not a few isolated cases who are seeking his help:

> Le loro lettere cominciarono ad arrivare dopo il primo numero del "Politecnico": furono due dopo quel primo numero, io volevo subito rispondere, ma le lettere si moltiplicavano, diventavano decine, sono diventate centinaia, e ora sono contento di non aver risposto subito perché, grazie a quello che ho imparato leggendole, ora posso certo rispondere meglio.[11]

> Their letters began to arrive after the first issue of *Il Politecnico*: They were two after that first number. I wanted to reply right away but the letters kept multiplying, they became dozens, they have become hundreds, and now I am glad that I did not answer immediately because, thanks to what I have learned in reading them, I can certainly give a better answer now.

By reading the letters, Vittorini learned that the profound "crisi di co-scienza" (crisis of conscience) that enveloped these young people has, despite their different experiences, a common denominator: they are accusing themselves of being "non uomini" (not men), and they want somebody to tell them otherwise – "cercano una smentita" (they are seeking a refutation) – and give them hope. Vittorini obliges. He reasons that their guilt can only be assuaged if they convince themselves that they have not been fascists but blind instruments and victims of fascism.[12] To see their victimhood requires an acute interpretative skill able to penetrate the thick veil of deception that conceals the difference between "fascismo sostantivo" (substantive fascism) and "fascismo aggettivo" (adjectival fascism). The first, he explains, is the *real* fascism – the one that counts: it is "fascism-the-noun" as substance and essence of capitalism that has reached its ultimate stage of industrial and financial development.[13] As an economic dictatorship, it defends the relations of production of bourgeois society by attacking the proletariat and disguising its materialistic nature through demagogic forms of propaganda. These forms are what he calls "adjectival fascism": the ideological smokescreen that made fascism-the-noun appear as a political program that would fight reactionary institutions and promote a social revolution eventually leading to a transformation "in senso collettivista" (along collectivist lines).

While the blindness of the young fascists made them "adjectival" participants in the exterior forms of the grand illusion, it also prevented them from seeing through it and, hence, kept them pure and uncontaminated from the pernicious, reactionary intrinsic nature of fascism-the-noun. What they did not understand, they could not be guilty of. Their inability to differentiate between the two "saved them," but now they are stunted by their own limitations: "Potremmo lasciarli al loro sentimento d'inferiorità? Sarebbe lasciare che non diventino mai 'uomini.' E che si corrompano; mentre in effetti sono puri" (Could we leave them with their feelings of inferiority? It would mean allowing them to never become "men," and to become corrupted when, in fact, they are pure).[14] Unless somebody holds up a mirror to them making them recognize who they are, they will fail to become men and their development will be corrupted. Luckily for them, the doting Vittorini is standing by to preclude such an eventuality. With the authorial (and editorial) gesture of answering their call, he offers, in effect, a discursive mirror that will make them see a textual reflection of an exemplary fascist-turned-anti-fascist. He will provide them with the big picture of interpretative reorganization – a "quadro della situazione," where their perceptual limitations, or narrow views of themselves, can be turned into a *delimitation* of a new, more encompassing, and more accurate, collective identity.

To discursively reform the young fascists, their adjectival status, *young*, will need to be naturalized into a substantive core group identity that can replace their former substantive: *fascists*. The strategy of substance replacement, indeed, begins in the title of the article which immediately establishes their new substantive while allegedly questioning the adjective: "Fascisti *i giovani*?" ("Are *the young* fascist?"). The answer, of course, is "no," and Vittorini does his best to make the "no" coincide with an implosion of his own question: reflecting on it, one would see a contradiction in terms, for *fascist* and *young* are at bottom inimical terms as the nature of one militates against the other. They can only be brought together as a result of a perceptual error.

His strategy of meaning replacement proves tricky because "the young" is hardly a stable or substantive category that can guarantee imperviousness to modifications or qualifications: it can always be repositioned syntactically and ideologically, rendering null the Vittorinian efforts to naturalize it into an oppositional term to fascism. The heterogeneity of "the young" makes it hard to group them under the rubric of an essential anti-fascist substantive, and in Vittorini's own description they, in fact, appear to be – literally – all over the map.

> Hanno ventiquattro, venticinque o anche solo venti anni, uno mi dice di averne diciotto, e sono di ogni classe sociale, l'operaia non esclusa, sebbene per la maggior parte dichiarino di studiare all'Università o di essersi appena laureati. Per metà ritornano da campi di internamento in Germania o da campi di prigionia; dell'altra metà c'è qualcuno che è stato soldato nell'esercito di Graziani, o nella X Mas. Ma non manca chi ha fatto il partigiano e si sente tuttavia ancora in colpa per essere stato "fino a un certo momento" fascista. Ognuno ha la sua data "fino alla quale" è stato "fascista": fino a gennaio '43, fino a febbraio '43, fino a marzo '43, e fino al 25 luglio o l'8 settembre '43, fino a un mese o l'altro del '44, uno addirittura "fino a ieri mattina," mi dice, scrivendomi il 5 novembre ultimo scorso.[15]

> They are twenty-four, twenty-five, or even only twenty years old, one tells me he is eighteen, and they come from every social class, including the working class, even though most of them state that they are studying at the university or that they have just graduated from it. Half of them came

back from internment camps in Germany or prison camps; some from the other half have been soldiers in the Graziani army or in the X Mas. There are also those who became *partigiani* but who feel nonetheless guilty to have been fascist "until a certain point." Each one has his own date "until which" he has been "fascist": until January '43, until February '43, until March '43, and until the 25th of July or the 8th of September '43, until this or that month in '44; one of them, writing this 5th of November, even tells me "until yesterday morning."

To make "the young" into a category that can withstand slippage into fascist semantic territory, Vittorini proceeds to elide their internal differences – possible cracks or fissures that can jeopardize the homogeneity – the purity of their new status of men. But how to tackle such a daunting task? How to subsume so many variables into one general, impermeable container? The Vittorinian solution is to declare that from a spiritual point of view differences among them don't count and that he is, on purpose, not differentiating:

> Ora io rispondo a tutti insieme. A bella posta non distinguo tra la crisi di chi dice di essere stato "non uomo" (cioè "fascista") fino al gennaio o luglio '43, e la crisi di chi dice di esserlo stato fino a un mese fa. Possono esserci differenze tra gli uni e gli altri. Certo ci sono. Ma spiritualmente non contano se non hanno evitato la crisi, o non hanno portato a superarla.[16]

> I am now replying to all of them together. On purpose I am not differentiating between the crisis of those who say they have been "not-men" (that is, "fascist") until January or July '43, and the crisis of those who say they have been so until a month ago. There could be differences between them. Certainly there are. But, spiritually, they do not count if they were of no use in avoiding the crisis or in helping to overcome it.

In other words, differences would only count if they had avoided or helped to overcome their crisis of conscience, but since they have not, they can be disregarded. The logic is obviously faulty but interesting, nevertheless, for its circularity points to a fundamental aporia, a point of discursive occlusion in Vittorini's collectivizing efforts of the young fascists: to acknowledge their past differences is to call into question their differentiating abilities, hence, to jeopardize their homogeneous status as "adjectival" fascists or participants of the fascism that "did not count." It was, after all, their perceptual inability to make distinctions that kept them pure, unlike those careerists who saw the "real fascism" and took full advantage of the possibility to distinguish themselves.

The young fascists were undistinguished and undistinguishing, undifferentiated and undifferentiating. So unremarkable, in fact, that even their different class connotation and educational background did not affect their fundamental simplicity: "*simple* militant workers," "*simple* militant students," "*simple* youths in good faith." *Simple* seems to be the adjective that guarantees their status of "adjectival" fascists: the term that occludes and sutures their differences while providing an essential core, a minimal unit around which their new identity as *uomini* can coalesce and develop.[17] It is also a term that grounds the Vittorinian binary system of *men* and *not men* for the quintessential Vittorinian new man, as we will see later, is in fact a model of simplicity through sacrificial self-abnegation. Before we consider the sacrificial implications of the Vittorinian man, however, we should explore further the strategy of simplification of the young fascists since it is a crucial discursive step in Vittorini's revisionist efforts. To recast their role under the regime (and by implication, of course, his own fascist past), Vittorini needs to blot out some of their individual variants: those unnecessary, superfluous details that might interfere with an unobstructed view of their essential similarities.

The occlusion of differences, effectively obscured behind their uniform simplicity, serves to naturalize their limitations and, hence, to link their present innocence to an equally uncontaminated past, to an undefiled and undefined point of origin that grounds their present right to be anti-fascists. They have not fundamentally changed: it was fascism that changed as it turned from revolutionary movement to reactionary regime. The logic of simplification as exoneration is clear, and it is not restricted to the young fascists and to himself. If what holds them together as a group despite their differences is their common simplicity, then other simple individuals can be part of the group. The line that separates the young fascists from the population at large is rather blurred and at times non-existent as, for example, in Vittorini's generous granting of blindness status to "tutto il popolo che ha avuto 'l'aberrazione' di accettare le sue [of fascism] forme, il suo metodo" (the entire people who acted in an "aberrant" fashion in accepting its [of fascism] forms, its method).[18] The sliding of the entire people ("tutto il popolo") into the collective group of adjectival fascists that he has carved out for the young fascists allows Vittorini to further the adjectival array collapsed under the banner of simplicity to include a *popular* element since, after all, *the people*'s acceptance of fascism derived from inability to see though its appearances (forms, methods). They might not have been technically young but they were equally blind.[19]

Although the attempt to exonerate "the people" through simplification and, ultimately, infantilization, is certainly not a strategy unique to Vittorini (as we have seen in my first chapter's critique of Luzzatto's problematic math), it is a strategy that Vittorini deploys in uniquely creative ways, especially as it intersects his long-standing, often vitriolic, polemic against bourgeois society. It is to the latter that we now turn.

Cultivating the Simple

Vittorini's discursive creation of a zone of collective simplicity is elastic and expansive, but its seemingly boundless inclusiveness has one notable exception: the bourgeoisie and its specialized, technical culture.[20] The logic that guides this aversion is best understood when viewed in contrast to Gadda's technocratic stance and portrayal of the unspecialized, incoherent peons. It is not an *esprit de géométrie* that guides my comparison here. If I point out the symmetries in the two authors' populist (Vittorini) and anti-populist (Gadda) stance it is because I believe that their respective discursive positioning of the *people* in relation to fascism sheds light on an important function of sacrificial discourse during the ventennio, namely, to articulate the mechanisms of social class mobility (and, of course, its interdiction) within the national body, by linking the function of specific social classes with those of corresponding parts of the physical body. Prioritizing those functions and identifying their hierarchical order for the proper functioning of the national whole involved excluding, and often forcefully expelling, problematic parts.

As I have argued in my previous chapter, Gadda's main bone of contention with the regime is its populist "allargamento delle basi" (expansion of the base): the entry of the masses into the state that threatens mechanisms of social mobility based on specialized, technical expertise. The "useful knowledge" of the professional cadres, traditionally associated with the bourgeois class, had been replaced during fascism with the high energy but useless work of immature social climbers. Dunces ("Donkeys") who had skipped grades and should have stayed below, achieved positions of command. Like the peons of *La cognizione*, their infantile verbal and bodily incoherence found an external point of identification in a sacrificial figure who would provide them with an echoing mirror, a model of cohesion while effectively displacing their voice *as labour*: the motherly tower matrix in the case of the peons, the Duce in the case of the fascist climbers/dunces (donkeys).

As I have argued, Gadda does not object to the fascist displacement of their class-based identity – on the contrary, his texts naturalize the fragmentation and incoherence of the labouring body: physical, "mechanical" labour should stay below, mental, "organizing" labour should stay above. The two realms reach their utmost level of efficiency when they specialize in their respective functions, that is, when they belong to different people. Gadda conflates organization from below with the following of priapesque instincts and loss of productive energy. What he vehemently objects to is the fact that fascism, while displacing and silencing the class-based identification of labourers, simultaneously provided a new cohesive principle of organization of those "fragmented" labourers in the exemplary, national, and indeed, collective figure of the Duce. It is this new mechanism of cohesion, not fascism as a political system, that Gadda's texts oppose with the focus on the "fragments below." The obsessive descriptions of lower parts in isolation, which effectively detaches them from the other parts, can be seen as Gadda's attempt to "freeze" them in their proper place, to discursively naturalize their separateness by focusing on their specialized function *as parts*.[21]

If Gadda's texts naturalize a fragmentary below, Vittorini's texts naturalize an undifferentiated below: a stable, homogeneous, essential *people* not riven by internal differences. Simplicity is the principle that overrides and subsumes categories potentially disruptive to internal unity and, at the same time, the term that differentiates it externally from other social classes: the bourgeoisie and the aristocracy. Social mobility is problematic for both authors but for different, if strongly related, reasons. For Gadda, "the people" should simply stay fragmented and below since moving upward would constitute trespassing into the territory of the head – the natural province of bourgeois professional culture: specialized, technical, and inherently mobile. Whereas Gadda's discursive strategy is to defend the bourgeoisie by insulating it from the people, Vittorini's strategy is to insulate the people from the bourgeoisie.

For Vittorini, the people should move upward *as people* – that is, not by trying to escalate the class ladder but by culturally stepping over it, as it were: devaluing bourgeois culture for what it values, for the premium it puts on the mobility potential of professional, specialized knowledge. Anti-bourgeois sentiment informed Vittorini's early novels and journalistic articles as well as his postwar writings as *Politecnico* editor, providing a thematic continuity between the two stages of his career. Common to both was also the idealistic belief in a classless society – whether it be the pre-war (fascist) version or the postwar (Marxist) one – that had "no place" for the bourgeoisie.[22] Devaluing bourgeois culture was, for Vittorini, an integral part of his project of "elevazione culturale del popolo" (cultural elevation of the people), a goal to which the *Politecnico* was committed as a laboratory and forum for a new culture formed through collaboration and "contatti con le masse" (contacts with the masses).[23] Popular participation would be a formative tool for re-establishing the popular interest in culture, the natural desire for culture that Vittorini thought the masses intrinsically possessed but now failed to properly recognize. Years of alienation and preoccupation with necessities had somehow disengaged the masses from their own natural propensity towards cultural pursuits. The *Politecnico* would promote a "cultura rigeneratrice della società" (culture that would regenerate society) by establishing a "legame tra le masse lavoratrici e i lavoratori stessi della cultura" (tie between the working masses and cultural workers themselves), an intellectual forum for an organic realignment of work, culture, and people.[24]

The goal of cultural regeneration was shared by the Italian Communist Party (PCI) in the years after the Second World War, but the question of how such renewal should be carried out became a thorny one and eventually led to a rift between Vittorini and Palmiro Togliatti, the Party leader. An acrimonious debate over the *Politecnico*'s editorial policy affected its circulation negatively, contributing to the demise of the periodical in December 1947, and motivated Vittorini's withdrawal from the PCI in 1951. As Stephen Gundle has pointed out, in his nuanced study of the cultural policies of the PCI, the openness of the *Politecnico* towards cultural influences outside the mainstream of Italian culture, such as psychoanalysis, existentialism, and the new American novel, was met with apprehension and disapproval by PCI officials and policy makers, who saw these as "foreign" trends potentially inimical to the Party's core values.[25] Indeed, the PCI's own provincial attitude in cultural matters, coupled with a long-standing uneasiness towards Marxist strains of positivism and rationalism, led to Togliatti's negative labelling of the contents of the *Politecnico* as "encyclopedic 'culture' in which an abstract search for the new, the different, and the surprising took the place of coherent choice and meaningful inquiry."[26] But Vittorini's "encyclopedia," if not conforming to Togliatti's editorial ideals, had, in fact, its own exclusionary logic of cultural selection: one that aimed precisely at leaving out cultural products that served specialized needs. Vittorini was, we might say, more concerned with fostering the right kind of cultural desire than in catering to needs.

Although Togliatti might have wished that the *Politecnico* advance a cultural agenda specifically geared towards and created for the working class, Vittorini was more interested, as indeed, he had been throughout fascism, in giving the people the "impractical" cultural library of the aristocracy: "pulling the people up" by giving them a cultural taste superior to that of the bourgeoisie. He believed that the type of social change that would lead to a classless society required an education of the masses geared not towards acquiring the tools of professional advancement but the tools of cultural elevation, or as he put it succinctly in a 1952 article titled "Questione di mela" ("The Question of the Apple"):

> *Quali i compiti e i fini della cultura?* Direi simbolicamente: gli stessi ch'ebbe Adamo nell'addentare la mela dell'albero proibito. Dunque "fini" e "compiti" che sono nell'interesse maggiore dell'uomo: per un suo piú alto "valore," per una sua piú elevata "condizione"; ma che possono anche essere in contrasto con la sua felicità contingente (a causa di tutte le lacerazioni che producono nella sua "condizione attuale").[27]

> *What are the duties and goals of culture?* I would say, symbolically: the same that Adam had in biting the apple of the forbidden tree. Those "goals and duties" that are in the best interest of man: that speak of his greater "value," of his higher "condition"; but that may also be in contrast with his contingent happiness (due to the disruptions they produce in his "current condition").

The contingent happiness of a better economic position (presumably, the lure of the apple in question) has less value than an overall enhancement in cultural conditions (presumably, the popular, classless paradise). Reaching a higher condition requires keeping the proverbial serpent of contingent desires in check and instilling in Adam loftier desires.

If the biblical serpent was present only as an unindicted co-conspirator in the article above, it had been very much indicted as the practical and mobile purveyor of bourgeois values by Vittorini during fascism. The problem of misguided desires in relation to popular culture had been clearly identified in a 1937 article for the Florentine journal *Il Bargello*, where Vittorini equated real culture with unnecessary culture, the kind of higher knowledge that should belong to the masses and that, let's say, an engineer, may feel authorized to ignore.[28]

> La questione, è che oggi non esiste *desiderio di cultura*. Non si concepisce la cultura come un'attività vera e propria dell'uomo, ma come mezzo d'attività, come una rotella che serva a mettere in moto altre rotelle. Così ci si limita a conseguirne il minimo indispensabile e specifico per quella data attività pratica che si intende esercitare. E un ingegnere si ritiene autorizzato a ignorare Tolstoj o Dostoevskij che non sono tecnica ma romanzi; Platone o Vico che non sono tecnica, ma filosofia; Gibbon, Colletta o Amari che non sono tecnica ma storia; Leopardi o Goethe che non sono tecnica ma poesia. Oggi si è colti nella materia che professionalmente ci riguarda. Ossia non si è colti affatto. Perché vera e propria cultura comincia dove finisce la cultura professionale, dove non si è piú praticamente interessati ad essere colti. Solo la cultura non necessaria è cultura. Solo la cultura che non serve, è cultura. Cioè, nel caso dell'ingegnere, non la tecnica ma la letteratura, la filosofia, la storia, insomma *il tutto insieme* della famosa "Biblioteca universale" Sonzogno.[29]

> The issue is that today there is no *desire for culture*. There is no understanding of culture as an activity intrinsic to man, but as a tool, like a wheel that moves other wheels. Thus, one acquires only the bare minimum that is needed and pertinent to the practical activity that one intends to pursue. So an engineer feels justified in ignoring Tolstoj or Dostoevskij that are not technical knowledge but novels; Plato or Vico that are not technical knowledge but philosophy; Gibbon, Colletta, or Amari that are not technical knowledge but history; Leopardi or Goethe that are not technical knowledge but poetry. Today, one is learned in the discipline of the chosen profession. That is, we are not learned at all. Because real culture begins where professional culture ends, where one is not interested in being learned for practical reasons. Only culture that is not necessary is culture. Only culture that is not useful is culture. That is, in the case of the engineer, not technical knowledge, but literature, philosophy, history – in short, the *all together* of the famous "Biblioteca universale" Sonzogno.

The *Biblioteca Universale Sonzogno*, an economic series of Casa Editrice Sonzogno, a Milanese publishing house (founded in 1861) that specialized in affordable and portable editions of works of Italian and foreign major authors, represented Vittorini's ideal of popular culture.[30] He equated the *Biblioteca* with an idyllic paradise lost to be regained, one in which the most disparate products of intellectual achievement were all gathered together, forming a plenitude of knowledge that was not only accessible to the masses but also enticing to them, satisfying their deeply felt "need for culture":

> Si trovava in quella "Bibilioteca" per dieci centesimi nei primissimi tempi, per una lira negli ultimi, la *Scienza Nuova* del Vico e il *Faust* di Goethe, i poemi di Puskin e il *Corano*, Boccaccio e Baudelaire e da Platone vi si seguiva il filo delle altezze umane toccate attraverso i secoli fino a un Verlaine, fino a un D'Annunzio. Vi si trovavano anche opere minori, come *La città del sole* di Campanella, o *L'elogio della pazzia* di Erasmo da Rotterdam, o i *Canti* di Petoefi, che nemmeno in edizioni a prezzi proibitivi da specialisti è possibile oggi avere in Italia. E c'era romanzo, c'era poesia, c'era filosofia, c'era storia, tutto insieme presentato come ugualmente necessario. Ma questo in sé era un fatto editoriale e non è questo in sé che ci preme. Noi dobbiamo ricordare, con rimpianto, la diffusione di quei volumetti, la febbre di averli, la passione per cui andavano da una mano all'altra: insomma il fatto culturale. Il fatto editoriale di quella "Biblioteca" a pochi soldi è semplicemente indizio dell'esigenza culturale di allora. Ed era esigenza che veniva dal popolo, cioè da tutti, in quanto tutti avevano la persuasione che *bisognava* essere colti.[31]

In the "Bibilioteca" we could find – for ten cents in the very early days, and for one lira towards the end – Vico's *Scienza Nuova* and Goethe's *Faust*, Puskin's poems, and the *Coran*, Boccaccio and Baudelaire, and from Plato one could follow a path to the heights of human achievement through the centuries, up to Verlaine or D'Annunzio. There were also minor works, such as Campanella's *The City of the Sun*, or Erasmus of Rotterdam's *In Praise of Folly*, or Petoefi's *Cantos*, that cannot be found nowadays in Italy even at the exorbitant price of the editions for specialists. And there was the novel, there was poetry, there was philosophy, there was history, presented all together as equally necessary. But this is an editorial fact, and not, in and of itself, what concerns us here. We remember, with regret, the circulation of those small volumes, the fever to possess them, the passion that accompanied them as they changed hands, in short, the cultural fact. The editorial policy of that affordable "Bibilioteca" is simply an indication of the need for culture during those times. And it was a need that was

coming from the people, that is, from everyone, since everyone was convinced of the *need* to be learned.

The editorial fact of "tutto insieme" (everything together) seems to
go hand in hand with the cultural fact of "tutti insieme" (everyone
together), with the passionate exchange of the precious (but inexpen-
sive) small volumes as they changed hands, the fever to possess them
and share them as fetishized tokens of the popular collective desire
for real, unnecessary culture. All those hands traditionally bound to
necessary tasks were equally bound to unnecessary high culture. They
were not confined to practical tasks but shared cultural needs and
imperatives.

Although Vittorini's depiction of the paradise lost of popular culture
represented by the *Biblioteca Universale Sonzogno* is historically and so-
ciologically inaccurate, it illustrates the assumptions guiding his critique of specialized culture as an obstacle to the popular attainment of
the heights of human achievement.[32] High culture, traditionally associated with the privileged classes, would be reached by the class traditionally associated with practical needs if those needs could somehow
be "elevated." But, how exactly do you elevate the people culturally
while retaining a belief in popular simplicity in the Vittorinian sense
of the word? How do you move the people upward without losing its
essential purity, that is, without transforming it into something other
than an undifferentiated and undifferentiating people (again, in the Vittorinian sense)? And even more problematic, how do you instil a taste
for unnecessary "real" culture to strata of the population whose daily
life is confronted by real necessities?

The Vittorinian solution to the admittedly intractable dilemma is a
strategy of cultural elevation as heroic redemption of "base needs,"
the sublimation of low selfish impulses into lofty desires accomplished
through the elimination of bourgeois temptations:

> "Ma cosa significa andare verso il popolo?" mi chiese un amico duro di
> mente. E io credetti di rispondergli: "Significa cercare il popolo in noi; io in
> me, tu in te; ed espellere il borghese che c'è in ognuno di noi. Perché anche
> nell'ultimo degli operai ci può essere un borghese da mettere alla porta."[33]

> "What does it mean to go to the people?" an obtuse friend asked me. And I
> replied: "It means looking for the people in us; I in myself, you in yourself;
> and to expel the bourgeois that is present in each of us. Because even in the

humblest of workers there could be a bourgeois who needs to be shown the door."

By expelling the bourgeois from the people, Vittorini figures, the lure of individual economic salvation would be replaced by the desire for collective salvation:

Essa [la borghesia] può dire: il mio regno è di tutti, perché può dire: diventate borghesi e godrete dei benefici del mio regno [. . .] Conquistati il tuo posto nel mondo e sarai salvo! [. . .] La vera libertà e` la mancanza assoluta di libertà. I nobili feudatari erano *liberi* nell'esercizio dei loro privilegi. I borghesi moderni sono *liberi* nell'esercizio dei privilegi che dà loro il denaro. La rivoluzione francese uccise la libertà dei nobili feudatari. Oggi resta da uccidere la libertà dei borghesi capitalisti. Le libertà sono i privilegi. E solo quando si saranno uccise tutte le libertà, voglio dire tutti i privilegi, si sarà trovata la vera libertà. La quale significa: ognuno sottomesso a tutti, alla collettività, allo Stato. Liberi sono quelli che danno, avrebbe detto Cristo [. . .] La questione è sempre quella posta da Cristo: redimersi dal peccato originale. E che cosa è il peccato originale se non l'individualismo, l'egoismo che divide ogni uomo dall'altro?[34]

The bourgeoisie will say: my realm is everybody's realm because it can say: become bourgeois and you can enjoy the benefits of my realm [. . .] Secure your place in the world and you will be saved! [. . .] True freedom is the absolute lack of freedom. Feudal nobles where *free* in exercising their privileges. Modern bourgeois are *free* in exercising the privileges provided by money. The French revolution killed the freedom of feudal nobles. What remains to be killed today is the freedom of bourgeois capitalists. Freedoms are privileges. Only when all freedoms will be killed – I mean all privileges – true freedom will be found, and it will have this meaning: each one subordinate to all, to the collectivity, to the state. Free are those who give, Christ would have said [. . .] The issue remains the same one presented by Christ: to be redeemed from original sin. And what is original sin if not individualism, egoism that separates each man from the other?

Redemption from the original sin of selfish acquisition requires that one be willing, instead, to *give* in the name of collective salvation. The bourgeois individualist paradise of the free market will need to be replaced by the desire for heroic deeds. A little forceful nudging would speed things up when "the hero in all of us" fails to naturally appear:

> Quando mai si è fatto qualcosa di buono col libero sviluppo? Perché non si lascia allora libero sviluppo al sentimento d'eroismo invece di imporre la leva militare? Se c'è un eroe vuol dire che tutti possiamo essere degli eroi, ·c'è una possibilità per tutti gli uomini di essere degli eroi, ma occorre una legge che costringa tutti gli uomini ad essere degli eroi.[35]

> When is the last time something good came out of the free market? Why instead of imposing military service don't we allow a free market for heroic sentiments? If a hero exists it means that we can all be heroes, that there is the possibility for all men to be heroes, but there needs to be a law that forces all men to be heroes.

Adventures abroad, such as the colonial occupation of Ethiopia, might have a heroic formative value as well, but only if they are undertaken with the right sentiment, that is, without an economic motive:

> Non vi è posto per l'egoismo sociale in Etiopia. Non vi è posto per le avventure economiche. Non vi è posto per chi tende a salvarsi INDI-VIDUALMENTE dalle difficoltà della vita. Tale è l'essenza del capitalismo: SALVARSI INDIVIDUALMENTE, fabbricarsi ognuno un castello di sicurezza personale. Mentre l'idea corporativa non ammette che le SALVEZZE COLLETTIVE ed è a quest'idea di salvezza collettiva, di sicurezza per tutto il popolo, che devono essere riservate, non ci stanchiamo di ripeterlo, le possibilità economiche dell'Etiopia italiana.[36]

> There is no place for social egoism in Ethiopia. There is no place for economic adventures in Ethiopia. There is no place for those intent on saving themselves INDIVIDUALLY from life's hardships. This is the essence of capitalism: INDIVIDUAL SALVATION, building one's castle of personal security. On the other hand, the corporative idea only allows COLLECTIVE SALVATION and, as we repeat tirelessly, it is for this collective salvation, for the safety of the entire people, that all economic potential of Italian Ethiopia should be reserved.

For the pre-*Politecnico* Vittorini, the project of cultural elevation of the people is hardly distinguishable from the ideal of political and social mobilization of the people (*popolo*) of the fascist revolution. Culture and

politics would coalesce in the fostering of a climate of spiritual elevation that could counter the pernicious allure of utilitarian and materialistic principles. The cultural revolution that Vittorini described in 1937
would promote a new organization of life which, in turn, would constitute "a positive springboard for the cultural elevation of the people."
The circular logic of the fascist permanent revolution seems to accom-
modate nicely Vittorini's cultural politics:

> Si tratta anche di restuire alla cultura il suo significato civile di attività
> umana necessaria e non utile; e si tratta di suscitare (questo in tutti, non
> soltanto nel popolo) il desiderio di essa come cultura generale, a prescin-
> dere dai cosiddetti scopi pratici. Si tratta infine di portare sul terreno di-
> retto del divenire culturale l'organizzazione della vita affinché nulla della
> vita si esaurisca in se stesso e tutto abbia efficacia per il divenire civile, per
> il divenire della civiltà che oggi possiamo, e per un pezzo ancora potremo
> chiamare fascista. La nostra rivoluzione è rivoluzione spirituale; deve
> dunque concretarsi in rivoluzione culturale [. . .] Non dobbiamo pertanto
> dimenticare che la nostra rivoluzione è rivoluzione in quanto è *risposta* e
> che abbiamo da rispondere a *tutti*, non a speciali categorie, che abbiamo
> da soddisfare un'esigenza di massa, che abbiamo da realizzare un pro-
> gramma di elevazione del popolo.[37]

The task is to give back to culture its civic meaning of human activity
that is necessary, not useful; and to induce (in everybody, not just the
people) this desire for it as general culture, aside from its so-called practical purposes. Finally, the task is to bring to the forefront of cultural
transformation the organization of life so that nothing in life is an end
in and of itself and everything is instrumental to civic transformation, to
the transformation of that civilization that today, and for a long time to
come, we can call fascist. Our revolution is a spiritual revolution; therefore, it must be realized as cultural revolution [. . .] We should not forget that our revolution is a revolution because it is an *answer* and that
we have to answer to *all*, not to special costituencies, and that we have to
fulfil people's needs, that we have to carry out a program of elevation of
the people.

The fascist revolution is by definition open-ended, that is, it aims at
creating a new man who is in a constant state of becoming. It is a spiritual quest that in order to retain a permanent revolutionary impetus has
to radically modify the role of culture and its impact on everyday life.

Culture has to become "open-ended," veering away from the here and now and towards joining the revolutionary trajectory in its permanent transformation. Instead of serving "scopi pratici," that is, activities that have individual utilitarian purpose, it would reorient and reorganize those very activities towards higher, collective, necessarily undefined, revolutionary goals.

The Mussolinian discursive device, that I have analysed in chapter 1, of linking an undefined but certain future to an equally undefined but critical past event, is deployed here by Vittorini to further his case against specialized culture. To go forward, the cultural revolution would have to go back, in the sense of restoring, that vague but idyllic point in time when the masses supposedly possessed a natural desire for "real" culture and all those hands would feverishly exchange books. The forward impetus of the fascist cultural revolution would be grounded retrospectively in a natural collective desire. It would be "an answer to all," a reply not aimed at addressing the needs of particular constituencies but an all-encompassing response to the popular demand for cultural elevation.

We have already examined the strategy guiding Vittorini's collective answers in his *Politecnico* letter to the young fascists. The 1946 collective address functioned to occlude their possible differences, hence, to naturalize and generalize their popular simplicity. Their undistinguishing nature (youth, blindness, stupidity) had saved them form the "real" fascism, but it also seemed to fail them now for they needed external guidance to recognize their innocence. Left to their own (inadequate) devices, they might believe that they had been fascists and never become men. If Vittorini's editorial intervention in 1946 aimed so insistently at saving "the people" *from* fascism, it was, I would suggest, not simply because Vittorini needed to distance himself from his own fascist past, but more precisely, because during his career as writer, editor, and columnist in the 1920s and 1930s, he had so frequently, and specifically, linked popular salvation *with* fascism. Vittorini's discursive operation can be viewed as a subtle erasure of his own fascist past that simultaneously retraces and attempts to "move to the left" the very rhetorical threads that he had previously used to define the Italian fascist *popolo*.

Fascism would protect the popolo against those who would corrupt its "natural" thinking, that intrinsic quality that was best exemplified by the young generations, as Vittorini explained in 1932. Far from being incompatible with fascism, as the later Vittorini will claim, the uncultivated "simple mind" of the young was apparently what the ideal fascist popolo should possess:

E gli impiegati di Ministero giudicano sempre gli uomini secondo il "pezzo grosso" che sono . . . Meschinità, meschinità di chi vive per quanto è "onorevole," per quanto è "decoroso," per quanto è di "figura" e "presenza," anzi che per quanto è "naturale." Perciò ha ragione Mussolini dove dice dei "giovani," cioè delle nuove generazioni, perché i giovani, oggi, sono tutti "natura". . . . E nel secondo decennio si vedrà anche questo. Lo "sborghesimento," prima di tutto del Partito, ciò che è urgente, poi la bonifica della mentalità dei borghesi stessi, che hanno tanto bisogno di essere ricondotti a pensare secondo natura, secondo la loro natura di Italiani. E non si dica che questo è parlare alla Rousseau. Questo è parlare alla Mussolini.[38]

Ministerial clerks always judge men according to whether they are "big shots" . . . The pettiness of those who live for what is "honourable," for what is "decorous," for what is "image" and "appearance," instead of what is "natural." Therefore, Mussolini is right to talk about "the young," that is, about the new generations, because the young today are all "nature". . . . And in the second decade we will see this as well. First of all, the "de-bourgeoisification" of the Party, which is urgent, then the reforming of the mentality of the bourgeois themselves, who are very much in need of being led back into thinking according to nature, according to their Italian nature. Let it not be said that this is speaking à la Rousseau. This is speaking à la Mussolini.

To think according to the "Italian nature" is to think like the fascist youth – with minds unreceptive to the values of bourgeois culture: to decorum, appearance, status, and everything that has to do with self-ish personal advancement and distinction. Those who do not possess "young minds" appear, in Vittorini's description, to fall by default either into the category of full-fledged bourgeois, or into the less clear-cut, but equally problematic category comprising groups that have been corrupted in some measure by bourgeois ideals. With the exception of the "natural" minds of the young, nobody is immune to the insidious lure. Interestingly, even the Fascist Party is said to be in urgent need of *sborghesimento* (de-bourgeoisification), the implication being that even card-carrying fascists are no longer real fascists when their ways diverge from the natural Italianness of thought of the young. Fascists, just like the bourgeois themselves, will have to undergo a reclamation (*bonifica*) of original thought that appears lost in the swampy lowlands of pettiness: they will have to be reformed and led back to their natural ways.[39]

Despite Vittorini's efforts to distance himself from Rousseau and to attribute the origin of his "back to nature" logic to Mussolini, the conceptual problem that he unwittingly highlights is, in fact, quintessentially Rousseauian since it constitutes the central subject of the novel *Emile*: the contradictions inherent in every pedagogical project.[40] In his famous essay ". . . That Dangerous Supplement," Jacques Derrida has encapsulated the Rousseauian preoccupation with the problem very succinctly: "Childhood is the first manifestation of the deficiency which, in Nature, calls for substitution (*suppléance*). Pedagogy illuminates perhaps more crudely the paradoxes of the supplement. How is a natural weakness possible? How can Nature ask for forces that it does not furnish? How is a child possible in general?"[41]

Derrida's gloss of Rousseau is useful for it illustrates the inescapable contradictions involved in the search for a stable, essentialist definition of a young mind and, by extension, of natural thought – that elusive characteristic that Vittorini strives to attribute to the Italian people. The problems associated with trying to define natural deficiency are the flip-side of the problems associated with the notion of natural self-sufficiency, that is, with establishing an ideal point in the formative process where lack can no longer be understood in negative terms. The two sets of problems, in fact, cannot logically be thought apart from each other, for every attempt to explain one invariably involves the other.

It is significant, however, that either one or the other side of the same impossible equation seems to occupy centre stage in Vittorini's discursive portrayals of the Italian people and of the young generations at different points in his career. Whereas the natural self-sufficiency of the young is underscored by the fascist Vittorini, their natural deficiency figures prominently in his postwar writings. In both cases, what keeps "the young" and "the people" in close discursive proximity, when not outright conflation, is the natural quality that Vittorini confers to both groups: they share a childlike simple mind that constitutes the guarantee of their cohesiveness as collective bodies.[42]

The fascist *uomo nuovo* (new man), whom Vittorini frequently extolled in the 1920s and 1930s, as well as his anti-fascist uomo nuovo, which culminates, as we will see, in Enne 2 (En 2), the protagonist of *Uomini e no*, are grounded in the discursive fiction of their popular, natural mind. If the fascist *popolo* had to shed the surplus parts of its collective body (the bourgeois parts) to go back to an ideal natural state represented by the young generations, the post-fascist *popolo* had to recognize the deficient nature of the young in order to properly assess its fascist past, that is, to "go back" and erase it by turning a lack into a natural barrier against fascism. Despite being respectively overburdened or undeveloped, Nature would ultimately serve as an ideological guarantor of a fascist status in the first case and an anti-fascist one in the second. In both cases, however, external intervention was needed to fine-tune the workings of nature or, as Derrida put it in his gloss of Rousseau, "to reconstitute Nature's edifice in the most natural way possible."[43]

When overburdened, nature's edifice would be reconstituted by excising the exogenous parts that sapped her strength. Those selfish elements that were in the business of taking instead of giving, should be shown, in Vittorini's words, the door of the edifice: "espellere il borghese che c'è in ognuno di noi. Perché anche nell'ultimo degli operai ci può essere un borghese da mettere alla porta" (to expel the bourgeois that is present in each of us. Because even in the humblest of workers there could be a bourgeois who needs to be shown the door). When underdeveloped, nature's weakness simply had to be turned around – turned into strength, if you will – by a discursive supplement that would transfigure, literally, a minus into a plus.

Vittorini himself had volunteered for the latter task in 1946. His collective answer would offer the discursive supplementation needed to "turn around" the young fascists. As for the former task of intervention upon nature, all he could do was acknowledge that the job had already been filled: "E non si dica che questo è parlare alla Rousseau. Questo è parlare alla Mussolini" (Let it not be said that this is speaking à la Rousseau. This is speaking à la Mussolini).

Heroic Temperament

We have already encountered the "supplement," in my first chapter, where we left it dressed, as it were, with Mussolini's uniform. As I argued, the rhetorical substitutions and construction of mimetic opponents served to underscore Mussolini's own unstable "properties," underpinning his capacity to embody the *pharmakon*: at once the agent responsible for the onset of national crises and their resolution. The inherent instability of the pharmakon, as we have seen, defies attempts to neatly inscribe it within a "summation of opposites" logic. Working against a stable *coincidentia oppositorum* is its sacrificial performative dimension that operates through the reiteration of locus, through movement and play that indefinitely postpone closure, and yet, gesture towards it by marking the discursive deployment of each sacrificial expulsion as a reconstitution of an original whole.

During fascism, the unity of the nation – idealized as a geographical, linguistic, political, and ideological community – was undoubtedly the privileged whole that would supersede, often by violent means, other possible communities or collective affiliations. Crucial to maintaining this privileged status, however, was not so much the institutionalized exercise of violence (or what we might think of as the reign of terror) but, rather, the ideological inscription of this privileged entity within a sacrificial economy of violence that would affirm its centrality while, at the same time, denying stability, finality, and closure to the process. The permanent revolution would go on indefinitely, requiring constant mobilization to protect but also to redraw the boundaries of the nation by colonial expansion. The same discourse that aimed to define national boundaries was, in effect, undercut by the very principle of expansion that required the outward repositioning of the border, hence, the constant destabilization of the original national whole.

The fascist *uomo nuovo* that the regime sought to create was likewise marked by a fundamental instability. If, on the one hand, it had to represent the norm to which all should aspire and conform, it also had to be exceptional in its heroic propensity, hence, radically departing from the norm. While the ideal fascist body was often represented, visually and rhetorically, as monolithic, whole, with contours inviolable and impenetrable like the national borders, the regime cultivated with equal if not greater zeal the image of the mutilated hero as the highest achievement in the life of the fascist subject. To give a limb for the fascist cause was considered the ultimate certification of a fascist status and second only to dying for the cause. In fact, the wholeness of the fascist body was often presented as the necessary prerequisite for mutilation. One needs to have in order to give.

Perhaps one of the most vivid illustrations of this bewildering logic was provided in a 1939 memo that Achille Starace, then chief of staff of the Fascist Voluntary Militia, sent to all the cabinet members and military commands where he ordered that greater effort be put in the medical care of the physically challenged and handicapped, so that they can be made ready for military service:

Dispongo pertanto che maggiore e più ampio impulso sia dato all'azione di recupero dei minorati fisici, perché si consegue un alto beneficio sociale e si apporta reale vantaggio ai singoli ed alle loro famiglie nonché alla Nazione, rendendo valido il braccio al lavoro e ridonando elementi riformati, fisicamente ripresi, al R. Esercito. E tale bonifica sociale deve riguardare non solo gli interventi operativi, per difetti o imperfezioni fisiche utilmente modificabili e le cure mediche per pregresse infermità sofferte, ma anche la profilassi e la cura dentaria che hanno la loro grande importanza sia nel campo della patologia individuale che nell'interesse dell'idoneità al servizio militare.

Ho impartito in merito esplicite disposizioni.

Dovrà costituire per gli Ufficiali Medici alto motivo di orgoglio il contributo ch'essi apportano alla tutela delle energie dei componenti l'Istituzione, alla quale hanno chiesto di appartenere, tenendo ben presente l'alto monito del DUCE "il Fascismo è religione" – Ad apostolato deve perciò elevarsi la propria opera.[44]

I order, therefore, that greater and more far-reaching efforts be put into the rehabilitation of the physically disabled, because individuals and their families, as well as the nation, receive considerable social benefit and real advantage in making one's arm fit for work and in giving back to the Royal Army reformed, physically reconstituted elements. Such social reclamation has to encompass not only surgical operations to correct physical defects and imperfections, and medical therapies to cure pre-existing infirmities, but also dental care and prophylaxis that are of great importance in the field of individual pathology as well as increasing readiness for military service.

I have given specific instructions to that effect.

The medical officers must feel very proud of their contribution in safeguarding the energies of the members of the institution that they have asked to join, bearing in mind the solemn injunction of the DUCE "Fascism is a religion" – hence, their efforts must rise to the level of apostolic mission.

As "apostles" of the nation, military doctors had to protect their institution's "energies" by reforming the physical parts of individuals who were "minorati" (disabled, literally "lessened") from birth or from previous infirmities, so that those "retaken" elements could be offered as gifts to the army – "ridonando elementi riformati, fisicamente ripresi, al R. Esercito" (giving back to the Royal Army reformed, physically reconstituted elements) – for, well, future "minorazioni" (disabling). The expenditure of national energies seemed to require a concerted recycling effort, where violence could be recharged by establishing as priority the individual's readiness to give, hence, by valuing the unity and integrity of the fascist body not per se but insofar as it makes future mutilation possible. The life of a fascist, according to Mussolini, had to be marked continually by willingness to sacrifice, without concern for personal safety or gain:

> La vita deve essere rischiata e rivissuta quotidianamente, continuamente, dimostrando che si è pronti a gettarla quando sia necessario.[45]

> Life must be put in jeopardy and re-experienced daily, continually demonstrating that one is ready to throw it away when necessary.

> Per noi fascisti la vita è un combattimento continuo, incessante, che noi accettiamo con grande disinvoltura, con grande coraggio, con la intrepidezza necessaria.[46]

> For us, fascist life is a continuous, incessant fight that we accept with great confidence, with great courage, with the necessary intrepid spirit.

> Sarete disposti a marciare incontro al pericolo, incontro alla morte, perché sentite che la vita è nulla quando sono in gioco i supremi interessi della Patria.[47]

> You are willing to march towards danger, towards death, because you feel that life is nothing when the supreme interests of the Fatherland are at stake.

> Bisogna accostarsi al martirio con devozione raccolta e pensosa, come il credente che si genuflette davanti all'altare di un dio.[48]

> One should approach martyrdom with composed and thoughtful devotion, like the believer who kneels in front of the altar of a god.

Sacrificial engagement would sustain and channel the nation's "energy" through idealistic tension, that ephemeral element that Mussolini often used as a code word for heroic and exceptional deeds as well as, significantly, for the day-to-day harmonious cooperation of different social groups.[49] Like violence, an individual or social class self-interest, when left unchannelled, that is, when not displaced and realigned with national interest, might devolve into chaos or disperse itself in unproductive ways.

Mussolini considered "altissima tensione ideale" (high idealistic tension) to be the most important condition for the effective realization of corporativism as an alternative system to the worldwide crisis of capitalism. Idealistic tension would be the cement of the ethical state, the crucial ingredient that would bind the economic and political discipline of the single party onto the totalitarian state, enabling the latter to absorb and redirect all the energy and interests of the people:

> Non vi è dubbio che, data la crisi generale del capitalismo, delle soluzioni corporative si imporranno dovunque, ma per fare il corporativismo pieno, completo, integrale, rivoluzionario, occorrono tre condizioni.
>
> Un partito unico, per cui accanto alla disciplina economica entri in azione anche la disciplina politica, e ci sia al di sopra dei contrastanti interessi un vincolo che tutti unisce, in fede comune.
>
> Non basta. Occorre, dopo il partito unico, lo Stato totalitario, cioè lo Stato che assorba in sé, per trasformarla e potenziarla, tutta l'energia, tutti gli interessi, tutta la speranza di un popolo.
>
> Non basta ancora. Terza ed ultima e più importante condizione: occorre vivere un periodo di altissima tensione ideale. (Vivi applausi).
>
> Noi viviamo in questo periodo di alta tensione ideale.
>
> Ecco perché noi, grado a grado, daremo forza e consistenza a tutte le nostre realizzazioni, tradurremo nel fatto tutta la nostra dottrina.
>
> Come negare che questo nostro, fascista, sia un periodo di alta tensione ideale? Nessuno può negarlo. Questo è il tempo nel quale le armi furono coronate da vittoria. Si rinnovano gli istituti, si redime la terra, si fondano le città.[50]

There is no doubt that, given the general crisis of capitalism, corporativist solutions will be imposed everywhere, but in order to reach a corporativism that is full, complete, integral, revolutionary, three conditions are needed:

A single party, so that economic discipline can work in unison with political discipline, and a bond that unites everybody in a common faith by subsuming contrasting interests. But this is not enough. Besides the single party, the totalitarian State is needed, that is, the State that encompasses, in order to transform it and magnify it, all the energy, all the interests, all the hopes of a people. It is still not enough. The third, last, and most important condition: It is necessary to live in a time marked by the highest idealistic tension. (*Loud applause.*)

We live in this time of high idealistic tension.

That is why, step by step, we will give strength and consistency to all of our accomplishments, turning our entire doctrine into deeds.

Can it be denied that this fascist time of ours is one of high idealistic tension? Nobody can deny it. This is the time when armament was crowned by victory. Institutions are reformed, land is reclamed, cities are founded.

Potentially divergent interests and desires would be depressurized and repolarized in the formation of a new organism, the totalitarian state, possessing a unitary will, absolute ethical value, and, apparently, even a personality:

> Il fascismo ha restituito allo Stato la sua attività sovrana – rivendicandone, contro tutti i particolarismi di classe e di categoria, l'assoluto valore etico; ha restituito al Governo dello Stato, ridòtto a strumento esecutivo dell'assemblea elettiva, la sua dignità di rappresentante della personalità dello Stato e la pienezza della sua potestà di imperio; ha sottratto l'amministrazione alle pressioni di tutte le faziosità e di tutti gli interessi.[51]

> Fascism has given back to the State its sovereign function – reclaiming, against all particularisms of class and profession, its absolute ethical value; it has given back to the Governance of the State that had been reduced to an executive instrument of the elective assembly, its dignity as representative of the State's character, and its full function in wielding authority. It has removed the administrative body from all the pressures of factionalism and partisan interests.

The organic state was described as an immense living organism characterized by internal harmony, by the effective cooperation of previously contrasting interests, and by the laborious voluntary contribution of each single individual who felt accomplished in being a living molecule of the larger social body:

> A questo vecchio Stato [liberale] che noi abbiamo sepolto con un funerale di terza classe, abbiamo sostituito lo Stato corporativo e fascista, lo Stato della società nazionale, lo Stato che raccoglie, controlla, armonizza e

contempera gli interessi di tutte le classi sociali, le quali si vedono egual-
mente tutelate. E mentre prima, durante gli anni del regime demo-liberale,
le masse laboriose guardavano con diffidenza lo Stato, erano al di fuori
dello Stato, erano contro lo Stato, consideravano lo Stato come un nemico
d'ogni giorno e di ogni ora, oggi non c'è italiano che lavori, che non cerchi
il suo posto nelle Corporazioni, nelle federazioni, che non voglia essere
una molecola vivente di quel grande, immenso organismo vivente che è lo
Stato nazionale corporativo fascista.[52]

To the old [liberal] State that we have buried with a third-class funeral,
we have substituted the corporative and fascist State, the State of national
society, the State that concentrates, controls, harmonizes, and tempers the
interests of all social classes, which are thereby protected in equal measure. Whereas, during the years of demo-liberal regime, the labouring
masses looked with diffidence upon the State, were outside the State and
against the State, and considered the State an enemy every day and every
hour, there is not one working Italian today who does not seek a place in
his Corporation or federation, who does not wish to be a living molecule
of that great, immense, living organization that is the national corporate
State of Fascism.

How then, was all this efficiency, integration, cooperation, and harmonious labour supposed to generate the heroic new man in a perpetual state of readiness for exceptional deeds? How was the orderly
living molecule to maintain the highest idealistic tension necessary for
the continual displacement of frictional class divisions? The harmonious integration of individual tasks and social roles that was to enable the entry of the masses into the fascist state would not seem to
be conducive to the formation of heroic temperaments or at least to
sustain them indefinitely and on a national scale as was the goal of the
regime. The solution, in typical Mussolinian fashion, was the recourse
to discursive deployment of sacrificial expulsions, as the ideological
dispositif that would recharge and calibrate the idealistic tension, keeping it just at the right level of readiness, like the bow ready to propel
the arrow:

L'arco della volontà deve essere sempre teso, perché spesso – il caso, la
fatalità, gli uomini – minacciano, compromettono, guastano l'opera che si
credeva compiuta.[53]

The arch of the will should always be kept in tension because chance, fate, men – often threaten, compromise, ruin the work that was thought complete.

In fascist terms, of course, completed work can never be such, because even when it comes to integrating social classes into a harmonious whole, Mussolinian logic dictates that one element should be expelled for the others to coalesce. Since the actual expulsion of an entire class that constituted a significant part of the Italian population would not have been very practical, the Duce settled for expelling the spirit or temperament that was typical of that class, from the fascist organism: the *spirito borghese* (bourgeois spirit) acquired all the traits of a veritable *bête noire*, remaining a favourite target of the Duce's invectives throughout the *ventennio*. The vitriolic attacks against bourgeois sentiment were paralleled in intensity and frequency only by those levelled against the anti-fascist opposition that we have examined in chapter 1. Like the perennially "lurking" anti-fascists, the bourgeois ethos seems to have occupied, in the Duce's speeches, the place reserved for the living dead: it was gone, and yet, it continued to be a threat, buried with the past, and yet, a dangerous menace for the future of the fascist nation. But, while the "camouflaging anti-fascists" were considered internal enemies that, at least in principle, could be physically located and expelled, the bourgeois spirit represented the ultimate internal enemy, dwelling not in some dark corner but in the very hearts and minds of Italians: an insidious presence that threatened "the fascist in every fascist," deflating the high tension of the new man and reducing him to a comfort-seeking "fascista imborghesito" (bourgeoisified fascist):

L'antifascismo è finito. I suoi conati sono individuati e sempre più sporadici. I traditori, i vociferatori, gli imbelli saranno eliminati senza pietà. Ma un pericolo tuttavia può minacciare il regime: questo pericolo può essere rappresentato da quello che comunemente viene chiamato "spirito borghese," spirito cioè di soddisfazione e di adattamento, tendenza allo scetticismo, al compromesso, alla vita comoda, al carrierismo. Il fascista imborghesito è colui che crede che oramai non c'è più nulla da fare, che l'entusiasmo disturba, che le parate sono troppe, che è ora di assettarsi, che basta un figlio solo e che il piede in casa è la sovrana delle esigenze. Non escludo l'esistenza di temperamenti borghesi, nego che possano essere fascisti. Il credo del fascista è *l'eroismo*, quello del borghese è *l'egoismo*.

Contro questo pericolo non v'è che un rimedio: il principio della rivoluzione continua. Tale principio va affidato ai giovani di anni e di cuore.
Esso allontana i poltroni dell'intelletto, tiene sempre desto l'interesse
del popolo: non immobilizza la storia, ma ne sviluppa le forze. La rivoluzione nel nostro pensiero è una creazione che alterna la grigia fatica
della costruzione quotidiana ai momenti folgoranti del sacrificio e della
gloria. Sottoposto a questo travaglio che segue la guerra, è già possibile
vedere, e sempre più si vedrà, il cambiamento fisico e morale del popolo
italiano.[54]

Anti-fascism is over. Its last sputterings are contained and more and more
sporadic. Traitors, rumour mongers, cowards, will be eliminated without
mercy. There is, however, a danger that can threaten the regime: this danger can be described as what is commonly called "bourgeois spirit," the
spirit of satisfaction and adaptability, the tendency to scepticism, to compromise, to comfortable living, to careerism. The bourgeoisified fascist is
one who believes that at this point there is nothing more to be done, that
enthusiasm is a nuisance, that there are too many parades, that it's time
to settle down, that one child is enough and that keeping one's foot in the
house is a sacrosanct prerogative. I do not deny the existence of bourgeois
temperaments, I deny that they are fascist. The creed of a fascist is *heroism*,
that of a bourgeois is *egoism*.

There is only one remedy against this danger: the principle of permanent revolution. Such principle should be entrusted to the young and
young at heart. It shuns the intellectually lazy, and always stirs popular
interest: it does not immobilize history, it bolsters its strengths, instead.
The revolution of our thought is a creation that alternates the drudgery of
daily construction to the dazzling moments of sacrifice and glory. As the
Italian people have been subjected to the turmoil that follows war, their
physical and moral change is already apparent, and will be even more so
in the future.

For the permanent revolution to create and maintain the *uomo nuovo*
in full heroic tension, it needs to continually expel those parasitical,
lazy, and egotistical parts, to keep on sacrificing them at "dazzling
moments" ("momenti folgoranti") so that the laborious and harmonic
whole of the remaining parts can be properly recharged and realigned.
And since the military occasion for the sacrificial dazzling moment
might not always be readily available, its spirit must be recreated and
repeated in the labouring tasks of everyday life:

Ognuno di voi deve considerarsi un soldato; un soldato anche quando non porta il grigioverde, un soldato anche quando lavora, nell'ufficio, nelle officine, nei cantieri o nei campi; un soldato legato a tutto il resto dell'Esercito; una molecola che sente e pulsa coll'intero organismo.[55]

Each one of you must consider himself a soldier; a soldier even when not wearing military fatigues, a soldier even when working at the office, in workshops, building sites or in the fields; a soldier tied to the rest of the Army; a molecule that feels and pulsates with the entire organism.

The fascist organism – of individuals, as well as of the nation – must be in a permanent state of mobilization, in war, as well as in peace:

Tutta l'atmosfera nella quale si svolge la vita del popolo italiano, ha carattere militare, deve avere e avrà un carattere sempre più militare: il popolo ha l'orgoglio di sapersi mobilitato permanentemente per le opere di pace e per quelle di guerra.[56]

The entire atmosphere surrounding the life of Italian people has a militaristic character, must have and will have a character that is more and more militarized: the people feel the pride of knowing they are permanently mobilized for works of peace as well as war.

Through permanent mobilization, the fascist organism can maintain its "heroic temperament" and forestall the otherwise inevitable stagnation: that dangerous state of low energy and stasis that might cause it to lose interest in military formations and become distracted by economic concerns or, even worse, by the economic mechanisms of social class formation:

Non è stato sempre il "combattimento" il fine ultimo di ogni nostra speranza? E non è il particolare temperamento dei fascisti quello di preferire il rischio di una vita eroica, alla stasi di un'esistenza insulsa?[57]

Has "fighting" not always been the ultimate goal of all our aspirations? And is it not the specific temperament of fascists to prefer the risk of heroic life over the stasis of a bland existence?

With the continual rhetorical expulsions of the bourgeois (or, rather, its temperament) from the organism of the *uomo nuovo*, Mussolini effectively put the notion of permanent mobilization at the service of permanent displacement of social class structure. The rhetoric of sacrifice provided the crucial discursive link between the two for it allowed a constant reiteration of the mechanism of expulsion – or displacement of the part, if you will – to be construed as the necessary step in the process of recovery of an original whole. This process would keep, at the same time, that elusive point of origin new by repeating the recovery mechanism over and over again in the present and, we may add, stretching it until the end of the regime. In fact, as late as 1939, Mussolini declared that the social revolution had just begun: "L'uomo delle squadre dice a colui che si attarda dietro le persiane che la rivoluzione non è finita, ma, dal punto di vista del costume, del carattere, delle distanze sociali, è appena cominciata" (The *squadrista* [member of fascist squad] tells the man who is still hesitating behind the window shutters that the revolution is not over, indeed, from the point of view of customs, of character, of social distance, it has just begun).[58]

Social distance was of particular concern to the regime, for it is invariably a reflection of relations among social classes and a potential referent for polarizing class consciousness. Although the regime did not seek to eliminate the economic class structure, it strove to deflect potential class conflict by emphasizing the harmonious cooperation of different social classes in the attainment of national goals.[59] Cooperation would be fostered by closer interaction among groups, or what Mussolini called "accorciare le distanze sociali" (reducing social distance). Reducing social distance did not mean that the fascist state favoured eliminating class-based economic differences; it meant, rather, that these differences should not count in ideological terms. They would be there, and yet, effectively displaced – sutured, as it were – in the equalizing act of giving a bodily part to the organic nation:

La collaborazione, cittadini, fra chi lavora e chi dà il lavoro, fra chi dà le braccia e chi dà il cervello; tutti gli elementi della produzione hanno le loro gerarchie inevitabili e necessarie; attraverso questo programma voi arriverete al benessere, la Nazione arriverà alla prosperità ed alla grandezza.[60]

Citizens – the collaboration between those who work and those who provide work, between those who give their arms and those who give their brain; all the production elements have their necessary and inevitable hierarchies; with this program you will find well-being, the Nation will attain prosperity and greatness.

Hierarchies among social groups were "inevitable" but differences among them had been "overcome," rendered invisible by a new condition of ideological proximity that effectively blurred the lines of separation:

> Che cosa in questo momento io vedo dinanzi a me? La Nazione. Vedo il popolo, che non ha più le classi e le categorie dai confini insuperabili.[61]

> What do I see at this moment in front of me? The Nation. I see the people no longer constrained by classes and categories with rigid boundaries.

The internal "superamento dei confini" or the overcoming of class differences would be paralleled, not surprisingly, by the external "superamento dei confini," that is, by the overcoming of national borders through colonial expansion.[62] With the sacrificial mobilization, or displacement, if you will, of bodily parts, the fascist organism would transform potentially disruptive internal tension into the "heroic tension" of imperial pursuits:

> Il popolo italiano, pur di non rimanere prigioniero nel mare che fu di Roma, sarebbe capace di sacrifici anche eccezionali.[63]

> The Italian people, to avoid being emprisoned by the sea that belonged to Rome, would be capable of sacrifices, even exceptional ones.

With the sacrificial expulsion of the sedentary and egotistical bourgeois from the national body, social distance could be reduced through the elision of a class (its temperament) and a new "intangible" hierarchy of social classes put into place. A new aristocracy would occupy the pinnacle of the sacrificial social ladder and its ascent serve as the cement, or ideological binding agent, for the other groups:

> Io considero i combattenti, i mutilati, le famiglie dei caduti, come l'aristocrazia grande, pura e intangibile della nuova Italia.[64]

> I consider the combatants, the amputees, the families of the fallen, the great, pure, and intangible aristocracy of the new Italy.

> [Medaglie d'oro]: Voi siete veramente il fiore purpureo della nostra razza, siete la vera aristocrazia della nuova generazione guerriera che sulla terra, sul mare e nel cielo, ha compiuto prodigi di eroismo.[65]

(Gold medals): You are truly the pinnacle of our race, you are the real aristocracy of the new generation of warriors that on land, at sea, and in the sky has performed heroic feats.

La realtà è, che al disopra delle tessere, degli statuti, dei regolamenti, dei programmi, al disopra dei simboli e delle parole, al di sopra della teoria e della pratica, al disopra dell'ideale e della polica, un cemento formidabile tiene legate le falangi fasciste; un vincolo sacro infrangibile tiene serrati i fedeli del Littorio: il cemento, il vincolo sacro dei nostri Morti.[66]

In reality, beyond party cards, statutes, regulations, programs, beyond symbols and words, beyond theory and practice, beyond ideals and politics, a formidable cement binds the fascist phalanxes; a sacred, unbreakable tie that holds together the faithful of the Littorio: the cement is the sacred obligation to our Dead.

Above all, and apparently keeping it all together, there was sacrifice: the mechanism that allowed the constant recharging of the ideological tension needed to create and maintain the *uomo nuovo* in a discursive position of heroic readiness. Just like the fascist nation, the new man would be able to overcome previous limits by climbing the ladder of ever higher heroic pursuits:

E in Europa, l'ho già detto e lo ripeto, c'è chi sale e c'è chi scende; il destino dell'Europa non è irrevocabilmente tracciato e definito. Io penso che fra coloro che salgono, fra coloro che montano all'orizzonte europeo ci sono gli italiani, ci siamo noi.[67]

I have already said it and I repeat it: In Europe there are those who are rising and those who are declining; the destiny of Europe is not irrevocably set and defined. I think that among those who are rising, among those appearing on the European horizon, are the Italians, we are.

In the end, of course, the heroic ladder began to wobble and coming over the European horizon was not the Italian nation or the other fascist allies but the smouldering wreckage of the Second World War. The edifice that was held together by the "vincolo sacro" (sacred tie) crumbled as it carried out the sacrificial expulsion of its most entrenched occupant: the Duce.

The Troubled Past

As we have seen with the 1946 letter to the young fascists, Vittorini's distancing efforts from a troubled past involved a textual erasure and delicate recasting of his position. Simplicity, I have argued, is the term that allowed him to transform a retrospective view on a tainted past into a sweeping point of departure for saving the people *as a group* – peeling them away from fascism, as it were, by naturalizing their perceptual inability to see through the regime's benign appearances. The people, it seems, never really had a choice between fascism and anti-fascism since, as Vittorini concluded, what they thought was their fascist belief was actually anti-fascism.

It is hard to envision a more skilful and encompassing justificatory strategy, one that manages at once to exonerate the people while retroactively morphing fascism into incipient anti-fascism. A nagging question, however, remains, dangling like a thread not completely tucked away in the discursive ideological fold: where did "the real" fascism go after the people had been saved from their own ideology? Or, to put it another way, whom does Vittorini leave in ideological Hell after rescuing the people, and are there lost unredeemable souls dwelling somewhere in his textual landscape? They are, in fact, not very hard to find for Vittorini had depicted them in his 1945 novel *Uomini e no* which remains to this day one of his most well-known and celebrated works, second perhaps only to *Conversazione in Sicilia* (*In Sicily*). Without taking anything away from the critical praise that has been lavished upon this text, I would like to suggest that if we keep the discursive strategy of the 1946 letter in mind when reading *Uomini e no*, its narrative assumes a more complex and problematic valence than is generally recognized.[68]

Vittorini's preoccupation with popular elevation that during fascism had often coincided with the regime's attempt to forge a more heroic and less bourgeois *uomo nuovo* is further complicated in *Uomini e no* by a reflective stance on what constitutes a man in the first place.[69] The protagonist Enne 2 (En 2) is a young leader of the resistance movement fighting the German occupation of Milan in 1944. Violent scenes of urban combat and poignant descriptions of German atrocities are interspersed with deeply introspective moments in which Enne 2 ponders the meaning of his actions and the ethical status of the choices that he and his companions face every day.

The brutality of war seems to contradict at every turn man's belief that actions can have ultimate moral purpose beyond their immediate scope. The description of the senseless killing of civilians in reprisals and the grisly display of corpses as warnings to the population provide a stark counterpoint to the much more intimate scenes of interaction between Enne 2 and his companions. Gestures, like offering a cigarette, or mundane activities such as riding a bicycle with a girlfriend, assume the lyrical tone of deeply human activities as they are set against the background of deeds that call into question the very definition of human behaviour. Indeed, it is the boundary that separates human from non-human, or man from not-man, that constitutes the central theme of the novel, that at times seems to veer into an existential dimension of ever deepening doubts and unbridled pessimism about the human condition.

There is, however, little doubt or existential languor in the novel about the status of the German occupiers as they are placed squarely into non-human territory. The constant association of Germans with their vicious dogs reinforces their non-human qualities as they are, effectively, transformed into "ideological animals." A scene where the dogs are fed an Italian prisoner makes this point quite literally as does the nickname of the German commander in charge of the occupation: Cane Nero (Black Dog).[70]

If moral dilemmas do not affect the Germans, who are represented as clearly beyond morality, they are acutely felt by the resistance fighters and their leader Enne 2, in particular. The concepts of salvation and perdition are constantly invoked by Enne 2 to denote, respectively, survivors and victims in the struggle for liberation: "to be saved" or "lost" (*salvarsi* or *perdersi*), one or the other will be their ultimate fate. The two terms also function as intermediate points of moral reflection and negotiation in their journey towards the *Liberazione*, which represents the end point of collective salvation from the hellish German occupation. Daily decisions to partake in dangerous operations or to aid fellow fighters alter the likelihood that they might be saved or lost as individuals, but these decisions might also change the likelihood of collective salvation, for their willingness to sacrifice – to lose themselves – might bring the *Liberazione* closer. Personal and collective interests are thus intertwined in ways that are often at odds with each other, requiring choices that are difficult even for committed, militant anti-fascists.

Enne 2, however, adopts one constant and overriding principle for tackling even the most intricate moral or practical choice: simplicity. Amid the chaos and disorientation of war, he will always search for and follow the simple path:

> Fumava, pensava alla sua cosa di dieci anni con Berta, e sapeva che Berta sarebbe tornata. Era sempre tornata, sempre ripartiva, poteva continuare così anche sempre, tornare, ripartire, e una volta poteva anche non ripartire più.
>
> Tra un anno ancora?
>
> Forse già la prima volta, o tra dieci anni ancora, egli lo sapeva, ma era come se non lo sapesse, o come se aspettare questo che sapeva fosse troppo complicato, e gli occorresse qualcosa di più semplice. Lo stesso con gli uomini che si perdevano: avrebbero continuato a perdersi, poi avrebbero finito di esser perduti, vi sarebbe stata una liberazione, egli lo sapeva; ma era come se non lo sapesse, o come se resistere fino ad averla non fosse abbastanza semplice mentre a lui occorreva qualcosa di molto semplice, molto semplice, a tal punto semplice da poter risolvere, semplicità per semplicità, ogni sua voglia di perdersi insieme ad ognuno che si perdeva.[71]

He was smoking, thinking of his ten-year-long thing with Berta, and he knew that Berta would return. She had always returned, and had always left again; it would continue like this forever, her coming, then leaving; and one time she might not leave again.

In a year from now?

It might be the next time, or ten years from now, he knew that, but it was as if he didn't know, or as if he knew that what he was waiting for would be too complicated, and he turned his thoughts to something simpler. It was the same thing with the men who went down: they would go on perishing, then they would cease perishing, there would be a liberation, he knew that; but it was as if he did not know it, or as if resisting until it came was not simple enough, and he needed something very simple, indeed, so simple it was able to dispel, for simplicity's sake, all his desire to go down alongside everyone else who was lost.

Enne 2 knows that the liberation is just a matter of time, but all the same he wants to sacrifice himself, his desire to "lose himself" overrides any tactical calculation: it is really not a matter of choice, it seems, but the most simple thing that he can do. The concern with simplicity dominates such a large portion of the novel, and is presented with such repetitive, obsessive regularity that it cannot be discounted as an incidental motif. Or, more accurately, we might think of it as incidental only in a strictly fetishistic sense, as a recurring detail that stands in the place of, and preserves as unsettled, a problem of knowledge.[72]

I am suggesting that simplicity functions in this text as a rhetorical suspensory belt, a thick veil that precludes ultimate verification, hence, allowing Vittorini to disavow the possibility that a conscious choice to resist or not to resist can be made. Since the simple course of action can mean different and, in fact, quite opposite things depending on the circumstances, to choose simplicity amounts, in effect, to avoid choosing. Notice how, in the following passage, a conversation between Enne 2 and Lorena (a fellow resistance fighter), simplicity overrides any other personal motivation or reason for doing what they do, subsuming alternatives into one seemingly overarching category:

"Lorena" disse Enne 2. "Tu sei in gamba, sei anche brava, sei una bella ragazza . . ."

"Che cosa ti piglia?"

"Lasciami parlare. Forse sei anche più diritta di ogni altra donna o uomo al mondo."

"Lo credi?"

"Tu puoi fare sempre quello che è più facile fare."

"Lo spero."

"Io pure" disse Enne 2 "vorrei fare quello che è più semplice."

"E non puoi farlo? Se lo vuoi puoi farlo."

"Invece no. Tu sei sulla sedia, sei venuta, ed è semplice. Non è semplice per te?"

"Certo che è semplice."

"Se tu fossi un'altra persona sarebbe semplice per tutti e due. Potremmo avere tutti e due quello che è più semplice. E persino andar via da Milano sarebbe semplice."

"Non è semplice andar via da Milano?"

"Per me? Per me no. Per te sarebbe semplice avere quello che vuoi, ed è semplice lo stesso non poterlo avere. Anche restar seduta tutta la notte su una sedia per te è semplice."

"È semplicissimo."[73]

"Lorena," En 2 began. "You are clever, you are good, you are a beautiful girl . . ."

"What's got into you?"

"Let me speak. Perhaps you are more upstanding than any woman or man in the world."

"Do you think so?"

"You are always able to do the thing that's simplest to do."

"I hope so."

"I too would like to do the simplest thing," said En 2.

"And can't you? If you want to you can do it."

"But I am not able. You are sitting on the chair, you've come here, and it is simple. Isn't it simple for you?"

"Of course it's simple."

"If you were another person it would be simple for both of us. We could both have what is simplest. And even leaving Milan would be simple."

"Isn't it simple to leave Milan?"

"For me? Not for me. For you it would be simple to have what you want, and for you it is also simple not to have it. Even staying on a chair the whole night is simple for you."

"It is very simple."

For Enne 2 simplicity is paramount. What is simple is what one is naturally inclined to do when faced with difficult choices: following one's instincts and desires rather than weighing costs and benefits and comparing possible outcomes. Or put another way, in *Uomini e no*, simplicity transforms a choice to be made by individuals into something already decided by nature and, hence, to be just recognized and acted on.

Enne 2's quest for simplicity culminates with his "decision" not to leave Milan. Leaving would have been the rational choice since the city had become dangerous for him after he was identified as a prominent militant anti-fascist and his picture was printed in newspapers. He would, instead, wait in his room, guns pointed at the door, for the arrival of Cane Nero, and mutual death would be assured:

L'operaio se ne andò, la voce di *Cane Nero* era davanti alla casa, c'era anche il suo scudiscio che fischiava, e *l'uomo Enne 2* era sicuro di fare la cosa più semplice che potesse fare.

Faceva una cosa come la cosa che avevano fatto lo spagnolo e Figlio-di-Dio. Si perdeva, ma combatteva insieme. Non combatteva insieme? Mica c'era solo combattere e sopravvivere. C'era anche combattere e perdersi. E lui faceva questo con tanti altri che l'avevano fatto [. . .]

Tolse la sicura alle due pistole.[74]

The worker went away; *Black Dog*'s voice was heard outside the building, along with his whistling whip, and *En 2 the man* was sure of doing the simplest thing he could do.

He was doing something like what the Spaniard and Son-of-God had done. He was going down, but along with it he was fighting. Wasn't he fighting along with it? There was more to it than fighting and surviving. There was also fighting and going down. And he was doing this along with the many others who had done it [. . .]

He released the safety catch on both pistols.

Vittorini ends the protagonist's life with a scene of heroic self-sacrifice in which Enne 2 "the man" brings about his own death in order to kill Cane Nero, "the ideological beast." The choice that Enne 2, in effect, has made of the moment and manner of his own death has been transformed, by the narrative insistence on simplicity, into an inevitable conclusion and a fulfilment of Enne 2's political role. Although this inevitability seems designed to solidify Enne 2 as a heroic anti-fascist, it also, I would argue, serves the more covert and crucial purpose of undermining the notion of resistance as a conscious choice that one can, in fact, make. If militant anti-fascism is not freely chosen but is a role that one recognizes and fulfils as "the simplest thing," then, by extension, a less militant, more widespread popular anti-fascism can also be construed as not a matter of choice but a matter of recognition and fulfilment. The people would just have to recognize that their simple ways are, in fact, an indication of their propensity for anti-fascism. Only through this recognition can they ground and fulfil their role as historical protagonists of the *Liberazione*.

The narrative of *Uomini e no*, subtly but significantly, enables the logic of the 1946 letter to the young fascists. By undermining choice and valorizing recognition, it prepares Vittorini's argument that the young fascists (and, hence, "the people") had been anti-fascists all along but they just did not know it, or failed to recognize it. The "adjectival" fascists will have to look back at their own past and separate themselves from the "real" fascism in order to become *uomini*. Vittorini had already provided them with a compelling portrait of *non-uomini*, a group ideologically damned that was unmistakably fascist: the Germans. Having placed them, literally, in the doghouse, the Germans represent a zone of abject ideological otherness that Italians would need to disavow in order to come to terms with their own problematic past.

Vittorini had considerable experience in identifying and expelling otherness as a process that would aid the formation of the Italian *uomo nuovo*. As we have seen in the first part of this chapter, the fascist *uomo nuovo* that he advocated during the years of the regime depended on successfully taking the bourgeois out of the *uomo*. It is not surprising, then, that his postwar *uomo nuovo* would require a similar operation of displacement of an abject part. In other words, to discursively portray the postwar new man as truly new and not just as a "fascista pentito" (repentant fascist), he needs to take the fascist past literally out of him.

The final scene of Enne 2's self-sacrifice represents an effort to give a dramatic narrative enactment to this difficult operation. Cane Nero is not simply the quintessential "beastly" fascist; he is also the embodiment of an Italian fascist past that Vittorini clearly prefers to recode as "German" in an effort to dispose of it more easily. If the quintessentially new man Enne 2 has "no choice" but to die while killing Cane Nero, it is because Cane Nero stands, in a larger sense, for the old fascist self, that tainted part that will need to be eliminated for Vittorini and his "young pupils" to make a fresh start in post-Liberation Italy.

Conclusion

This book has attempted to trace sacrificial discourse in political and literary texts of the *ventennio*. I have argued that while often found in political and religious narratives, "sacrifice" acquired a distinctive set of meanings and ideological functions in the context of Italian fascism. Repeated introduction and narrative dramatizations of a sacrificial scene were fundamental to the regime's ability to sustain a revolutionary ethos beyond its early movement phase and to its efforts to create a fascist subject who would view self-effacement as the highest personal achievement. The rhetoric of sacrifice proved to be a crucial tool for justifying the control and deployment of violence, bridging the gap between physical force and its verbal counterpart, and between potential and actual force.

Readiness to sacrifice was a central tenet of the regime's efforts to create a state of permanent mobilization. In addition to furthering the militaristic ethos of the regime, it provided a discursive platform for recharging and channelling violence in ways that supported social cohesion and integration.

The sacrificial propensity of the fascist subject was assiduously cultivated by the regime that established and rhetorically reiterated its centrality in the forging and maintenance of heroism, an indispensable quality of the fascist "new man," perhaps its single most important trait. Potentially divisive internal tensions stemming from social class differences were displaced by the discursive emphasis on heroic tension, a state of sacrificial mobilization that required the expulsion of bourgeois characteristics from the body politic. This body was understood both as a collective entity in which social groups with different functions coalesced organically (as parts of a physical body would) and in individual terms, as an ideal comprising physical and temperamental traits, to which the new man should aspire in order to achieve fascist self-identity and socialization.

A discursive economy of sacrificial giving was meant to foreclose egoistic calculations, thereby preventing expenditure of energies and resources deemed to weaken national cohesion or to deflate the militaristic will of the people. This discourse was articulated and amplified in specific ways that this book has sought to illustrate: crisis and resolution, and social contact between the Duce and the masses and among different classes, were key rhetorical fields. Not only were these fields long-lived, spanning the twenty-year duration of the regime, but they were also frequently deployed and adapted to different contexts and needs. Both fields depended on the discursive articulation of a sacrificial scene that governed the relation between parts and the whole by sanctioning the expulsion or segregation of undesirable elements such as anti-fascist and bourgeois tendencies from the national collectivity.

Furthermore, this sacrificial substratum was central to the notion of discourse itself during the ventennio as it undergirded the relation between subject and voice. Fostering the voluntary sacrifice of individual voice and the acquisition of a collective "echoing" voice by the fascist subject set boundaries on the content and, more importantly, on the modalities of speech. The rhetoric of anti-rhetoric, in a paradoxical fashion illustrated, or modelled, by the Duce in countless speeches, valorized silence, construed not as an absence of communication but as a cornerstone of a fascist discursive style in which the constant limiting of verbal expression to an essential minimum was viewed performatively.

Sacrificial self-limitation was compensated ideologically by the subject's acquisition of a fascist identity that was learned, practised, and consolidated in the creation and repetition of an echoing posture – the acceptance of the voice of the Duce as one's own. Fascist silence was, in fact, not silent at all but a figure of sacrificial submission, shorthand for the substitution of individual speech and self-expression with a collective, totalizing voice. Social contact, as defining the relation between Duce and the fascist subject, and as bridging (shortening) the social distance among classes, was to constitute the end product of a substitution that was performed discursively.

I have argued that sacrificial rhetoric was used to displace differences and deflect potential class conflict within the nation. It was central to creating a fascist subject who would labour in silence – a new man able to master the skill of selfless expression required for joining the collective national voice.

I have also attempted to draw the broader implications of the rhetoric of sacrifice in shaping the discourse about fascism, its legibility and, indeed, historical intelligibility, after the ventennio. The retrospective appraisal of fascism that unfolds in the writings of two major literary figures of the interwar years, Carlo Emilio Gadda and Elio Vittorini, points not only to the centrality of sacrifice in fascist rhetoric, but also to its pivotal role (and I mean pivotal literally since both writers distanced themselves eventually from their "fascist past") in constructing representations of a new, post-fascist Italian society that was entering "adulthood" and leaving behind a state of "infantile immaturity." Sacrifice emerged as the discursive ground on which ideological shifting, replacing, and recasting were carried out, a perimeter that both writers, albeit in different ways, patrolled to reposition themselves in relation to the dictatorship, and to distance the nation from its very recent and troubled past. In both cases, it was by depicting a sacrificial labouring body that the question of which social classes a collective, national voice should represent, and which it should exclude, was articulated.

By following a trajectory internal to the fascist and anti-fascist writings of the two authors, I have sought to bring into relief this strangely and obsessively manipulated body, to shed light on the reasons for its silencing, fragmentation, dispersal, infantilizing, and for Vittorini, retrieval and revalorization.

For Gadda, sacrifice interfered with crowd control. His texts attempt to establish a barrier against the encroachment of lower classes into the bourgeois society he sharply criticized but where he ultimately felt most at home. Not coincidentally, it is by staging an elaborate scene of domestic trespass that his famous novel, La cognizione del dolore, set in a thinly disguised fascist Italy, attempts to come to terms with the mechanisms of social advancement, or entry of the lower classes into the state that fascism had brought about and that Gadda had resisted. It is these mechanisms, inextricably bound to the sacrificial rhetoric of the regime, that his narrative opposes – and not fascism itself. By highlighting Gadda's resistance to sacrifice, I have sought to render Gadda's "anti-fascism" legible, that is, to discern the logic that guides his otherwise opaque textual representations of labouring bodies – bodies that are physically deformed and verbally incoherent.

This legibility is crucial to our understanding of Gadda's literary production and of equal importance for the scope of this book. It shows how the rhetoric of sacrifice was used to articulate the properties of a national, collective voice and to negotiate the "correct" distance among social classes during fascism, as well as marking an "after" – a "turning away from" or repositioning in relation to an uncomfortable fascist past. The textual trajectory maps the development of this turn as it was enabled by the articulation of sacrificial economies. Sacrifice was not just a theme in Gadda's writing but a central structuring principle of his narrative, one that motivated and, indeed, animated some of his most famous literary creations. This exploration has benefited our understanding of the works of a major literary figure, and also illustrated from within, as it were, the discursive mechanisms that bound sacrificial rhetoric to fascism. Gadda's own attempts to untangle them make him an analytical ally of sorts (albeit a very recalcitrant one) as we are compelled to ponder the ideological and textual reasons behind such sustained efforts on his part.

In his technical articles, written in the mid-1930s in praise of urban renewal depopulation schemes, Gadda shared, indeed, reproduced, the fascist rhetoric of silencing the labouring body that was a fundamental part of the regime's sacrificial discourse. As the first two chapters of this book have illustrated, the fascist rhetoric of sacrifice was characterized by the inseparability of the moment of violence, which encompassed the silencing of the labouring body, from the compensatory moment of acquiring a fascist identity. Displacement was always followed by replacement. Gadda, however, could not abide the compensatory aspect of sacrifice that corresponded to the "entry" of the masses into the state.

His ideological landscapes attempt to come to terms with "open spaces," and the social contact that might ensue therein, either by controlling it or by registering the painful failure to do so.

Whether in the novelistic settings of the late 1930s and early 1940s featuring bleak geographical features and alienated inhabitants of a fictional South American country that closely resembles Italy under fascism, or in the openly anti-fascist parody written from the mid-1940s to the mid-1950s, of the Duce's speeches cast as sexual outpourings hurled at the adoring Italian masses, Gadda returns insistently to the image of a fragmentary, scattered, and incoherent labouring body that is threatening to coalesce around newfound mechanisms of ideological inclusion provided by the fascist rhetoric of sacrifice.

Female bodies, particularly mothers, were placed at the very centre of Gadda's ideological landscapes and functioned as anchors of his representations of fascist Italy. The maternal body was cast as the ultimate labouring body, a veritable sacrificial matrix responsible for the ideological reproduction of fascist ideology. In Gadda's misogynist portrayals, mothers are painted as "loose" gatekeepers and chief facilitators of the regime: they fail to protect "private spaces" by engaging in sacrificial transactions that allow incoherent bodies to trespass and occupy spaces where they do not belong. Fascism's misguided invitation of the excluded masses of workers into the totalitarian state is sexualized in Gadda's narrative representations as the dangerous entry of "lower parts" into a national body. Their lack of verbal and corporeal coherence is underscored in Gadda's writings as an attempt to deny them a narrative frame or enclosure that could potentially serve as an acknowledgment of their maturity (as a class) in his/story.

If Gadda's fascism unravels, and is reversed into anti-fascism, precisely on the question of sacrifice, it is because sacrifice had been central to fascist articulations of a national collective body.

In the last chapter of this book, we encounter, again, in the writings of another major writer of modern Italy, Elio Vittorini, sustained attempts to deal with the "immaturity" of labouring bodies in relation to fascism. If for Gadda the infantilization of the labouring classes ultimately serves the ideological purpose of insulating, of placing distance (or an empty space, as it were) between the bourgeoisie and the encroaching masses, for Vittorini, infantilization is used to protect the masses against the corrupting temptations of bourgeois values. The fragmentary and scattered "below," which Gadda's texts naturalize as a way to delegitimize their social mobility, are reaggregated in Vittorini's texts by subsuming internal differences under the banner of simplicity. Internal unity, cohesiveness, and the possibility of cultural elevation of the people were given simplicity as a common denominator, a quality of thought or temperament that Vittorini associated with "the young."

During fascism he had held the fascist youth as the model for a quintessentially Italian new man, extolling their natural propensity for personal sacrifice and heroism that flowed spontaneously from minds resistant to the corrupting, selfish bourgeois values. After the war, the "simple mind" of the young was, effectively, recast as a natural barrier against fascism, thereby expanding retrospectively the ranks of historic anti-fascism. The displacement of an abject part, whether it was the incipient or lingering bourgeois that needed to be expelled from the fascist hero, or an uncomfortable fascist past that, after the war, needed to be cancelled from the conscience of newly minted anti-fascists, is a rhetorical operation that allows Vittorini to replace the content of his new man, to take him seamlessly into a new place and time: post-liberation Italy.

In tracing this complex operation of recoding, the last chapter of this book confirms and expands the argument made in chapter 3 regarding the continued impact of fascist sacrificial rhetoric after the regime's demise. For Vittorini, too, sacrifice is linked to the question of controlling, or negotiating the legibility of the ventennio. His case, however, allowed us to probe this link in the opposite ideological direction. While Gadda's anti-populism grounds his negative view of sacrifice, Vittorini's populism shapes the positive valence he attaches to it.

By naturalizing the spirit of self-sacrifice of the *uomo nuovo* in his postwar narrative, Vittorini enables a retrospective appraisal of fascism that absolves "the people" of historical responsibility.

Vittorini's own ideological repositioning from fascism to anti-fascism is rendered more coherent by a rhetorical strategy that attempts to transport the new man outside of his fascist birthplace and ultimately represent him as a resistance fighter in his acclaimed novel *Uomini e no.* The incoherent labouring bodies Gadda tried so hard to keep out of the house find a new respectable dwelling and dignified role in Vittorini's post-fascist Italy.

Appendix

Discorso del 3 gennaio

Signori!

Il discorso che sto per pronunziare dinanzi a voi forse non potrà essere, a rigor di termini, classificato come un discorso parlamentare.

Può darsi che alla fine qualcuno di voi trovi che questo discorso si riallaccia, sia pure attraverso il varco del tempo trascorso, a quello che io pronunciai in questa stessa Aula il 16 novembre.

Un discorso di siffatto genere può condurre, ma può anche non condurre ad un voto politico.

Si sappia ad ogni modo che io non cerco questo voto politico. Non lo desidero: ne ho avuti troppi. (*"Bene!"*).

L'articolo 47 dello Statuto dice:

"La Camera dei deputati ha il diritto di accusare i ministri del re e di tradurli dinanzi all'Alta corte di giustizia."

Domando formalmente se in questa Camera, o fuori di questa Camera, c'è qualcuno che si voglia valere dell'articolo 47. (*Vivissimi prolungati applausi. Moltissimi deputati sorgono in piedi. Grida di: "Viva Mussolini!" Applausi anche dalle tribune*).

Il mio discorso sarà quindi chiarissimo e tale da determinare una chiarificazione assoluta.

Voi intendete che dopo aver lungamente camminato insieme con dei compagni di viaggio, ai quali del resto andrebbe sempre la nostra gratitudine per quello che hanno fatto, è necessaria una sosta per vedere se la stessa strada con gli stessi compagni può essere ancora percorsa nell'avvenire. (*Approvazioni; commenti*).

Sono io, o signori, che levo in quest'Aula l'accusa contro me stesso. Si è detto che io avrei fondato una *Ceka*. Dove? Quando? In qual modo? Nessuno potrebbe dirlo!

Veramente c'è stata una *Ceka* in Russia, che ha giustiziato, senza processo, dalle centocinquanta alle centosessantamila persone, secondo statistiche quasi ufficiali. C'è stata una *Ceka* in Russia, che ha esercitato il terrore sistematicamente su tutta la classe borghese e sui membri singoli della borghesia. Una *Ceka*, che diceva di essere la rossa spada della rivoluzione.

Ma la *Ceka* italiana non è mai esistita.

Nessuno mi ha negato fino ad oggi queste tre qualità: una discreta intelligenza, molto coraggio e un sovrano disprezzo del vile denaro. (*Vivissimi, prolungati applausi*).

Se io avessi fondato una *Ceka*, l'avrei fondata seguendo i criteri che ho sempre posto a presidio di quella violenza che non può essere espulsa dalla storia. Ho sempre detto, e qui lo ricordano quelli che mi hanno seguito in questi cinque anni di dura battaglia, che la violenza, per essere risolutiva, deve essere chirurgica, intelligente, cavalleresca. (*Approvazioni*).

Ora i gesti di questa sedicente *Ceka* sono stati sempre inintelligenti, incomposti, stupidi. (*"Benissimo!"*).

Ma potete proprio pensare che nel giorno successivo a quello del Santo Natale, giorno nel quale tutti gli spiriti sono portati alle immagini pietose e buone, io potessi ordinare un'aggressione alle 10 del mattino in via Francesco Crispi, a Roma, dopo il mio discorso di Monterotondo, che è stato forse il discorso più pacificatore che io abbia pronunziato in due anni di Governo? (*Approvazioni*). Risparmiatemi di pensarmi così cretino. (*Vivissimi applausi*).

E avrei ordito con la stessa intelligenza le aggressioni minori di Misuri e di Forni? Voi ricordate certamente il discorso del 7 giugno. Vi è forse facile ritornare a quella settimana di accese passioni politiche, quando in questa Aula la minoranza e la maggioranza si scontravano quotidianamente, tantoché qualcuno disperava di riuscire a stabilire i termini necessari di una convivenza politica e civile fra le due opposte parti della Camera.

Discorsi irritanti da una parte e dall'altra. Finalmente, il 6 giugno, l'onorevole Delcroix squarciò, col suo discorso lirico, pieno di vita e forte di passione, l'atmosfera carica, temporalesca.

All'indomani, io pronuncio un discorso che rischiara totalmente l'atmosfera. Dico alle opposizioni: riconosco il vostro diritto ideale ed anche il vostro diritto contingente; voi potete sorpassare il fascismo come esperienza storica; voi potete mettere sul terreno della critica immediata tutti i provvedimenti del Governo fascista.

Ricordo e ho ancora ai miei occhi la visione di questa parte della Camera, dove tutti intenti sentivano che in quel momento avevo detto profonde parole di vita e avevo stabilito i termini di quella necessaria convivenza senza la quale non è possibile assemblea politica di sorta. (*Approvazioni*).

E come potevo, dopo un successo, e lasciatemelo dire senza falsi pudori e ridicole modestie, dopo un successo così clamoroso, che tutta la Camera ha ammesso, comprese le opposizioni, per cui la Camera si aperse il mercoledì successivo in un'atmosfera idilliaca, da salotto quasi (*approvazioni*), come potevo pensare, senza essere colpito da morbosa follia, non dico solo di far commettere un delitto, ma nemmeno il più tenue, il più ridicolo sfregio a quell'avversario che io stimavo perché aveva una certa *crânerie*, un certo coraggio, che rassomigliavano qualche volta al mio coraggio e alla mia ostinatezza nel sostenere le tesi? (*Vivi applausi*).

Che cosa dovevo fare? Dei cervellini di grillo pretendevano da me in quella occasione gesti di cinismo, che io non sentivo di fare perché repugnavano al profondo della mia coscienza. (*Approvazioni*). Oppure dei gesti di forza? Di quale forza? Contro chi? Per quale scopo?

Quando io penso a questi signori, mi ricordo degli strateghi che durante la guerra, mentre noi mangiavamo in trincea, facevano la strategia con gli spillini sulla carta geografica. (*Approvazioni*). Ma quando poi si tratta di casi al concreto, al posto di comando e di responsabilità si vedono le cose sotto un altro raggio e sotto un aspetto diverso. (*Approvazioni*).

Eppure non mi erano mancate occasioni di dare prova della mia energia. Non sono ancora stato inferiore agli eventi. Ho liquidato in dodici ore una rivolta di Guardie regie, ho liquidato in pochi giorni una insidiosa sedizione, in quarantott'ore ho condotto una divisione di fanteria e mezza flotta a Corfù. (*Vivissime approvazioni*).

Questi gesti di energia, e quest'ultimo, che stupiva persino uno dei più grandi generali di una nazione amica, stanno a dimostrare che non è l'energia che fa difetto al mio spirito.

Pena di morte? Ma qui si scherza, signori. Prima di tutto, bisognerà introdurla nel Codice penale, la pena di morte; e poi, comunque, la pena di morte non può essere la rappresaglia di un Governo. Deve essere applicata dopo un giudizio regolare, anzi regolarissimo, quando si tratta della vita di un cittadino! (*Vivissime approvazioni*).

Fu alla fine di quel mese, di quel mese che è segnato profondamente nella mia vita, che io dissi: "Voglio che ci sia la pace per il popolo italiano"; e volevo stabilire la normalità della vita politica.

Ma come si è risposto a questo mio principio? Prima di tutto, con la secessione dell'Aventino, secessione anticostituzionale, nettamente rivoluzionaria. (*Vive approvazioni*). Poi con una campagna giornalistica durata nei mesi di giugno, luglio, agosto, campagna immonda e miserabile che ci ha disonorato per tre mesi. (*Applausi vivissimi e prolungati*). Le più fantastiche, le più raccapriccianti, le più macabre menzogne sono state affermate diffusamente su tutti i giornali! C'era veramente un eccesso di necrofilia! (*Approvazioni*). Si facevano inquisizioni anche di quel che succede sotto terra: si inventava, si sapeva di mentire, ma si mentiva.

E io sono stato tranquillo, calmo, in mezzo a questa bufera, che sarà ricordata da coloro che verranno dopo di noi con un senso di intima vergogna. (*Approvazioni*).

E intanto c'è un risultato di questa campagna! Il giorno 11 settembre qualcuno vuol vendicare l'ucciso e spara su uno dei nostri migliori, che morì povero. Aveva sessanta lire in tasca. (*Applausi vivissimi e prolungati. Tutti i deputati sorgono in piedi*).

Tuttavia io continuo nel mio sforzo di normalizzazione e di normalità. Reprimo l'illegalismo.

Non è menzogna. Non è menzogna il fatto che nelle carceri ci sono ancor oggi centinaia di fascisti! (*Commenti*). Non è menzogna il fatto che si sia riaperto il Parlamento regolarmente alla data fissata e si siano discussi non meno regolarmente tutti i bilanci, non è menzogna il giuramento della Milizia, e non è menzogna la nomina di generali per tutti i comandi di Zona.

Finalmente viene dinanzi a noi una questione che ci appassionava: la domanda di autorizzazione a procedere con le conseguenti dimissioni dell'onorevole Giunta.

La Camera scatta; io comprendo il senso di questa rivolta; pure, dopo quarantott'ore, io piego ancora una volta, giovandomi del mio prestigio, del mio ascendente, piego questa Assemblea riottosa e riluttante e dico: siano accettate le dimissioni. Si accettano. Non basta ancora; compio un ultimo gesto normalizzatore: il progetto della riforma elettorale.

A tutto questo, come si risponde? Si risponde con una accentuazione della campagna. Si dice: il fascismo è un'orda di barbari accampati nella nazione; è un movimento di banditi e di predoni! Si inscena la questione morale, e noi conosciamo la triste storia delle questioni morali in Italia. (*Vive approvazioni*).

Ma poi, o signori, quali farfalle andiamo a cercare sotto l'arco di Tito? Ebbene, dichiaro qui, al cospetto di questa Assemblea e al cospetto di tutto il popolo italiano, che io assumo, io solo, la responsabilità politica, morale, storica di tutto quanto è avvenuto. (*Vivissimi e reiterati applausi. Molte voci: "Tutti con voi! Tutti con voi!"*).

Se le frasi più o meno storpiate bastano per impiccare un uomo, fuori il palo e fuori la corda! Se il fascismo non è stato che olio di ricino e manganello, e non invece una passione superba della migliore gioventù italiana, a me la colpa! (*Applausi*). Se il fascismo è stato un'associazione a delinquere, io sono il capo di questa associazione a delinquere! (*Vivissimi applausi. Molte voci: "Tutti con voi!"*).

Se tutte le violenze sono state il risultato di un determinato clima storico, politico e morale, ebbene a me la responsabilità di questo, perché questo clima storico, politico e morale io l'ho creato con una propaganda che va dall'intervento ad oggi.

In questi ultimi giorni non solo i fascisti, ma molti cittadini si domandavano: c'è un Governo? (*Approvazioni*). Ci sono degli uomini o ci sono dei fantocci? Questi uomini hanno una dignità come uomini? E ne hanno una anche come Governo? (*Approvazioni*).

Io ho voluto deliberatamente che le cose giungessero a quel determinato punto estremo, e, ricco della mia esperienza di vita, in questi sei mesi ho saggiato il Partito; e, come per sentire la tempra di certi metalli bisogna battere con un martelletto, così ho sentito la tempra di certi uomini, ho visto che cosa valgono e per quali motivi a un certo momento, quando il vento è infido, scantonano per la tangente. (*Vivissimi applausi*).

Ho saggiato me stesso, e guardate che io non avrei fatto ricorso a quelle misure se non fossero andati in gioco gli interessi della nazione. Ma un popolo non rispetta un Governo che si lascia vilipendere! (*Approvazioni*). Il popolo vuole specchiata la sua dignità nella dignità del Governo, e il popolo, prima ancora che lo dicessi io, ha detto: Basta! La misura è colma!

Ed era colma perché? Perché la sedizione dell'Aventino ha sfondo repubblicano! (*Vivi applausi; grida di: "Viva il re!"; i ministri e i deputati sorgono in piedi; vivissimi, generali, prolungati applausi, cui si associano le tribune*). Questa sedizione dell'Aventino ha avuto delle conseguenze perché oggi in Italia, chi è fascista, rischia ancora la vita! E nei soli due mesi di novembre e dicembre undici fascisti sono caduti uccisi, uno dei quali ha avuto la testa spiaccicata fino ad essere ridotta un'ostia sanguinosa, e un altro, un vecchio di settantatré anni, è stato ucciso e gettato da un muraglione.

Poi tre incendi si sono avuti in un mese, incendi misteriosi, incendi nelle Ferrovie e negli stessi magazzini a Roma, a Parma e a Firenze.

Poi un risveglio sovversivo su tutta la linea, che vi documento, perché è necessario di documentare, attraverso i giornali, i giornali di ieri e di oggi: un caposquadra della Milizia ferito gravemente da sovversivi a Genzano; un tentativo di assalto alla sede del Fascio a Tarquinia; un fascista ferito da sovversivi a Verona; un milite della Milizia ferito in provincia di Cremona; fascisti feriti da sovversivi a Forlì; imboscata comunista a San Giorgio di Pesaro; sovversivi che cantano *Bandiera rossa* e aggrediscono i fascisti a Monzambano.

Nei soli tre giorni di questo gennaio 1925, e in una sola zona, sono avvenuti incidenti a Mestre, Pionca, Vallombra: cinquanta sovversivi armati di fucili scorrazzano in paese cantando *Bandiera rossa* e fanno esplodere petardi; a Venezia, il milite Pascai Mario aggredito e ferito; a Cavaso di Treviso, un altro fascista è ferito; a Crespano, la caserma dei carabinieri invasa da una ventina di donne scalmanate; un capomanipolo aggredito e gettato in acqua a Favara di Venezia; fascisti aggrediti da sovversivi a Mestre; a Padova, altri fascisti aggrediti da sovversivi.

Richiamo su ciò la vostra attenzione, perché questo è un sintomo: il diretto 192 preso a sassate da sovversivi con rotture di vetri; a Moduno di Livenza, un capomanipolo assalito e percosso.

Voi vedete da questa situazione che la sedizione dell'Aventino ha avuto profonde ripercussioni in tutto il paese. Allora viene il momento in cui si dice basta! Quando due elementi sono in lotta e sono irriducibili, la soluzione è la forza. (*Vive approvazioni. Vivi applausi. Commenti*).

Non c'è stata mai altra soluzione nella storia e non ce ne sarà mai.

Ora io oso dire che il problema sarà risolto. Il fascismo, Governo e Partito, sono in piena efficienza.

Signori!

Vi siete fatte delle illusioni! Voi avete creduto che il fascismo fosse finito perché io lo comprimevo, che fosse morto perché io lo castigavo e poi avevo anche la crudeltà di dirlo. Ma se io mettessi la centesima parte dell'energia che ho messo a comprimerlo, a scatenarlo, voi vedreste allora. (*Vivissimi applausi*).

Non ci sarà bisogno di questo, perché il Governo è abbastanza forte per stroncare in pieno definitivamente la sedizione dell'Aventino. (*Vivissimi, prolungati applausi*).

L'Italia, o signori, vuole la pace, vuole la tranquillità, vuole la calma laboriosa.

Noi, questa tranquillità, questa calma laboriosa gliela daremo con l'amore, se è possibile, e con la forza, se sarà necessario. (*Vive approvazioni*).

Voi state certi che nelle quarantott'ore successive a questo mio discorso, la situazione sarà chiarita su tutta l'area. (*Vivissimi e prolungati applausi. Commenti*).

Tutti sappiamo che ciò che ho in animo non è capriccio di persona, non è libidine di Governo, non è passione ignobile, ma è soltanto amore sconfinato e possente per la patria. (*Vivissimi, prolungati e reiterati applausi. Grida ripetute di: "Viva Mussolini!." Gli onorevoli ministri e moltissimi deputati si congratulano con l'onorevole Presidente del Consiglio. La seduta è sospesa*).

Discorso pronunciato alla Camera dei deputati, nella tornata del 3 gennaio 1925 (ore 15–16.10, 16.35–18.25). (Dagli Atti del Parlamento italiano. Camera dei deputati. Sessione cit. Legislatura cit. Discussioni. Vol. III: dal 3 gennaio al 30 marzo 1925 – Roma, Tipografia della Camera dei deputati, 1925; pagg. 2028–32). *Opera Omnia* 21, 235–41.

Speech of 3 January

Gentlemen!

The speech that I am about to give in your presence may not be classified, strictly speaking, as a parliamentary speech.

Perhaps in the end some of you will find that this speech is connected, even after some length of time, to the one I gave in this very same room on 16 November.

A speech of this kind can lead, but it can also not lead, to a political vote.

In any case, let it be known that I am not seeking this political vote. I don't wish to have it: I have had too many. (*"Good!"*)

Article 47 of the Statute states:

"The House of Representatives has the right to accuse the king's ministries and to summon them in front of the High Court of Justice."

I formally ask if in this Chamber, or outside of it, there is someone who wants to invoke article 47. (*Loud, sustained applause. Many deputies rise. Shouts: "Long live Mussolini!" Applause from the gallery as well.*)

My speech will be extremely clear and will therefore lead to an abso·lute clarification.

You understand that after a long journey with travelling companions, who, by the way, will always deserve our gratitude for what they have done, it is necessary to stop so that we can see if the same road, with the same companions, can be travelled again in the future. (*Agreement; comments.*)

It is I, gentlemen, who raise in this Chamber the accusation against myself! Some said that I have founded a Cheka. "Where? When? How? No one can say!"

Actually there was a Cheka in Russia that put to death, without trial, between one hundred and fifty and one hundred and sixty thousand people, according to statistics that are practically official. There was a Cheka in Russia that terrorized systematically the entire bourgeois class and single members of the bourgeoisie – a Cheka that claimed to be the red sword of the revolution.

But the Italian Cheka never existed.

To this day, nobody has denied that I possess these three qualities: a modicum of intelligence, much courage, and a supreme disdain for vile money. (*Loud, sustained applause.*)

If I had founded a Cheka I would have done it following the criteria that I have always placed in command of that violence which cannot be expelled from history. Those of you following me during the harsh battles of the past five years will remember what I have always said: that to be decisive, violence has to be surgical, intelligent, chivalric. (*Agreement.*)

Now, the actions of this so-called Cheka have always been unintelligent, uncoordinated, stupid. (*"Very Good!"*)

Can you really think that on the day following Holy Christmas, a day when all souls are inclined to good and pious sentiments, I could give the order for an assault at ten in the morning in Via Francesco Crispi, in Rome, after my speech at Monterotondo – a speech that was perhaps the most conciliatory I have given during my two years of Rule? (*Agreement.*) Spare me from thinking me so idiotic. (*Loud applause.*)

And would I have used the same intelligence to plan the lesser assaults on Misuri and on Forni? Certainly, you remember the speech of June 7. Perhaps you recall that week of fiery political passions, when in this room the minority and majority groups clashed daily, to such an extent that some had lost hope that the conditions for a political and civil coexistence could be found between the two opposing sides in the Chamber.

Provoking statements from one side and the other. Finally, on the 6th of June, the Honourable Delcroix pierced, with his soaring speech, full of life and passion, the viscous atmosphere of a gathering thunderstorm.

On the following day, I deliver a speech that completely clears the air. I say to the opposition: I recognize rights both as ideal and as contingent; you can move beyond fascism as an historical experience; you can subject to immediate criticism all the measures taken by the fascist Government.

I remember, and I still have in front of my eyes, the vision of this side of the Chamber, where everyone was keenly aware that in that moment I had spoken profound words of wisdom and established the conditions for a necessary coexistence: without it no political assembly of any kind is possible. (*Agreement*.)

How could I, after a success – let me say this without ridiculously false modesty – after such an astounding success recognized by the entire Chamber, including the opposition –, one that led to an idyllic atmosphere, almost like a salon (*Agreement*), when the Chamber opened on the following Wednesday – unless I had been seized by raging madness, how could I have entertained the thought, let alone of committing a crime, but of inflicting a most insignificant wound to that adversary whom I respected because he had a certain audacity, a certain courage, that at times resembled my courage and obstinacy in defending a point of view? (*Loud applause*.)

What was I supposed to do? On that occasion, some pea brains expected cynical acts from me, ones that I did not feel I should engage in because they were deeply offensive to my conscience. (*Agreement*.) Acts of force? What kind of force? Against whom? To what end?

When I think about these gentlemen who, during the war while we were eating in the trenches, were the ones who strategized by moving pins on the map. (*Agreement*.) But when we are at the helm, in positions of responsibility dealing with concrete situations, we see things in a different light and from a different perspective. (*Agreement*.)

And yet, I had ample opportunity to demonstrate my energy. I did not fail to rise to the occasion. In twelve hours, I put down an uprising of Royal Guards; in a few days, I put down a treacherous rebellion; in forty-eight hours, I led an infantry contingent and half the fleet at Corfu. (*Very strong agreement*.)

These energetic acts – the latter impressed even one of the greatest generals of a friendly nation – demonstrate that I do not lack for fighting spirit. The death penalty? This is a joke, gentlemen. First of all, the death penalty would need to be written into the penal code and in any case the death penalty cannot be used by a Government as retaliation. It has to be applied after a regulated – highly regulated – judicial process since we are dealing with a citizen's life! (*Very strong agreement*.)

It was at the end of that month – a month that has left a profound mark on my life – that I said: "I want peace for the Italian people," and I wanted to bring normalcy to political life.

But what was the response to my position? To start with, the Aventine Secession, an unconstitutional secession, clearly revolutionary. (*Strong agreement.*) Followed by a press campaign that lasted during June, July, and August – a wretched, dirty campaign that brought us three months of dishonour. (*Loud, sustained applause.*) The most outlandish, horrifying, gruesome lies have been spread unsparingly in all the newspapers! There was certainly an abundance of necrophilia! (*Agreement.*) There was even speculation about what happens beneath the earth: there were fabrications, known to be lies, and lying nonetheless.

But I remained calm, serene, in the midst of this tempest that will be remembered by those succeeding us with a profound sense of shame. (*Agreement.*)

And we see one of the results of this campaign! On 11 September, somebody wants revenge for the man killed and shoots one of our very best men – who died poor. He had sixty lire in his pockets. (*Loud, sustained applause. All deputies rise.*)

Nevertheless, I continue in my efforts to normalize and to achieve normalcy. I supress illegality.

It is not a lie. It is not a lie that to this day there are still hundreds of fascists in jail! It is not a lie that the Parliament reopened on schedule and that, just as regularly, budgets were discussed; the swearing in of the Militia is not a lie and the appointment of generals for all the local headquarters is not a lie.

And then we were faced with an issue that we found compelling: the request for an authorization to proceed with the consequent resignation of the esteemed Council.

The Chamber erupted; I understand the meaning of this reaction; nevertheless, after forty-eight hours, I am once again persuasive, with my influence and prestige, I persuade this unruly, reluctant Assembly and I say: Let the resignations be accepted. They are accepted. It is still not enough; I then make one last effort at normalcy: the plan for electoral reform.

What is their reaction to all this? Their reply is to step up the campaign. They say: fascism is a horde of barbarians occupying the nation; it is a movement of bandits and plunderers! They present it as a moral question, and we know the sad story of moral questions in Italy. (*Strong agreement.*)

Besides, gentlemen, why are we chasing butterflies? Well, then, I hereby declare, before this Assembly and before the entire Italian people that I alone take the political, moral, historical responsibility for everything that has happened. (*Loud and sustained applause. Many shouts: "We are with you! We are with you!"*)

If sentences, more or less mangled, are enough to hang a man, bring out the gallows and the noose! If fascism has been nothing more than castor oil and cudgel, instead of the superb ardour of the best Italian youth, then I am guilty! (*Applause.*) If fascism has been a criminal organization, I am the leader of this criminal organization! (*Loud applause. Many shouts: "We are with you!"*)

If all violence has been the result of a particular historical, political, and moral climate, then the responsibility is mine because I created it with constant propaganda from the time of intervention until the present.

In the last few days, many citizens, not just fascists, have been wondering: is there a government? (*Agreement.*) Do we have men or do we have puppets? Do these men have dignity as men? And do they also have one as a government? (*Agreement.*)

On purpose I wanted things to reach that extreme point, and, relying on my experience of life, I tested the Party during these months. Just like when assessing the quality of certain metals one has to strike them with a mallet, I tested the character of certain men. I have seen what they are worth and understood why they slink away the moment the seas get rough. (*Loud applause.*)

I tested myself, and please know that I would not have taken those measures if the interests of the nation had not been at stake. The people do not respect a government that accepts insult! (*Agreement.*) The people want a government that reflects their own dignity, and the people said, even before I did: "Enough! We reached the limit!"

And why did we reach the limit? Because the Aventine sedition has a republican connotation! (*Loud applause; shouts: "Long live the king!"; All ministers and deputies rise. Loud, general, sustained applause. Applause from the gallery as well.*) This Aventine sedition had consequences because nowadays, in Italy, fascists are still risking their lives! In just the two months of November and December eleven fascists were killed: one of them had his head beaten to a bloody pulp, and another – a seventy-three-year old – was killed and thrown from a high wall.

And then there were three fires in one month: mysterious fires, fires in the railways and their depots in Rome, Parma, and Florence.

Then a widespread flare-up of subversive activity. I will show you the evidence – since nowadays it is necessary to show the newspaper reports – yesterday's and today's newspapers: a Militia squad leader severely injured by subversives in Genzano; an assault attempt to the fascist headquarters in Tarquinia; a fascist injured by subversives in Verona; a militiaman injured in the province of Cremona; fascists injured by subversives in Forlì; a communist ambush in San Giorgio di Pesaro; subversives attacking fascists in Monzambano and singing "*Bandiera rossa.*"

Just in the three days of this January 1925, in just one area, there were incidents in Mestre, Pionca, Vallombra: fifty subversives armed with rifles run about town singing "*Bandiera rossa*" and exploding firecrackers; in Venice, militiaman Mario Pascai assaulted and injured; in Cavaso di Treviso, another fascist injured; in Crespano, the Carabinieri station stormed by twenty or so female hotheads; a first lieutenant assaulted and thrown in the water in Favara di Venezia; fascists assaulted by subversives in Mestre; in Padua, more fascists assaulted by subversives.

I draw your attention to this because it is indicative: subversives hit train 192 with rocks and broke windows; in Moduno di Livenza a First Lieutenant was assaulted and beaten.

This situation shows you that the Aventine sedition had deep repercussions in the entire country. Well, then, the time has come to say: enough! When two elements are locked in a struggle and are irreconcilable, the solution is force. (*Strong agreement. Loud applause. Comments.*)

In all of history there was never another solution and there will never be.

Now, I dare say that the problem will be solved. Fascism, the government and the Party, are fully functional.

Gentlemen!

You were deceiving yourselves! You thought that fascism was finished because I held it down, that it was dead because I punished it and I was even so cruel as to say it. But if I were to use the one-hundredth part of the energy that I put in restraining it to unleash it, then you would see. (*Loud applause.*)

That will not be necessary because the Government is strong enough to put down the entire Aventine sedition permanently. (*Loud, sustained applause.*)

Italy – gentlemen – wants peace, wants tranquility, wants industrious calm. We will give her this tranquility, this industrious calm, with love if possible and with force if necessary. (*Strong agreement.*)

You can be certain that in the forty-eight hours following my speech, the situation will be totally clarified. (*Loud, sustained applause.*)

We all know that my intentions are not driven by personal quirks or the unbridled desires of government but by an immense and powerful love of our homeland. (*Loud, sustained, repeated applause. Repeated shouts of "Long live Mussolini!"*)

The Honorable ministers and many deputies congratulate the Honorable Prime Minister. The session is adjourned.

Speech given to the the House of Representatives, during the session of 3 January 1925 (time: 15–16.10, 16.35–18.25). (From Atti del Parlamento italiano. Camera dei deputati. Sessione cit. Legislatura cit. Discussioni. Volume III: dal 3 gennaio al 30 marzo 1925 – Roma, Tipografia della Camera dei deputati, 1925; pp. 2028–32). Translation mine.

Primo Discorso per il Decennale

Camerati!

Esattamente dieci anni fa, il 16 ottobre 1922, in una riunione da me convocata e tenutasi a Milano in via San Marco 46, fu decisa l'insurrezione.

Tutti coloro che parteciparono a quella storica riunione sono presenti. Uno solo è assente: Michele Bianchi, che ricordiamo sempre con profondo rimpianto. (*Applausi. Si grida: "Presente!"*).

La discussione fu animata e tutti i punti di vista furono esposti. Ma alla fine si raggiunse l'unanimità assoluta per le misure da prendersi immediatamente, le quali consistevano nel passaggio dei poteri dalla Direzione al quadrumvirato, nella formazione delle colonne che dovevano marciare su Roma, in altri dettagli riguardanti la mobilitazione delle camicie nere e nei poteri da dare al quadrumvirato.

Se noi rileggiamo taluni discorsi politici del tempo, possiamo oggi essere sorpresi davanti all'apparente discrezione dei nostri obiettivi. Ma un esercito, quando si mette in marcia, deve partire nelle migliori condizioni possibili, suscitare il minore numero possibile di inquietudini e di disagi.

Recenti esperienze politiche in taluni paesi di Europa ci dicono che allora, come sempre, la nostra forza fu accompagnata dalla saggezza. L'insurrezione sta alla rivoluzione come la tattica sta alla strategia. L'insurrezione non è che un momento della rivoluzione. La rivoluzione totalitaria doveva cominciare dopo. E cominciò infatti nel gennaio 1923, quando furono creati la Milizia Volontaria per la Sicurezza Nazionale e il Gran Consiglio.

È tempo di dire una cosa che forse sorprenderà voi stessi, e che cioè, fra tutte le insurrezioni dei tempi moderni, quella più sanguinosa è stata la nostra.

Poche decine di morti richiedette l'espugnazione della Bastiglia, nella quale di prigionieri politici non c'era più nessuno. Le migliaia, le decine di migliaia di morti vennero dopo, ma furono volute dal terrore.

Quanto poi alle rivoluzioni contemporanee, quella russa non ha costato che poche decine di vittime. La nostra, durante tre anni, ha richiesto vasto sacrificio di giovane sangue, e questo spiega e giustifica il nostro proposito di assoluta intransigenza politica e morale.

Siamo alla fine del primo decennio. Voi non vi aspetterete da me il consuntivo. Io amo piuttosto di pensare a quello che faremo nel decennio prossimo. (*Applausi*). Del resto basta guardarsi attorno, per convincersi che il nostro consuntivo è semplicemente immenso. Ma avviandoci al secondo decennio occorrono delle direttive di marcia. Comincerò da quella che personalmente mi riguarda. Io sono il vostro capo (*applausi vivissimi; grida di: "Viva il Duce!"*) e sono, come sempre, pronto ad assumermi tutte le responsabilità! (*Applausi*). Bisogna essere inflessibili con noi stessi, fedeli al nostro credo, alla nostra dottrina, al nostro giuramento e non fare concessioni di sorta, né alle nostalgie del passato, né alle catastrofiche anticipazioni dell'avvenire.

Tutti coloro che credono di risolvere la crisi con rimedi miracolistici sono fuori di strada. O questa è una crisi ciclica, "nel" sistema, e sarà risolta; o è una crisi "del" sistema ed allora siamo davanti a un trapasso da un'epoca di civiltà ad un'altra. Là dove si è voluto esasperare ancora di più il capitalismo facendone un capitalismo di Stato, la miseria è semplicemente spaventosa. (*Applausi*).

Si è posto anche il problema dei giovani. Il problema dei giovani si pone da sé. Lo pone la vita, la quale ha le sue stagioni, come la natura. Ora, nel secondo decennio bisogna fare largo ai giovani. Nessuno è più vecchio di colui che ha la gelosia della giovinezza. Noi vogliamo che i giovani raccolgano la nostra fiaccola, si infiammino della nostra fede e siano pronti e decisi a continuare la nostra fatica. Occorre fascistizzare ancora più quelli che io chiamo gli angoli morti della vita nazionale, non farsi troppo assorbire dalla ordinaria amministrazione fino al punto di rinunziare a quella che è la gioia e l'ebbrezza del rischio, essere pronti a tutto quello che può costituire il compito più severo di domani.

Voi vi riunite oggi in Roma, in questa Roma che noi volemmo, per rialzarla nell'amore e nell'orgoglio degli italiani e nell'ammirazione del mondo. Vi riunite in questa piazza che è il cuore di Roma e quindi il cuore d'Italia (*vivissimi applausi*), non solo perché c'è palazzo Venezia, costruito da una di quelle città che noi possiamo chiamare imperiali, come Genova, Pisa, Amalfi, Ravenna ed anche Firenze, che diffuse l'imperialismo immortale del suo genio; non già perché in quel palazzo che voi vedete è morta la madre di Napoleone appena novantasei anni or sono – di quel Bonaparte tagliato nella razza possente dei Dante e dei Michelangelo, che non imparò mai a pronunciare correttamente il francese, quel Bonaparte al quale noi siamo grati per aver acceso la prima fiaccola della unità della patria, e per aver chiamato alle armi gli italiani, che egli stesso definì fra i migliori soldati d'Europa – ma perché qui c'è l'ara del Milite Ignoto e l'ara dei caduti fascisti.

Il Milite Ignoto è il simbolo dell'Italia una, vittoriosa, fascista, una dalle Alpi di Aosta romana fino al mare di Trapani, che vide la disfatta delle navi cartaginesi. Egli è la testimonianza suprema di ciò che fu, la certezza infallibile di ciò che sarà!

Discorso pronunciato a Roma, in piazza Venezia, la mattina del 16 ottobre 1932, davanti a venticinquemila gerarchi del P.N.F. (Da *Il Popolo d'Italia*, N. 248, 18 ottobre 1932, XIX). *Opera Omnia* 25, 134–6.

First Speech for the Tenth Anniversary

Comrades!

Exactly ten years ago, on 16 October 1922, in a meeting that I arranged and that took place in Milan in via San Marco 46, the insurrection was decided upon.

All those who participated in that historic meeting are present. Only one is absent: Michele Bianchi, whom we remember always with profound regret. (*Applause. Shouts: "Present!"*)

It was a lively discussion and all viewpoints were heard. But in the end we reached absolute unanimity regarding the immediate measures to be taken: the transfer of powers from the Directorate to the quadrumvirate, the formation of columns that were to march on Rome, and other details pertaining to the mobilization of Blackshirts and to the powers that were to be granted to the quadrumvirate.

If we reread certain political speeches of the time, we can be surprised by the apparent modesty of our objectives. But when an army begins to march, it has to start under the best conditions and create the least possible apprehension and hardship.

Recent political experience in some European countries demonstrates that our forcefulness, then as now, has been accompanied by wisdom. Insurrection is to revolution what tactics is to strategy. The insurrection is only a small part of the revolution. The totalitarian revolution was to begin later. In fact, it began in January 1923 when the Voluntary Militia for National Security and the Grand Council were created.

It is time to say something that perhaps will surprise you, that is, of all the insurrections of modern times, ours has been the bloodiest.

The storming of the Bastille required the loss of a few dozen, among which no political prisoners remained. Losses in the thousands, tens of thousands, came afterwards, but they were part of the strategy of terror.

As for contemporary revolutions, the Russian one only had a few dozen victims. Ours, in the course of three years, required great sacrifice of the blood of our youth, and this explains and justifies our stance of absolute political and moral intransigence.

We are at the end of the first decade. You would not expect from me a balance sheet. I prefer, rather, to think about what we will do in the next decade. (*Applause.*) And besides, one only needs to look around to be convinced of our immense achievements. But as we turn towards the second decade, marching orders are needed. I will begin with one that touches me personally. I am your leader (*Sustained applause; shouts of "Long live the Duce!"*) and, as always, I am ready to assume all responsibility! (*Applause.*) We need to be inflexible with ourselves, faithful to our belief, to our doctrine, to our vow of no compromise of any sort, be it in the name of nostalgia towards the past, or of catastrophic expectations for the future.

All those who believe in resolving the crisis with miracle remedies are misguided. This is either a cyclical crisis "within" the system and, hence, it will be resolved; or it is a crisis "of" the system, in which case we are witnessing a transition from one epoch of civilization to another. In places where capitalism has been pushed to the extreme, and has become State capitalism, there is terrible poverty. (*Applause.*)

We also face the problem of youth. The problem of youth arises by itself. Life poses it, since it has its seasons, like nature. Now, in the second decade, we need to give way to the young. No one is older than he who is jealous of youth. We want our youth to carry our torch, to burn with our faith and be ready and willing to continue our work. We need to fascistize even more what I call the dead corners of national life, avoiding excessive involvement in ordinary administration which leads to giving up the joy and thrill of risk, to be ready for all that may be required to face tomorrow's more demanding tasks.

You are assembled here in Rome today, in the Rome that we wanted to be seen again with love and pride by Italians and admired by the world. You are assembled in this square that is the heart of Rome and, hence, the heart of Italy (*Loud applause*), not only because there is Palazzo Venezia here, built by one of those cities that we can call imperial, like Genoa, Pisa, Amalfi, Ravenna, and even Florence that spread the immortal imperialism of its genius; not only because in the palace that you see died, just ninety-six years ago, the mother of Napoleon – that Bonaparte who is made of the same powerful stock as the race of Dante and Michelangelo, who never learned to pronounce French correctly, that Bonaparte we give thanks to for lighting the first torch of a united homeland, and for calling to arms Italians, whom he regarded among the best soldiers of Europe – but also because here is located the tomb of the Unknown Soldier and the tomb of the fascist fallen.

The Unknown Soldier is the symbol of Italian unity, victorious, fascist; one from the Alps of Roman Aosta to the sea of Trapani which saw the utter defeat of Carthaginian ships. He is the supreme witness of what was and the infallible certainty of what will be!

Speech given in Rome's piazza Venezia on the morning of 16 October 1932 before twenty-five thousand party officials of the P.N.F. (From *Il Popolo d'Italia*, no. 248, 18 October 1932, XIX). *Opera Omnia* 25, 134–6. Translation mine.

Alla "Decima Legio"

Ho voluto che la ripresa dei miei contatti con le gerarchie del Partito cominciasse da voi, o camerati di Bologna: primo, perché avete dato il più alto contributo di sangue alla causa della rivoluzione fascista; secondo, perché siete degni di chiamarvi "Decima legio," cioè la legione fedelissima, sulla quale Cesare poteva in ogni momento contare; terzo, per l'importanza che nella vita politica, economica e morale della nazione ha Bologna e la terra che dal Po all'Adriatico la circonda. Dopo questo rapporto altri ne seguiranno per le gerarchie delle altre regioni e il Partito procederà così alla sua integrale mobilitazione, dal centro all'estrema periferia.

Ci incontriamo in un momento tempestoso che rimette in gioco non solo la carta dell'Europa, ma, forse, quella dei continenti.

Niente di più naturale che questi eventi grandiosi e le loro ripercussioni in Italia, abbiano provocato una emozione anche fra noi. Ma di questo speciale comprensibile stato d'animo ha approfittato la minima, ma ciò nondimeno miserabile zavorra umana, che si era ridotta a vivere negli angiporti, nei ripostigli e negli angoli oscuri. Si deve a questa zavorra la diffusione delle "voci" che hanno circolato, molte delle quali, le più ridicole, mi riguardavano personalmente.

Il fenomeno era destinato ad esaurirsi, altrimenti con mia somma mortificazione, avrei dovuto dubitare di una cosa nella quale ho sempre fermamente creduto, e cioè che il popolo italiano è uno dei più intelligenti della terra.

Senza drammatizzare le cose, perché non vale assolutamente la pena, la conclusione che se ne deve trarre si riassume in queste parole: ripulire gli angolini dove, talora mimetizzandosi, si sono rifugiati rottami massonici, ebraici, esterofili dell'antifascismo. Non permetteremo mai, né a loro né ad altri, di portare nocumento alla salute fisica e morale del popolo italiano.

Il popolo italiano sa che non bisogna turbare il pilota, specie quando è impegnato in una burrascosa navigazione, né chiedergli ad ogni istante notizie sulla rotta.

Se e quando io apparirò al balcone e convocherò ad ascoltarmi l'intero popolo italiano, non sarà per prospettargli un esame della situazione, ma per annunziargli, come già il 2 ottobre del 1935 o il 9 maggio del 1936, decisioni, dico decisioni, di portata storica.

Per ora non è il caso. La nostra politica è stata fissata nella dichiarazione del 1° settembre e non v'è motivo di cambiarla. Essa risponde ai nostri interessi nazionali, ai nostri accordi e patti politici ed al desiderio di tutti i popoli, compreso il germanico, che è quello di almeno localizzare il conflitto. ·

Del resto, liquidata la Polonia, l'Europa non è ancora effettivamente in guerra. Le masse degli eserciti non si sono ancora urtate. Si può evitare l'urto col rendersi conto che è vana illusione quella di voler mantenere in piedi o, peggio ancora, ricostituire posizioni che la storia e il dinamismo dei popoli hanno condannato.

È certo col saggio proposito di non allargare il conflitto che i Governi di Londra e di Parigi non hanno sin qui reagito di fronte al "fatto compiuto" russo; ma ne consegue che hanno compromesso la loro giustificazione morale tendente a revocare il fatto compiuto germanico.

In una situazione come l'attuale, piena di molte incognite, una parola d'ordine è sorta spontaneamente fra le masse dell'autentico popolo italiano: prepararsi militarmente per parare ad ogni eventualità; appoggiare ogni tentativo di pace e lavorare vigilanti, in silenzio.

Questo è lo stile del fascismo; questo deve essere ed è lo stile del popolo italiano.

(Il Duce ha parlato con voce chiara e ferma, scandendo le parole nei punti e nei passaggi più salienti. Al termine del discorso, che è stato frequentemente interrotto da applausi e da ovazioni, i gerarchi rinnovano al Duce una più ardente dimostrazione di affetto, circondandolo e volendo ognuno maniferstargli da vicino la propria dedizione e la fede indefettibile.)

Discorso pronunciato a Roma, nella sala delle Battaglie di palazzo Venezia davanti alle gerarchie del fascismo bolognese. (Da *Il Popolo d'Italia*, Nn. 247, 248, 252, 261, 266, 267, 4, 5, 9, 18, 23, 24 settembre 1939, XXVI). *Opera Omnia* 29: 311–13.

To the Tenth Legion

As I renew my contact with Party officials I wanted to begin with you, comrades from Bologna: first, because you have made the supreme sacrifice in blood to the cause of the fascist revolution; second, because you are worthy of your name – Tenth Legion, the most faithful legion – the one Caesar could always count on; and third, for the importance that Bologna and its surrounding lands – from the river Po to the Adriatic Sea – have in the political, economic, and moral life of the nation. After this meeting others will follow for the officials of the other regions so that the Party will be fully mobilized from centre to periphery.

We meet at this tempestuous time when not only the map of Europe but, perhaps, even that of all the continents is in play.

Naturally, these momentous events and their repercussions in Italy have provoked an emotional response among us as well. But this special, understandable sentiment has been exploited by that insignificant, but no less miserable, human flotsam, who had been living in alleys, closets, and dark corners. We owe to this flotsam the spreading of "rumours" that were going around, many of which, including the most ridiculous, concerned me personally.

This phenomenon was destined to disappear, otherwise I would have had to doubt, with profound mortification, what I have always firmly believed, namely, that Italians are one of the most intelligent people on earth.

Without attributing too much importance to this incident, which it does not deserve, the conclusion that we must reach can be summarized in these words: clean out the corners, where, sometimes camouflaged, the anti-fascist junkyard of masons, Jews, and lovers of all things foreign has taken refuge. We will never allow them or anyone else to harm the physical and moral health of the Italian people.

The Italian people realize that the pilot must not be disturbed, especially when he is engaged in navigating stormy seas, nor must he be asked questions every moment about the route.

If and when I shall appear on the balcony and call on the entire Italian people to hear me, it will not be to discuss the situation but to announce decisions – and I mean decisions – of historic importance such as that of 2 October 1935 or 9 May 1936.

There is no need for it now. Our policy was set in the 1 September declaration and there is no reason to change it. It reflects our national interests, our political agreements and pacts, and the desire of all peoples, including the German one, to at least localize the conflict.

Besides, with Poland liquidated, Europe is not yet actually at war. Army formations have not yet clashed. The clash can be avoided by recognizing that it is a vain illusion to try to maintain or, worse still, to reclaim positions that history and the dynamism of peoples have doomed.

In order to contain the conflict, the governments of London and Paris have wisely until now not reacted to the Russian fait accompli, but as a consequence they compromised their moral justification to take action against the German fait accompli.

In the present moment of uncertainty the marching orders that arise spontaneously from the Italian masses are: to prepare our military forces for any eventuality, to support any possible peace effort, to work in silence while keeping a watchful eye. This is the style of fascism; this must be and is the style of the Italian people.

(The Duce spoke with a clear and firm voice, emphasizing words to mark the most important points and transitions. At the end of the speech, which was frequently interrupted by applause and ovations, Party officials gave an even stronger demonstration of affection towards the Duce by surrounding him, with each one wanting to get close to express his personal dedication and boundless faith.)

Speech given in Rome, in the Hall of Battles of Palazzo Venezia in front of Party officials from Bologna's PNF. (From *Il Popolo d'Italia*, Nn. 247, 248, 252, 261, 266, 267, 4, 5, 9, 18, 23, 24 September 1939, XXVI). Opera Omnia 29, 311-13. Translation mine.

Notes

Introduction

1 Benito Mussolini, "Preludio al Machiavelli," April 1924, in *Scritti e discorsi di Benito Mussolini*, 12 vols. (Milan: Hoepli, 1934–40), 5: 109. References to Mussolini's *Scritti e discorsi* will hereafter appear as *SD*. All translations of *SD* are mine. In the version of the "Preludio" printed in *SD*, the word *atonismo* appears instead of *atomismo*. I believe it to be a typographical error, since *atonismo* seems out of context, while *atomismo* is a term frequently used by Mussolini in relation to social structure. For discussion of the uses of Machiavellian themes and principles during Italian fascism, see Joseph Femia, "Machiavelli and Italian Fascism," *History of Political Thought* 25, no. 1 (2004): 1–15.

2 Ruth Ben-Ghiat, *Fascist Modernities: Italy, 1922–1945* (Berkeley: University of California Press, 2001); Guido Bonsaver, *Censorship and Literature in Fascist Italy* (Toronto: University of Toronto Press, 2007); Gigliola Gori, *Italian Fascism and the Female Body: Sport, Submissive Women, and Strong Mothers* (New York: Routledge, 2004); Claudia Lazzaro and Roger J. Crum, *Donatello among the Blackshirts: History and Modernity in the Visual Culture of Fascist Italy* (Ithaca: Cornell University Press, 2005); Ellen Nerenberg, *Prison Terms: Representing Confinement during and after Italian Fascism* (Toronto: University of Toronto Press, 2001); Robin Pickering-Iazzi, *Politics of the Visible: Writing Women, Culture, and Fascism* (Minneapolis: University of Minnesota Press, 1997); Karen Pinkus, *Bodily Regimes: Italian Advertising under Fascism* (Minneapolis: University of Minnesota Press, 1995); Jeffrey T. Schnapp, *Staging Fascism: 18BL and the Theater of Masses for Masses* (Stanford: Stanford University Press, 1996); Barbara Spackman, *Fascist Virilities. Rhetoric, Ideology, and Social Fantasy in Italy* (Minneapolis: University of Minnesota Press, 1996); Marla Stone,

The Patron State: Culture and Politics in Fascist Italy (Princeton: Princeton University Press, 1998); and Mary Ann Frese Witt, *The Search for Modern Tragedy: Aesthetic Fascism in Italy and France* (Ithaca: Cornell University Press, 2001).
3 English translation of *Il culto del Littorio: La sacralizzazione della politica nell'Italia fascista* (Rome: Laterza, 1993).

1: Discursive Ritual and Sacrificial Presentation

1 Cited in Renzo De Felice, *Mussolini il fascista* (Turin: Einaudi, 1966), 1: 725–6.
2 Ibid., 726.
3 Emilio Gentile, *The Sacralization of Politics in Fascist Italy* (Cambridge: Harvard University Press, 1996); Mabel Berezin, *Making the Fascist Self: The Political Culture of Interwar Italy* (Ithaca: Cornell University Press, 1997); Simonetta Falasca-Zamponi, *Fascist Spectacle: The Aesthetics of Power in Mussolini's Italy* (Berkeley: University of California Press, 1997). In *Making the Fascist Self*, Berezin defines ritual as "the analytic term that most appropriately captures the numerous public spectacles which occupied public space in fascist Italy" (7). Taking "internal colonization" as "the governing metaphor of the political process that underlay the Italian fascist cultural project" (7), her analysis seeks to explain the political process by essentially denying explicative properties to textual elements such as metaphor: "In contrast to the usual scholarly practice of analyzing ritual as text, my analysis focuses on the formal properties of ritual action as constitutive of meaning. In so doing, I conceptualize rituals as emotive practices or actions whose meaning lies in the repetition of patterns" (7). In *Fascist Spectacle*, Falasca-Zamponi argues: "Mussolini's aspirations to transform Italy and create it anew was yet another variation on the theme of the God-like artist-creator. And although fascism relied on people's feelings and sentiments (much as art came to appear as the refuge from instrumental-rational society), it still strove to neutralize the senses, to knock them out" (12). Once we assume that the people were "knocked out," either by violence or by spectacles and rituals that impeded their rational faculties, we can no longer critically assess the relation between cultural, collective understandings embedded in Italian society and ideological meanings. Paradoxically, studies like Berezin's and Falasca-Zamponi's that seek to explain the ideological resonance of cultural practices – the regime's ability to create consensus by deploying resources from the cultural milieu – actually sever the relationship between ideology and culture by characterizing the resonance of spectacles and nrituals as "emotive" and "non-rational." Shared, cultural

understandings, are no longer "understood" but are simply "shared" in "communities of feelings" (Berezin, 7), or "celebrations [that] united people in a common cult" (Falasca-Zamponi, 13).

4 Originally published in 1936, the classic essay on the subject is Walter Benjamin, "The Work of Art in the Age of Mechanical Reproduction," in *Illuminations* (New York: Schocken, 1985), 217–51. See the following contributions to the aesthetics/ideology debate: Martin Jay, "'The Aesthetic Ideology' as Ideology; or What Does It Mean to Aestheticize Politics?" *Cultural Critique* 21 (Spring 1992), 41–61; Terry Eagleton, *The Ideology of the Aesthetic* (Oxford: Basil Blackwell,1990); Josef Chytry, *The Aesthetic State: A Quest in Modern German Thought* (Berkeley: University of California Press, 1989); Susan Buck-Morss, "Aesthetics and Anaesthetics: Walter Benjamin's Artwork Essay Reconsidered," *New Formations* 20 (Summer 1993), 123–43; Paul de Man, *Aesthetic Ideology*, edited by Andrzej Warminski (Minneapolis: University of Minnesota Press, 1996).

5 As Barbara Spackman has noted in *Fascist Virilities* (114–19), the discounting of and failure to analyse fascist rhetoric is typically coupled with/compensated by the attribution of "quasi-magical" qualities to the Duce and his charismatic/rhetorical power of persuasion. Far from leading to a deeper understanding of the mechanisms that underpinned consensus, the "empty-rhetoric" paradigm posits a fundamental lack of substance and irrationality of fascist rhetoric while, at the same time, claiming its effectiveness as an instrument of ideological manipulation.

6 Sergio Luzzatto, *Il corpo del duce: Un cadavere tra immaginazione, storia e memoria* (Turin: Einaudi, 1998). The English translation of this work by Frederika Randall, *The Body of Il Duce: Mussolini's Corpse and the Fortunes of Italy* (New York: Metropolitan, 2005), omits several passages that appeared in the original Italian version. All citations from this book are from the translated edition unless otherwise indicated.

7 Luzzatto, *The Body of Il Duce*, 52.

8 Mario Isnenghi has also pointed to the specularity of the two bodies Mussolini/Matteotti and their body/cadaver symbolic interplay in "Il corpo del Duce," in *Gli occhi di Alessandro: Potere sovrano e sacralità del corpo da Alessandro Magno a Ceausescu*, ed. Sergio Bertelli and Cristiano Grottanelli (Florence: Ponte alle Grazie, 1990), 170–83.

9 Luzzatto, *Il corpo del duce*, 22; emphasis in original, translation mine.

10 Mussolini, "Discorso del 3 gennaio," *Opera Omnia*, edited by Edoardo and Duilio Susmel, 36 vols. (Florence: La Fenice, 1951–63), 21: 235–41. The complete speech is included here in the Appendix. References to Mussolini's

Opera Omnia will hereafter appear as *OO*; references to the "Discorso del 3 gennaio" will hereafter appear as DG. All translations of *Opera Omnia* are mine.

11 Stanley. G. Payne, *A History of Fascism, 1914–1945* (Madison: University of Wisconsin Press, 1995), 114.

12 Cesare Rossi, *Il delitto Matteotti nei procedimenti giudiziari e nelle polemiche giornalistiche* (Milan: Ceschina, 1965), 224.

13 Spackman, *Fascist Virilities*, 132–43. Spackman's analysis sheds light on the relationship between ideological formations and rhetorical strategies as it traces the fascist exploitation of a particular model of sexual difference to bind its heterogeneous ideologems. Indeed, the two moments of "force" and "consent," which from Machiavelli to Benjamin and even in recent studies of fascism continue to stage a fantasy of rape, anchor Mussolini's representation of violence as fundamentally gendered and eminently rhetorical.

14 Ibid., 133.

15 René Girard, *Violence and the Sacred* (Baltimore: Johns Hopkins University Press, 1977).

16 René Girard, *"To Double Business Bound": Essays on Literature, Mimesis, and Anthropology* (Baltimore: Johns Hopkins University Press, 1978), xiii–xiv. For discussion of the fascist "deification" of Mussolini, see Emilio Gentile, *Il culto del Littorio*, 261–97; Pier Giorgio Zunino, *L'ideologia del fascismo: Miti, credenze e valori nella stabilizzazione del regime* (Bologna: Il Mulino, 1985), 202–10; Falasca-Zamponi, *Fascist Spectacle*, 42–88.

17 In her discussion of the fascist representation of violence, Falasca-Zamponi argues that "Fascism's discourse of fascist victims radically eliminated the victims of fascism" (*Fascist Spectacle*, 37). On one level this is certainly true. Fascism's own "martyrs" supplanted the "other dead" in gaining the status of privileged victims within fascist discourse. But we should also notice that this occlusion is often dependent, rhetorically, on a logic of simultaneous reintroduction and displacement. For example, the fascist rhetorical invocation of violence against the forces of anti-fascism often served precisely to "bring back to life" the spectre of these "other dead" as mimetic doubles to "fascist martyrs," hence, valorizing the latter's sacrifice and symbolic capital. See the sarcastic Mussolinian remarks on the "utility" and "formative role" of the oppositional forces, reprinted in Eugenio Adami, *La lingua di Mussolini* (Modena: Società Tipografica Modenese, 1939), 71. For a discussion of Mussolini's portrayal of Italy as the victim of other nations during the Ethiopian war, see Falasca-Zamponi, *Fascist Spectacle*, 148–82.

18 Girard, *Violence and the Sacred*, 11; emphasis in original.
19 Spackman has pointed out the link between violence against the opposi-
    tion and the criterion of intelligence in the "Discorso del 3 gennaio," in *Fas-
    cist Virilities*, 141–2. See also 144 for a discussion of how the same criterion
    is redeployed by Mussolini in the context of demographic policies.
20 Paul de Man, "Excuses," in *Allegories of Reading: Figural Language in Rous-
    seau, Nietzsche, Rilke, and Proust* (New Haven: Yale University Press, 1979),
    299. Spackman has referred to this essay in her analysis of the "Discorso
    del 3 gennaio" (*Fascist Virilities*, 132–43) in arguing that the effect of
    excuses in the speech is to sever guilt from responsibility while increas-
    ing the amount of violence. I agree with Spackman that the excusing of
    violence has the effect of increasing the violence of the speech. I draw,
    however, opposite conclusions regarding the rhetorical relation between
    guilt and responsibility in the speech, which I see as one of inseparabil-
    ity and mutual reinforcement through the hide/reveal binomial structure
    provided by excuses.
21 de Man, "Excuses," 286.
22 Girard, "To Double Business Bound," xiii.
23 Ibid., xiii–xiv.
24 As Pier Giorgio Zunino (*L'ideologia del fascismo*, 11–62) has cogently argued
    in his critique of this view, the portrayal of "fascism without ideas" carries
    with it the corresponding assumption – equally unsupported by historical
    evidence – of "fascism wholly reducible to the exercise of violence." Far
    from leading to a deeper understanding of fascism, the "empty rhetoric/
    people pretended axiom," and its equivalent, "rhetoric as manipulation/
    people were duped," rest on a subjectivist conception of ideology in which
    myths and symbols are psychologized and reduced to an obfuscation of
    reality.
25 Jacques Derrida, *Dissemination* (Chicago: University of Chicago Press,
    1981), 130.
26 Ibid., 127.
27 Such as the binding of socialist Matteotti with the formerly socialist Mus-
    solini – now fascist Mussolini. Two excellent analyses of the "polarity
    binding" function of fascist discourse are Ernesto Laclau, "Fascism and
    Ideology," in *Politics and Ideology in Marxist Theory: Capitalism, Fascism,
    Populism* (London: Verso, 1977), and Alice Y. Kaplan, *Reproductions of Banal-
    ity: Fascism, Literature, and French Intellectual Life* (Minneapolis: University
    of Minnesota Press, 1986).
28 For Mussolini's use of physiological metaphors, see Augusto Simonini, *Il
    linguaggio di Mussolini* (Milan: Bompiani, 1978), 142–4; Francesca Rigotti,

"Il medico-chirurgo dello Stato nel linguaggio metaforico di Mussolini," in *Cultura e società negli anni del fascismo* (Milan: Cordani, 1987), 501–17; and Spackman's discussion of Mussolini's portrayal of himself as "master hygienist" and metaphorical doctor, in *Fascist Virilities*, 145–8.

29 I am indebted on this point to Laclau's theorization of the relational aspect of ideological meaning – located not in isolated ideas or concepts but in their articulation within a particular discourse (in "Fascism and Ideology") as well as to Spackman's application of Laclau's formulation (in *Fascist Virilities*).

30 Mussolini, "Contro la neutralità," 13 Dec. 1914, in *SD* 1: 20.

31 Ibid., 24. Here Mussolini joins and redeploys the pre-existing rhetorical field of the myth of the "two Italies": the need for recovering the "true" Italian tradition that had been obscured and misinterpreted. For an analysis of this field in pre-war Italian culture, see Walter L. Adamson, "The Language of Opposition in Early Twentieth-Century Italy: Rhetorical Continuities between Prewar Florentine Avant-gardism and Mussolini's Fascism," *Journal of Modern History* 64 (March 1992), 22–51. See also Zunino's comments in *L'ideologia del fascismo*, 105. On the significance of the First World War for fascist ideology, see Emilio Gentile, *Le origini dell'ideologia fascista 1918–1925* (Bologna: Il Mulino, 1996), and Mario Isnenghi, *Il mito della grande guerra* (Bologna: Il Mulino, 1989). Falasca-Zamponi (*Fascist Spectacle*, 29) discusses the critique of parliamentary representation in relation to violence and its role as "the engine of history, the element that would fight mediocrity and lack of differentiation."

32 Mussolini, "Intransigenza assoluta," 22 June 1925, in *SD* 5: 117.

33 Mussolini, "Discorso di Udine," 20 Sept. 1922, in *OO* 18: 413.

34 Mussolini, "59a Riunione del Gran Consiglio del Fascismo," 12 Feb. 1925, in *OO* 21: 255–6.

35 Mussolini, "La situazione economica," 26 May 1934, in *SD* 9: 98.

36 Zunino, *L'ideologia del fascismo*, 354. See his discussion of "the hypothetical pace and the inevitable war," 344–55.

37 Mussolini, "Il discorso di Genova 'Chi si ferma è perduto,'" 14 May 1938, in *SD* 11: 287.

38 Mussolini, "Discorso di Milano," 1 Nov. 1936, in *SD* 10: 208.

39 Spackman, *Fascist Virilities*, 129–30. For an analysis of a different deployment of the figure of martyrdom in pre-fascist Italy, see Barbara Spackman, "*Il verbo (e)sangue*: Gabriele D'Annunzio and the Ritualization of Violence," *Quaderni d'italianistica* 4 no. 2 (1983): 218–29. On the subject of fascist commemoration of "martyrs," see also Gentile, *The Sacralization of Politics in*

Fascist Italy, and Berezin's discussion of fascist commemoration as ritual genre, in *Making the Fascist Self*.

40 Renzo De Felice, *Mussolini il duce* (Turin: Einaudi, 1974–81), 1: 302.

41 For a detailed analysis of how the economic crisis affected various economic groups and sectors of the population, see ibid., 54–101.

42 Ibid., 304–5.

43 Mussolini, "Primo Discorso per il Decennale," 16 Oct. 1932, in *OO* 25: 134. Hereafter, references to this speech will be given in the text as PD. The complete speech is included here in the Appendix.

44 Emphasis added.

45 Emphasis added.

46 For a discussion of the fascist cyclical conception of history and crisis and its relation to Oswald Spengler's influence, see Zunino, *L'ideologia del fascismo*, 131–6. On the "morality" and "necessity" of the crisis from a fascist point of view, see the 1932 essay by Nello Quilici, "Crisi o rivoluzione?" republished in Renzo De Felice, ed., *Autobiografia del fascism: Antologia di testi fascisti 1919–1945* (Bergamo: Minerva Italica, 1978), 383–6.

47 De Felice, *Mussolini il duce*, 1: 307.

48 Mussolini, "Alla 'Decima Legio,'" 23 Sept. 1939, in *OO* 29: 312. Hereafter, references to this speech will be given in the text as DL. This is the official version of the speech, published in *Il Popolo d'Italia* on 24 Sept. 1939; emphasis added. The complete speech is included here in the Appendix.

49 This historical account draws largely on the interpretation presented in Payne, *History of Fascism*, 212–44.

50 De Felice, *Mussolini il duce*, 1: 597-601.

51 Payne, *History of Fascism*, 220..

52 Ibid., 228.

53 Ibid., 232.

54 Ibid., 243–4.

55 Mussolini, "Alla 'Decima Legio.'" This excerpt is from an unofficial version of the speech, reprinted in its entirety in Angelo Michele Imbriani, *Gli italiani e il Duce: Il mito e l'immagine di Mussolini negli ultimi anni del fascismo (1938–1943)* (Naples: Liguori, 1992), 212–13.

56 Simona Colarizi and Renzo De Felice see those comments as an attempt by Mussolini to reawaken bellicose sentiments. Both historians claim, at the same time, that the attempt actually produced opposite effects. Simona Colarizi, *Storia d'Italia*, vol. 23, *La seconda guerra mondiale e la Repubblica* (Turin: UTET, 1984), 81, and De Felice, *Mussolini il duce*, 2: 690–5. Angelo Michele Imbriani (*Gli italiani e il Duce*, 65–6) minimizes the importance of those comments. Enzo Santarelli sees them as a diversionary tactic to avoid

issues of foreign policy while mobilizing the Fascist Party. Enzo Santarelli, *Storia del fascismo*, 3 vols. (Rome: Editori Riuniti, 1973), 3: 159–61.

57 Nicola Gallerano, "Gli italiani in guerra 1940–43: Appunti per una ricerca," *Italia contemporanea*, no. 160 (Sept. 1985), 89–91; translation mine.

58 Imbriani, *Gli italiani e il Duce*, 61.

59 Ibid., 43.

60 Ibid., 42–3.

61 Ibid., 47–8.

62 Ibid., 49.

63 Ibid., 74–5.

64 Ibid., 83–4.

65 Ibid., 89; emphasis in original.

66 Ibid., 90.

67 A collection of letters illustrating popular sentiment during the spring and summer of 1940 can be found in Aurelio Lepre, *Le illusioni, la paura, la rabbia: Il fronte interno italiano 1940–1943* (Naples: Edizioni Scientifiche Italiane, 1989).

2: Sacrificial Turns and Their Rhetorical Echoes

1 Hermann Ellwanger, *Sulla lingua di Mussolini* (Milan: Mondadori, 1941), 67–8.

2 Paolo Valesio introduced the term "the rhetoric of anti-rhetoric." For a sustained discussion of the subject, see his *Novantiqua: Rhetorics as a Contemporary Theory* (Bloomington: Indiana University Press, 1980).

3 Ellwanger, *Sulla lingua di Mussolini*, 26. This work is a translation of the original German edition: *Studien zur Sprache Benito Mussolinis* (Florence: Sansoni, 1939). Among the publications of his mentor, Emil Winkler, are the following: *Sprachtheoretische Studien* (Leipzig: Wilhelm Gronau, 1933) and *Grundlegung der Stilistik* (Bielefeld: Velhagen and Klasing, 1929). For additional fascist studies of Mussolini's rhetorical style, see Lorenzo Bianchi, *Mussolini scrittore e oratore* (Bologna: Zanichelli, 1937), and Andrea Gustarelli, *Mussolini, scrittore ed oratore* (Milan: Vallardi, 1935).

4 Ellwanger, *Sulla lingua di Mussolini*, 24.

5 Ibid., 30.

6 Ibid.

7 Ibid., 30–1.

8 Emphasis added.

9 On this point, I am indebted to Spackman's characterization of the fetishization of the Duce as a "fetishization of the people/nation *in the*

leader" and to her discussion of how the Duce "insistently and throughout the regime presents himself as the embodiment and conduit of the people's will" (*Fascist Virilities*, 90–1).

10 Kenneth Dean and Brian Massumi, *First and Last Emperors: The Absolute State and the Body of the Despot* (New York: Autonomedia, 1992), 138; cited in Karen Pinkus, *Bodily Regimes: Italian Advertising under Fascism* (Minneapolis: University of Minnesota Press, 1995), 16.

11 Pinkus, *Bodily Regimes*, 16.

12 Ibid., 18.

13 Ellwanger, *Sulla lingua di Mussolini*, 26–7.

14 Ibid., 28.

15 Ibid., 27. The importance of examples in the ideological "education" of the masses is frequently stressed by Mussolini: "In questo periodo il Partito deve essere più che mai il motore della vita della nazione, il sangue che circola, l'aculeo che sprona, la campana che batte, l'esempio costante. L'esempio. Non vi è alcuna cosa al mondo che possa superare in efficacia l'esempio" (Now more than ever, the Party must be the engine of national life, the blood that circulates, the spur that prods, the bell that tolls, the constant example. The example. There is nothing in the world that can surpass the efficacy of example). "Gli imperiosi doveri dell'ora," 24 June 1943, in *OO* 31: 196.

16 Adami, *La lingua di Mussolini*, 36.

17 Ibid., 37.

18 Ibid., 38.

19 Pinkus, *Bodily Regimes*, 7.

20 Mario Appelius, "Vincere," from *Vincere* (Rome: Editrice La Vittoria, 1940), reprinted in De Felice, ed., *Autobiografia del fascismo*, 495–6.

21 Mussolini, "Al congresso dei sindacati fascisti," 6 May 1928, in *OO* 23: 139. In the same speech, Mussolini also reiterates the government's commitment to "go to the masses": "Prima di essere criminoso, è semplicemente idiota pensare che un Governo cosciente dei suoi fini, com'è il Governo fascista, non vada con cuore aperto verso le masse del popolo italiano" (Aside from the fact that it would be criminal, it is simply idiotic to think that a Government as conscious of its goals as the fascist Government would not go to the masses of Italian people with an open heart) (141).

22 Mussolini, "Al popolo di Mantova," 24 Oct. 1925, in *OO* 21: 417.

23 Mussolini, "Intransigenza assoluta," 22 June 1925, in *OO* 21: 357; cited in Ellwanger, *Sulla lingua di Mussolini*, 32.

24 See Louis Althusser, "Ideology and Ideological State Apparatuses (Notes Towards an Investigation)," in *Lenin and Philosophy and Other Essays*,

translated by Ben Brewster (New York: Monthly Review Press, 1971), 127–86.

25 Judith Butler, *The Psychic Life of Power: Theories in Subjection* (Stanford: Stanford University Press, 1997), 115.

26 Ibid., 115–16; emphasis in original.

27 Ibid., 116–17; emphasis in original.

28 Fritz Haug, as paraphrased by Slavoj Zizek, "The Spectre of Ideology," in *Mapping Ideology*, ed. Slavoj Zizek (London: Verso, 1994), 14.

29 Mussolini, cited in Ellwanger, *Sulla lingua di Mussolini*, 33.

30 Ellwanger, *Sulla lingua di Mussolini*, 34; emphasis in original.

31 Ibid., 35; emphasis added.

32 Ibid., 33. See also "Agli avvocati," 29 May 1935, in *OO* 27: 82: "Ora che vi ho così parlato, non voglio aggiungere altro. Desidero tuttavia che voi portiate l'eco di questa mia parola a tutti i camerati avvocati di tutte le parti d'Italia" (Now that I have spoken to you in this manner, and I do not want to add anything else. However, I would like you to bring the echo of my words to all the lawyer comrades in every part of Italy). The insistence on "echo" can be found even in Mussolinian speeches delivered during the Italian Social Republic (*Repubblica Sociale Italiana*, 1943–45). See "La grande primavera della patria è imminente," 17 Dec. 1944, in *OO* 32: 140: "Io so già che la eco delle manifestazioni milanesi è giunta ai legionari delle quattro divisioni che, addestrate in Germania sotto una severa disciplina e una forte preparazione, si accingono a liberare il suolo della patria" (I already know that the echo of the Milanese events has reached the legionnaires of the four divisions that, trained in Germany under strict discipline and with thorough preparation, stand ready to liberate the national soil).

33 Mussolini, "Al popolo di Vercelli," 27 Sept. 1925, in *OO* 21: 391. Note the insistence on "vibrations" that precedes the "echo" reference in the same speech: "Questa vostra adunata è veramente significativa. Io mi sento vostro, carne della vostra carne, spirito del vostro spirito. Ho l'immodestia di dire che vibro della vostra passione e che mi nutro della vostra fede. In questi giorni ho avuto sotto gli occhi lo spettacolo del nostro popolo in armi, del nostro glorioso esercito (*'Viva l'Esercito!'; applausi*), al quale vi prego di mandare il più vibrante saluto" (Your gathering is very significant. I feel that I am yours, flesh of your flesh, spirit of your spirit. I say, rather immodestly, that I vibrate with your passion and that your faith nurtures me. In these days, I have seen with my own eyes the spectacle of our people in arms, of our glorious army (*"Long live the Army!"; applause*), that I beg you to greet with the most vibrant salute) (391). Erasmo Leso has noted that "vibrant" was "a word dear to Mussolini," and he cites

many examples from official speeches, in "Osservazioni sulla lingua di Mussolini," in *La lingua italiana e il fascismo*, ed. Erasmo Leso et al. (Bologna: Consorzio Provinciale Pubblica Lettura, 1978), 15–62. I find the following two particularly interesting: "nelle città gentili della Toscana ho sentito – dico ho sentito – vibrare attorno a me il consenso formidabile di quel popolo anonimo e minuto che è la base granitica della Patria" (in the genteel Tuscan cities I felt – and I mean I felt – vibrating around me the formidable consensus of that anonymous, little people that is the bedrock of the Fatherland"). In Leso, "Osservazioni," 32. "Una città che lavora come Milano, non può permettersi il lusso di un'attività politica chiacchierona e superficiale. V'è troppo diffuso il senso della responsabilità. Ma quando gli avvenimenti incalzano e precipitano, allora, sotto la Milano industriosa, trafficante, lavoratrice, spunta la vecchia Milano del '48, del '51 e '53, la Milano che seppe tutto 'osare' contro gli austriaci che la tenevano schiava. Allora passa per le strade e le piazze della metropoli, una formidabile vibrazione alla quale nessuno resiste: la città si muove, ormai, e si mette – come sempre – alla testa" (A labouring city like Milan cannot afford the luxury of political activity that is garrulous and superficial. The sense of responsibility is too widespread there. But when events are imposing and are precipitous, then, from under the industrious, bustling, laborious Milan rises the old Milan of '48, of '51 and '53, the Milan that risked all against the Austrians who kept her enslaved. Then, a formidable vibration that no one can resist goes through the streets and the piazzas of the metropolis: The city moves, at last, and places itself – as always – at the helm.) In Leso, "Osservazioni, 18–19.

34 See Kaja Silverman, *The Acoustic Mirror: The Female Voice in Psychoanalysis and Cinema* (Bloomington: Indiana University Press, 1988). See also Mladen Dolar's discussion of the "acoustic mirror" in relation to narcissism and the Lacanian mirror-phase, in "The Object Voice," in *Gaze and Voice as Love Objects*, ed. Renata Salecl and Slavoj Zizek (Durham: Duke University Press, 1996), 13–16; Michel Chion, *The Voice in Cinema*, edited and translated by Claudia Gorbman (New York: Columbia University Press, 1999); and Joan W. Scott, "Fantasy Echo: History and the Construction of Identity," *Critical Inquiry* 27 (2001): 284–304. Butler (*The Psychic Life of Power*, 112) notes the possibility of reading Althusser's scene of interpellation as "a visual rendering of an auditory scene – a mirror stage or, perhaps more appropriately, an 'acoustic mirror' – that permits the misrecognition without which the sociality of the subject cannot be achieved." Slavoj Zizek stresses the complementarity of Althusser and Lacan, in *The Sublime Object of Ideology* (London: Verso, 1989).

35 Jacques Lacan, "The Mirror Stage as Formative of the Function of the I as Revealed in Psychoanalytic Experience," in *Écrits: A Selection*, translated by Alan Sheridan (New York: Norton, 1982), 1–7.

36 Adriana Cavarero also critically engages the infant-mother vocal bond, albeit from a philosophical perspective, in her book, *A più voci: Filosofia dell'espressione vocale* (Milan: Feltrinelli, 2003).

37 Silverman, *The Acoustic Mirror*, 100.

38 Mussolini, "Al popolo di Casale," 27 Sept. 1925, in *OO* 21: 390.

39 Mussolini, "Al popolo di Vercelli," 27 Sept. 1925, in *OO* 21: 393.

40 I am indebted here to Mladen Dolar's description ("The Object Voice," 14) of the voice of the nymph Echo as a "voice without a body" in the story of Narcissus: "But his curious 'affair' with the nymph Echo, who could only echo his words and couldn't speak by herself, is a story of a failed love and a failed narcissism – the voice returned is not his own voice, and he would rather die than abandon himself to the other ("'Ante,' ait, 'emoriar, quam sit tibi copia nostri,'" says Ovid). And when the nymph dies, only her voice is left, which still makes echo to our own, the voice without the body, the remainder, the trace of the object."

41 Ugo Ojetti, *Cose viste*, 1923; cited in Renzo De Felice and Luigi Goglia, *Mussolini: Il Mito* (Rome: Laterza, 1983), 109.

42 Ellwanger, *Sulla lingua di Mussolini*, 61–2.

43 Giuseppe Ardau, *L'eloquenza mussoliniana* (Milan: Mondadori, 1929), 59.

44 Mussolini, "Al sindaco di Castellammare di Stabia," 17 Sept. 1924, in *OO* 21: 71; emphasis added. Notice also the reference to internal turmoil (*travaglio*) as the necessary link between obedience and command in the following speech: "parlo per i fascisti di tutta Italia, i quali, se un dogma debbono avere, questo deve portare un solo chiaro nome: disciplina! Solo obbedendo, solo avendo l'orgoglio umile ma sacro di obbedire, si conquista poi il diritto di comandare. Quando il travaglio sia avvenuto nel vostro spirito, potete imporlo agli altri. Prima, no. Di questo debbono rendersi ben conto i fascisti di tutta Italia" (I am speaking for all Italian fascists: if there is a dogma they should respect, it can have only one clear name – discipline! Only by obeying, only by having the humble but sacred pride of obeying, does one earn the right to command. It is when the turmoil has occurred in your spirit that you can impose it upon others, not before. All Italian fascists should realize this). Cited in Ardau, *L'eloquenza mussoliniana*, 114–15.

45 Mussolini, "Al popolo dell'Aquila," 12 Oct. 1924, in *OO* 21: 113.

46 Butler, *The Psychic Life of Power*, 118; emphasis in original.

47 Mussolini, "Al popolo di Vercelli," 27 Sept 1925, in *OO* 21: 390; emphasis added.
48 This void can also be thought in terms of "melancholic loss" since Mussolini's sacrificial guilt undergirds his symbolic expulsion and, of course, simultaneous "retrieval" of the lost object of desire, the Duce himself. The classic essay on melancholia is Sigmund Freud, "Mourning and Melancholia," in *The Standard Edition of the Complete Psychological Works of Sigmund Freud*, edited and translated by James Strachey, 24 vols. (London: Hogarth, 1953–74), 14: 237–58. On this subject, see also Eric Santner, *Stranded Objects: Mourning, Memory, and Film in Postwar Germany* (Ithaca: Cornell University Press, 1990); Alexander and Margarete Mitscherlich, *The Inability to Mourn: Principles of Collective Behavior*, translated by Beverly R. Placzek (New York: Grove Press, 1975); Jessica Benjamin, *The Bonds of Love: Psychoanalysis, Feminism, and the Problems of Domination* (New York: Pantheon, 1988); Nicolas Abraham and Maria Torok, *The Wolf Man's Magic Word: A Cryptonymy*, translated by Nicholas Rand (Minneapolis: University of Minnesota Press, 1986).
49 Mussolini, "Al popolo di Vercelli," 390–1; emphasis added.
50 Franco Ciarlantini, *Mussolini immaginario* (Milan: Sonzogno, 1933), 107–8; emphasis added.

3: Gadda's Sacrificial Topographies

1 Gadda's technical writings can be found (with some overlap in coverage) in the following works and collections: *Le meraviglie d'Italia, Gli anni*, in *Opere di Carlo Emilio Gadda*, vol. 3, *Saggi giornali favole e altri scritti I*, edited by Liliana Orlando, Clelia Martignoni, and Dante Isella (Milan: Garzanti, 1991); *Pagine di divulgazione tecnica*, in *Opere di Carlo Emilio Gadda*, vol. 5, *Scritti vari e postumi*, edited by Andrea Silvestri et al. (Milan: Garzanti, 1993); *Azoto e altri scritti di divulgazione scientifica*, edited by Vanni Scheiwiller, Andrea Silvestri, and Dante Isella (Milan: Scheiwiller, 1986); *I Littoriali del Lavoro e altri scritti giornalistici 1932–1941*, edited by Manuela Bertone (Pisa: ETS, 2005).
2 Gadda, "I nuovi edifici della Città del Vaticano," *L'Ambrosiano*, 8 Aug. 1934, 3; republished in *I Littoriali del Lavoro*, 53–60. All translations of this work are mine. In 1932–34, Gadda had supervised the construction of the Vatican's new power plant, described in his essay, "Gli impianti tecnici del Vaticano: La centale termoelettrica," in *Opere*, vol. 5, *Scritti vari e postumi*, 108–13.

3 Gadda, "I nuovi edifici della Città del Vaticano," 56.
4 Ibid., 57.
5 Ibid., 56.
6 Gadda, "I nuovi borghi della Sicilia rurale," *Nuova Antologia*, 1 Feb. 1941, 281–6; "La colonizzazione del latifondo siciliano," *Le Vie d'Italia*, 3 March 1941, 335–43. Both articles are republished in *I Littoriali del Lavoro*, 109–31.
7 Gadda, "I nuovi borghi della Sicilia rurale," 117.
8 Ibid.
9 Ibid., 120.
10 Carlo Emilio Gadda, *La cognizione del dolore* (Turin: Einaudi, 1963). Hereafter, referred to as *La cognizione*. All translations in English of this work, unless otherwise indicated, are from Carlo Emilio Gadda, *Acquainted with Grief*, translated by William Weaver (New York: Braziller, 1969), hereafter, referred to as *AG*.
11 *La cognizione*, 31; translation mine.
12 Ibid.
13 Ibid., 37–8; translation mine.
14 Although Robert S. Dombroski's analysis of *La cognizione* is by no means exclusively, or even primarily guided by a psychoanalytic critical framework, his reading is sensitive to the psychoanalytic implications of Gadda's narrative and points to them frequently. See Robert S. Dombroski, *Creative Entanglements: Gadda and the Baroque* (Toronto: University of Toronto Press, 1999), and his "Carlo Emilio Gadda: Travesties," in *Properties of Writing: Ideological Discourse in Modern Italian Fiction* (Baltimore: Johns Hopkins University Press, 1994), 107–36. For a reading of *La cognizione* that focuses on Freudian motifs in "Mourning and Melancholia," see Carla Benedetti, "The Enigma of Grief: An Expressionism against the Self," in *Carlo Emilio Gadda: Contemporary Perspectives*, ed. Manuela Bertone and Robert S. Dombroski (Toronto: University of Toronto Press, 1997), 159–76. See also Guido Lucchini, "Gadda's Freud," in Bertone and Dombroski, *Carlo Emilio Gadda*, 177–94.
15 *La cognizione*, 44 (*AG*, 4–5).
16 Ibid., 135 (*AG*, 99).
17 Gianfranco Contini in his "Saggio introduttivo" to *La cognizione* has remarked on the topographical analogies between the Italian landscape and the fictitious, but transparently similar Maradagàl (8).
18 *La cognizione*, 48 (*AG*, 8–9); emphasis added.
19 Ibid., 3.
20 Ibid., 58 (*AG*, 19).
21 Ibid., 119–20 (*AG*, 82–3).

22 Ibid., 180 (*AG*, 146).

23 Ibid., 23 (*AG*, 201).

24 Ibid., 236 (*AG*, 204). On the sex of the bells, I obviously disagree with Dombroski, who sees them unequivocally as male genitals because of the phallic shape of the *batacchio* (clapper). See his *Properties of Writing*, 118–19. As I will later point out, we need to distinguish between the "male" phallic tower and the clearly "female" bells.

25 *La cognizione*, 175 (*AG*, 142). Mother's painful loss and sense of betrayal is amplified by this passage's literary reference to Ugo Foscolo's *Ultime lettere di Jacopo Ortis* (Milan: Mondadori, 1986), "Da' colli Euganei, 11 Ottobre 1797": "Il sacrificio della patria nostra è consumato." *Last Letters of Jacopo Ortis*, translated by Douglas Radcliff-Umstead (Chapel Hill: University of North Carolina Press, 1970), "From the Euganean Hills, 11 October 1797": "Our country's sacrifice has been completed." The historical event in question is, of course, Napoleon's ceding of Venice to Austria in the infamous Treaty of Campoformio of 1797.

26 *La cognizione*, 177–8 (*AG*, 144).

27 Ibid., 172 (*AG*, 138).

28 Ibid., 134 (*AG*, 98).

29 Ibid., 123 (*AG*, 86).

30 Pinkus, *Bodily Regimes*, 16.

31 *La cognizione*, 124–5 (*AG*, 87–8); emphasis added.

32 For a comprehensive study of the concept of "phallic mother," see Marcia Ian, *Remembering the Phallic Mother: Psychoanalysis, Modernism, and the Fetish* (Ithaca: Cornell University Press, 1991). The classic essay on the subject is, of course, Sigmund Freud, "Fetishism" (1927), in *Sexuality and the Psychology of Love*, ed. Philip Rieff (New York: Macmillan, 1963), 204–9. I believe that Gadda's "tower-matrix" does not fit neatly into the Freudian account of the castration complex since Gadda's narrative image of the "composite phallus" does not seem to be organized around the principle of fetishist compensation, or disavowal of "lack" but, rather, around a supplementary logic of acquisition. Gadda's narrative seems less interested in the possibility that "if mother does not have it, my own too is in danger," than in the reassuring thought of *father* having *it* (female's genitals) too after all.

33 *La cognizione*, 110–11 (*AG*, 73); emphasis added.

34 Robert S. Dombroski, *L'esistenza ubbidiente: Letterati italiani sotto il fascismo* (Naples: Guida, 1984), 110–11. Again, while agreeing with Dombroski that this scene is phallic (because of the tower), I think that his misreading of the sex of the bells obscures the "active" involvement of Mother in the

scene itself. Dombroski writes: "Oggi, come può un lettore minimamente influenzato dalla dottrina freudiana ignorare le immagini così trasparentemente sessuali della diatriba? Cioè la 'libera associazione' (in realtà, 'associazione organizzata') che trasforma le campane in enormi, mostruosi peni che eiaculano il loro suono sulla ricca e verde campagna. Le campane sono 'furibonda sicinnide,' le colline, 'baccanti androgine' che si aprono alla 'lubido municipalistica d'ogni incanutito offerente' e agli sfrenati desideri esibizionistici della volontà autoritaria" (Nowadays, how can a reader minimally influenced by Freudian doctrine ignore the images so transparently sexual of the tirade? That is, the "free association" (in reality "organized association") that transforms the bells into enormous, monstrous penises that ejaculate their sound on the lush, green countryside. The bells are "furious sicinnis," the hills "androgynous bacchantes" that avail themselves to the "municipal lubido of every grey-haired offerer" and the unbridled exibitionist desires of the authoritanian will). *L'esistenza ubbidiente*, 106; my translation. I reread Gadda's contorted passage a few times, and it seems to me that the "baccanti androgine" (androgynous bacchantes) are the *campane* (bells) and not the *colline* (hills). This small revision, in fact, produces a quite different scene of who is "offering" what to whom.

35 Carlo Emilio Gadda, *Eros e Priapo (da furore a cenere)* [*Eros and Priapus*] (Milan: Garzanti, 1975), 38–9; emphasis added. I have used and slightly modified (to reflect the Italian text more closely) Robert S. Dombroski's translation of this passage in *Creative Entanglements*, 132. All subsequent translations from *Eros e Priapo* are mine.

36 *Somaro* (or its synonym *asino*) in Italian means both donkey and dunce, as the term is used when referring to the braying animal as well as to "dense" students.

37 *Eja, eja, alalà* was a salutation originally coined by Gabriele D'Annunzio. The Vate claims to have invented it one night in August 1918. On that occasion, he was reportedly at an airfield, and the military officials saluted him with the traditional "Hurra! Hurra! Hurra!" that the Italian Navy had borrowed and adapted from the English "Hip, hip, hooray!" *Eja, eja, alalà* was later adopted by the fascist Blackshirts, who also used its shortened version "Alalà" when charging opponents, as a way to distinguish themselves from the Italian Army battle cry "Savoia!" Achille Starace, widely considered the regime's choreographer, later incorporated it into the official salutation to Mussolini: "Hail to the Duce, founder of the Empire! Eja, eja, alalà!" ("Saluto al Duce, fondatore dell'Impero! Eja, eja, alalà!").

38 Dombroski, *L'esistenza ubbidiente*, 111; my translation.

39 Mussolini, 23 Oct. 1925, cited in *Il "Duce" visto da Mussolini*, ed. E. Tedeschi
    (Milan: Bietti, 1965), 340; my translation.

40 Mussolini, "Discorso agli ufficiali," 27 Aug. 1932, in *SD* 8: 98.

41 For an extended and nuanced discussion of female "receptivity" as a figure
    for the rape of the masses, see Spackman, *Fascist Virilities*.

42 *Eros e Priapo*, 75.

43 Ibid., 58. In *La cognizione* (185; *AG*, 152) there is a similar scene: "Già altra
    volta era accaduto che [Gonzalo] s'infuriasse, per quella inadempienza dei
    polli del Serruchón porco: e aveva accusato il gallo di morosità genetica e
    di perversione, le galline d'esser lesbiche e tr . . .; poi la furia s'era schiarita
    in una reminescenza di Livio 'gallinam in marem, gallum in foeminam se
    si vertisse . . .' E, atrocemente, sghignazzando, aveva brindato alla salute
    del gallo! Ma non disse affatto alla salute, disse una parte del corpo: aveva
    inneggiato, (irridendo lei, la mamma), al gallo bardassa, meglio di tutti i
    padri della Keltiké lurida, aveva urlato, 'cosí non generava dei Keltikesi'
    (In the past, on other occasions, he had become infuriated at these default-
    ing hens of the lousy Serruchón: and he had accused the rooster of genetic
    non-fulfilment and of perversion, the hens of being lesbians and whores;
    then his fury had calmed down with a recollection of Livy, "gallinam in
    marem, gallum in foeminam se si vertisse." And, atrociously, snickering,
    he had drunk the rooster's health! But he hadn't actually said to his
    heath, he had mentioned a part of the body: he had sung the praises
    (mocking her, his Mama) of the scoundrelly cock, better than all the
    fathers of lousy Keltiké, he had yelled, "that way they wouldn't generate
    any Keltikese").

44 *Eros e Priapo*, 61.

45 The description of the "borsetta da signora" (lady's purse) that occurs
    in *Eros e Priapo* (127–8) leaves no doubt that Gadda attributes a central
    oiko-nomical role to Mother's reproductive "exchanges" during fascism:
    "Nella borsa di pelle, detta borsetta, ma in realtà borsona delle gentili
    signore, possiamo distinguere, quando la nostra impudenza e stoltezza
    ce lo consente, delle 'grandi labbia': dentro, all'aprir quelle, te tu vi scorgi
    delle 'piccole labbia' con interior nottolino-clitoride: dentro ancora avvi
    un'intima borsicina e dentro la borsicina il borsellino con reparti vari quasi
    i ventricoli e le orecchiette cardiache d'un nascituro. L'operazione di estra-
    zione d'una lira frusta dai penetrali del borsellino puoi quindi pensare in
    quali tempi o tempucoli si adempia (alle banche, all'esattoria, alla posta)
    e con quale delizia del fegato degli aspettanti à la queue. Questo quarto
    d'ora di apertura di quattro coppie di successive labbia non è in realtà che
    un atto trasposto e un atto trasferito: per il quale la titolare della ficoborsa

o vulvomarsupio, non potendo esibire agli astanti la sua propria gentil
persona, esibisce loro, con tanto di grinta ferma e quel tono signorile che la
distingue, tutte le sue seconde e terze borsicine emboitées l'una nell'altra
in una successione interiorizzante. Come a dire: 'Vedete, gua', la mi' gente
e 'l mi' poppolo, che cos'è una signora vera.' E la vi pesca e ripesca dentro
a non più finire. E tra infiniti moccichini e crayoni la ne ripiglia finalmente
fuora la liruccia frusta con un numero da meno alla serie e la vi richiude il
francobollo stampigliato 'Vinceremo!'" (In the leather handbag, known as
a purse, but in reality a big pouch of the genteel ladies, we can distinguish,
when our impudence and folly allow us to do so, the "labia majora":
inside which, when opening those, you discover the "labia minora" with
internal clitoris-latch: inside that we find an intimate purse and inside
the intimate purse the change purse with various dividers almost like the
ventricles and the little cardiac valves of a future child. The extraction
operation of a worn-out lira from the inner folds of the change purse –
you can surmise how much, or little, time it would take (at the bank, the
council tax office, the post office) and the delightful rage of those in line.
This quarter-hour of opening four pairs of successive *labia* is in reality
a transposed and transferred act: through which the proprietor of the
vagino-purse or vulva-pouch, not being able to show to those present her
genteel persona, shows them, with that touch of firm determination and
ladylike tone that distinguishes her, all the second and third embroidered
folds, one inside the other in interior succession. As if to say: "My fellow people and compatriots, look – this is a real lady." And she endlessly
fumbles and fumbles again through it. And among all the crayons and
mucousy handkerchiefs she finally takes out the worn-out puny lira with
a discoloured serial number and she puts in a stamp with the inscription
"Victory is ours !").

46 *La cognizione*, 240 (*AG*, 208).
47 My use of the term "vocalized below" here is fully indebted to Barbara
    Spackman's *Decadent Genealogies: The Rhetoric of Sickness from Baudelaire to
    D'Annunzio* (Ithaca: Cornell University Press, 1989).
48 *La cognizione*, 236 (*AG*, 204).
49 *Eros e Priapo*, 42–3.
50 Ibid., 143.
51 Ibid., 141.
52 Ibid., 144.
53 Ibid., 143.
54 Ibid., 142.
55 *La cognizione*, 220 (*AG*, 188).

56 Gadda's anti-populism and anti-socialism have been noted by various critics. My point here is not that his anti-populism is remarkable or even unique among writers of his generation. Rather, that his anti-populism and anti-fascism cannot be thought apart from each other. To do so would play into Gadda's own ideological revisionist placement of himself, as the keeping apart of these two terms renders his "detachment" illegible and, hence, more unassailable. An interesting essay on the question of Gadda's "nonconformist" fascism that also explores the racist overtones of Gadda's anti-fascism is Peter Hainsworth, "Fascism and Anti-fascism in Gadda," in Bertone and Dombroski, eds., *Carlo Emilio Gadda*, 221–41.

57 Butler, *The Psychic Life of Power*, 116. See also my discussion of "speaking properly" in relation to Mussolini's dialogue with the masses in the previous chapter.

58 According to Mussolini, in the fascist economic body – the corporation – discipline and control coincided: "Il corporativismo è l'economia disciplinata, e quindi anche controllata, perché non si può pensare ad una disciplina che non abbia un controllo" (Corporativism is disciplined, and hence, controlled, economy, because discipline without control is inconceivable). "Discorso del XIV novembre per lo stato corporativo, in *SD* 8: 271.

59 I am indebted here to Pinkus' discussion (*Bodily Regimes*, 119–24) of the hands' status as "hands" in fascist iconography and advertising which she sees as the visual translation of Marx's distinction between *Kopf-* and *Handarbeit*, albeit operating with the opposite logic, as fascism sought to separate rigidly the two terms.

60 Mussolini, "Per il Piazzale della Vittoria a Vicenza," 23 Sept. 1924, in *SD* 4: 277.

61 Mussolini, "Discorso ai medici," 28 Jan. 1932, in *SD* 8: 22. This speech, like so many others, ends with an invitation to "amplify" the echo of the Duce's words: "Camerati, ho finito. Portate l'eco di queste mie parole a tutti i vostri colleghi raccolti nelle città e disseminati negli ottomila comuni d'Italia e dite loro che io conto anche e sovrattutto sui medici italiani per quanto riguarda la difesa del Regime e gli sviluppi della Rivoluzione Fascista" (Comrades, I have finished. Let the echo of these words of mine carry to all your colleagues gathered in the cities and disseminated in the eight thousand towns of Italy and tell them that I am counting also and especially on Italian doctors for the defence of the Regime and the expansion of the Fascist Revolution).

62 Mussolini, in Emil Ludwig, *Colloqui con Mussolini*, translated by Tomaso Gnoli (Milan: Mondadori, 1970), 132.

63 Mussolini, in Emil Ludwig, *Talks with Mussolini*, translated by Eden and
   Cedar Paul (Boston: Little, Brown, 1933), 126–7.
64 Mussolini, "Al popolo di Cremona," 19 June 1923, in *SD* 3:170–1.
65 Mussolini, in Ludwig, *Colloqui con Mussolini*, 196.
66 Mussolini, in Ludwig, *Talks with Mussolini*, 204.
67 Mussolini, "Celebrazione della Vittoria," 4 Nov. 1925, in *OO* 21: 442–3.
68 On the mussolinian *massa/gregge* motif, see also Ludwig, *Colloqui con Mussolini*, 127 (*Talks with Mussolini*, 120): "La massa per me non è altro che
   un gregge di pecore, finché non è organizzata. Non le sono affatto ostile.
   Soltanto nego che essa possa governarsi da sola. Ma se la si conduce,
   bisogna reggerla con due redini: entusiasmo e interesse. Chi si serve solo
   di uno dei due, corre pericolo. Il lato mistico e il politico si condizionano
   l'un l'altro. L'uno senza l'altro è arido, questo senza quello si disperde nel
   vento delle bandiere" (For me, the masses are nothing but a herd of sheep,
   so long as they are unorganised. I am nowise antagonistic to them. All
   that I deny is that they are capable of ruling themselves. But if you would
   lead them, you must guide them by two reins, enthusiasm and interest. He
   who uses one only of these reins is in grave danger. The mystical and the
   political factors condition each other reciprocally. Either without the other
   is arid, withered, and is stripped of its leaves by the wind).

   The description of the ideal fascist community based on hierarchy in contrast with the aggregation of a "mere herd" is also of interest: "Ecco quel
   che il fascismo vuol fare della massa: organizzare una vita collettiva, una
   vita in comune, lavorare e combattere in una gerarchia senza gregge. Siamo
   decisi ad attuare l'umanesimo e la bellezza della vita in comune" (You see,
   then, what we Fascists want to make out of the masses. We want to organ-
   ise their collective life; to teach them to live, to work, and to fight in a great
   fellowship – but in a hierarchy, not in a mere herd. We want the humanity
   and the beauty of a communal life). Mussolini, in Ludwig, *Colloqui con
   Mussolini*, 130 (*Talks with Mussolini*, 124).

69 In *Eros e Priapus* (151–2), the insistence on listing and defining particular occupations as a way of separating the single components of the
   "popolo" is accompanied by Gadda's explicit endorsement of *a-populismo*
   (non-populism).
70 *Eros e Priapo*, 199. For a discussion and critical revisitation of Gadda's view
   of machines, in the context of his initial flirtation and later rejection of
   Futurism, see Norma Bouchard, "(Re)Considering Gadda and Futurism,"
   Italica 79, no. 1 (2002): 23–43.
71 Amorous compliment.

72 *Eros e Priapo*, 198; emphasis added.
73 For Gadda's uneasy relation with mothers, see also Manuela Bertone, "Murderous Desires: Gaddian Matricides from *Novella seconda* to *La cognizione del dolore*," in Bertone and Dombroski, eds., *Carlo Emilio Gadda*, 111–31, and Margaret Baker, "The Women Characters of Carlo Emilio Gadda," in *Visions and Revisions: Women in Italian Culture*, ed. Mirna Cicioni and Nicole Prunster (Providence: Berg, 1993), 53–69.
74 *La cognizione*, 205 (*AG*, 172–3).
75 Ibid., 264 (*AG*, 232–3).

4: The Redemption of Vittorini's *New Man*

1 Elio Vittorini, *Uomini e no* (Milan: Mondadori, 1973). All translations in English of this work, unless otherwise indicated, are from Elio Vittorini, *Men and Not Men*, translated by Sarah Henry (Marlboro: Marlboro Press, 1985), hereafter referred to as *MN*. Occasionally, I have modified slightly Henry's translation to reflect the Italian text more closely.
2 For critical surveys of Vittorini's life and career, see Raffaele Crovi, *Il lungo viaggio di Vittorini: Una biografia critica* (Venice: Marsilio, 1998); Anselmo Madeddu, *Vittorini da Robinson a Gulliver* (Siracusa: Edizioni dell'Ariete, 1997); and Guido Bonsaver, *Elio Vittorini: The Writer and the Written* (Leeds: Northern Universities Press, 2000)
3 *Vita di Pizzo-di-Ferro detto Italo Balbo*, published in 1931 (Turin: Libreria del Littorio) under the names Curzio Malaparte and Enrico Falqui. Reprinted in Lorenzo Greco, *Censura e Scrittura: Vittorini, lo pseudo-Malaparte, Gadda* (Milan: Il Saggiatore, 1983), 186; my translation. Greco demonstrates with his detailed analysis and argument that the real author of Italo Balbo's biography was Vittorini.
4 Elio Vittorini, *Conversazione in Sicilia* (Manchester: Manchester University Press, 1978); *In Sicily*, translated by Wilfrid David (New York: New Directions, 1949).
5 For the initial phase of Vittorini's literary career, see Ettore Catalano, *La forma della coscienza: L'ideologia letteraria del primo Vittorini* (Bari: Dedalo, 1977); Anna Panicali, *Il primo Vittorini* (Milan: Celuc, 1974); see in particular Panicali's first chapter, "L'apprendistato rondesco-selvaggio," where she discusses Vittorini's "Sermone dell'ordinarietà" (1926–28), *Il Brigantino del Papa* (1928), and *Ritratto di re Giampiero* (1927).
6 Here is an example of the tendency to marginalize, when not altogether blot out, Vittorini's fascist past: In January 2003, the Italian newspaper *La Repubblica*, as part of its ongoing series *La Biblioteca di Repubblica*, offered

a free book ("Supplemento al numero odierno") to its readers – a special edition of Vittorini's *Uomini e no* (Milan: Mondadori, 2003). On the book jacket, the place usually reserved for brief biographical and professional information that "sum up" the author, appears the "blurb" that I am recopying and translating below. Notice how Vittorini's fascist days are completely expunged, as it flows from his humble origins directly into the Vittorini anti-fascist member of the Resistance:

> Elio Vittorini nacque a Siracusa nel 1908 e morì a Milano nel 1966. Figlio di un ferroviere, dopo i primi studi lasciò nel 1924 la Sicilia e si trasferì in Venezia Giulia, dove prese a lavorare come operaio edile. Nel 1930 si stabilì a Firenze, dove rimase fino al 1938 collaborando a varie riviste, tra cui *Solaria*, *Il Bargello*, *Campo di Marte*. Si spostò quindi a Milano, dove entrò in contatto con i gruppi antifascisti, iscrivendosi al Partito comunista clandestino, e partecipando poi alla Resistenza. Nel dopoguerra fu redattore capo dell'*Unità* e direttore di *Milano sera*. Dal 1945 al 1947 diresse il periodico *Il Politecnico*, prima settimanale poi mensile, sul quale animò numerose polemiche sui rapporti fra politica e cultura. Uscito dal Pci nel 1951, curò per l'editore Einaudi la collana *I gettoni* e successivamente, dal 1960, la collana *La Medusa* di Mondadori. Nel 1959 fondò insieme a Italo Calvino la rivista *Il Menabò*. Esordì alla narrativa nel 1931, con i brevi racconti di *Piccola borghesia*, seguiti dal romanzo *Il garofano rosso*, uscito a puntate su *Solaria* nel 1933–34 e in volume nel 1948. Del 1939 è *Conversazione in Sicilia*, cui seguono *Uomini e no* (1945), *Il Sempione strizza l'occhio al Fréjus* (1947), *Le donne di Messina* (1949), *Erica e i suoi fratelli* (1956), *Le città del mondo* (incompiuto, uscito postumo nel 1969). Di grande importanza l'antologia *Americana*, da lui curata nel 1941, e i saggi raccolti in *Diario in pubblico* (1957) e *Le due tensioni* (1967, postumo).

Elio Vittorini was born in Siracusa in 1908 and died in Milan in 1966. Son of a railroad worker, after his early schooling he left Sicily in 1924 and moved to Venezia Giulia, where he began to work as a construction worker. In 1930, he moved to Florence, where he remained until 1938 working as contributor to various journals, including *Solaria*, *Il Bargello*, and *Campo di Marte*. He then moved to Milan, where he came in contact with anti-fascist groups, becoming a member of the clandestine Communist Party and later participating in the Resistance. In the postwar period, he was editor-in-chief of *L'Unità* and managing editor of *Milano sera*. From 1945 to 1947 he directed the weekly, then monthly, *Il Politecnico*, where he spearheaded numerous debates on the relation between politics and culture. After leaving the PCI, in 1951, he edited the series *I gettoni* for the publishing house Einaudi, and, starting in 1960, Mondadori's series *La Medusa*. In 1959, he founded with Italo Calvino the journal *Il Menabò*. He made his literary debut in 1931 with the short stories of *Piccola borghesia*, followed by the novel *Il garofano rosso*, published in instalments in *Solaria* during 1933–34 and as a book in 1948; 1939 is the year of *Conversazione in Sicilia*, followed by *Uomini e no* (1945), *Il Sempione strizza l'occhio al Fréjus* (1947), *Le donne di Messina* (1949), *Erica e i suoi fratelli* (1956), and *Le città del mondo* (unfinished, published posthumously in 1969). Of great importance is the anthology *Americana*, which he edited in 1941, and the essay collections *Diario in pubblico* (1957) and *Le due tensioni* (1967, posthumous).

7 Elio Vittorini, "Fascisti i giovani?" in *Il Politecnico*, no. 15 (5 Jan. 1946); Emphasis of "simple" added; other emphasis in original. Reprinted in the anthology *Il Politecnico*, ed. Marco Forti and Sergio Pautasso (Milan: Rizzoli, 1980), 69–73. All translations of this work are mine.

8 Vittorini, "Fascisti i giovani?" 73.

9 For analyses of the cult of youth in fascist Italy from different perspectives, see the following: Barbara Spackman, "Fascist Puerility," *Qui Parle* 13, no. 1 (2001), 13–28; Laura Malvano, "The Myth of Youth in Images: Italian Fascism," in *A History of Young People in the West*, vol. 2, *Stormy Evolution to Modern Times*, ed. Giovanni Levi and Jean-Claude Schmitt (Cambridge: Harvard University Press, 1997), 232–56; and Bruno Wanrooij, "The Rise and Fall of Italian Fascism as a Generational Revolt," *Journal of Contemporary History* 22 (1987): 401–18.

10 Anna Panicali, *Elio Vittorini: La narrativa, la saggistica, le traduzioni, le riviste, l'attività editoriale* (Milan: Mursia, 1994), 231.

11 Vittorini, "Fascisti i giovani?" 69.

12 "Non dobbiamo dunque dire a ogni giovane che egli ha il diritto (in quanto giovane, e cioè in quanto cresciuto sotto il fascismo) a convincersi di non essere colpevole? Non dobbiamo anzi aiutare ogni giovane a convincersi di non essere colpevole? E l'unico modo per aiutarli a convincersi di non esser colpevoli è di mostrar loro quello che in realtà sono stati: strumenti sì del fascismo, ciechi dinanzi a quello che il fascismo era, vittime di quello che sembrava, deboli, non forti, ma non fascisti." Vittorini, "Fascisti i giovani?" (Shouldn't we tell each youth that he has the right [as a youth, that is, growing up under fascism] to be convinced that he is not guilty? Shouldn't we actually help each youth be convinced that he is not guilty? The only way to help them be convinced that they are not guilty is by

showing them what they have been in reality: yes, pawns of fascism, blind
to what fascism was, victims of what it seemed to be – weak, not strong,
but not fascist) (ibid., 70).

13 The view that fascism represented a dictatorial evolution of bourgeois capitalism is by no means unique to Vittorini. As Stanley G. Payne (*A History
of Fascism*, 443) points out in his concise but useful overview of interpretations of fascism: "The notion that fascism is primarily to be understood as
the agent of 'capitalism,' 'big business,' 'finance capital,' the 'bourgeoisie,'
'state monopoly capitalism,' (Stamokap), or some conceivable combina-
tion thereof is one of the oldest and most widely disseminated interpretations, having for many decades served as the official Communist theory
of fascism." More comprehensive studies of the interpretations of fascism
are: Renzo De Felice, *Le interpretazioni del fascismo* (Rome: Laterza, 1974);
A. James Gregor, *Interpretations of Fascism* (Morristown, NJ: General Learning Press, 1974); Francesco Perfetti, *Il dibattito sul fascismo* (Rome: Bonacci,
1984). A useful "state of the field" discussion and overview of critical approaches is Roger Griffin, ed., *International Fascism: Theories, Causes and the
New Consensus* (London: Oxford University Press, 1998).

14 Vittorini, "Fascisti i giovani?" 73.

15 Ibid., 69.

16 Ibid.

17 Vittorini confirmed his reliance on the "magical" power of adjectives in
"Fondamenti della letteratura: Fede nella parola," originally published as
preface to his novel *Il garofano rosso* (Milan: Mondadori, 1948), reprinted in
Elio Vittorini, *Diario in pubblico (1929–1956)* (Milan: Bompiani, 1970), 333–4:
"È in ogni uomo di attendersi che forse la parola, *una parola, possa trasfor-
mare la sostanza di una cosa*. Ed è nello scrittore di crederlo con assiduità e
fermezza. È ormai nel nostro mestiere, nel nostro compito. *È fede in una
magia: che un aggettivo possa giungere dove non giunse, cercando la verità, la ragione*; o che un avverbio possa recuperare il segreto che si è sottratto a ogni
indagine. Ma è l'ottimismo che se ne va sempre per ultimo, e che dunque
serve, sovente, di piú lungo aiuto" (Each man has a tendency to believe
that perhaps *words, one word, can transform the substance of a thing*. It is the
constant and steadfast belief of a writer. It is part of our job, of our task. *It
is faith in magic: that an adjective can go where reason, searching for truth, cannot*; or that an adverb can reclaim the secret that had eluded every investigation. Optimism is always the last thing to go and is, therefore, most
helpful in the long run); emphasis added. All translations of Elio Vittorini,
Diario in pubblico, are mine.

18 Vittorini, "Fascisti i giovani?" 70.

19 Another interesting description that links "impaired sight" to the necessity of "coming to terms" is in "Giovani dopo la tempesta," *Il Politecnico* (May 1946), reprinted in Elio Vittorini, *Diario in pubblico*, 225: "C'è oggi nel mondo, non solo in Italia, una disperazione di vivere che sembra togliere, proprio ai piú giovani, ogni possibilità, anche semplicemente storica, di lottare. Durante il fascismo c'era almeno risentimento, negli scrittori che la mostravano. Oggi ci sono occhi che nemmeno guardano, tanto li offusca stanchezza o pianto. Ma sono occhi, sono uomini. Sono una realtà con la quale dobbiamo pur fare i conti" (Nowadays in the world, not just in Italy, a feeling of living in despair seems to deprive the youngest of every possibility, even one that is simply in line with history, to fight. During fascism there was at least resentment in writers that showed angst. Today there are eyes that do not even see, clouded as they are by fatigue or crying. But they are eyes, they are men. They are a reality we must come to terms with).

20 Anna Panicali, in *Il primo Vittorini* (7–8), traces Vittorini's anti-bourgeois sentiment to his early writings and in particular to "Sermone dell'Ordinarietà" (1926–28): "In questo contesto – tutto malapartiano ma anticipato stilisticamente nella poetica xenofoba rondesca – Elio Vittorini viene proponendo il suo primo antiborghesismo politico: il borghese italiano è la personificazione della straordinarietà perché si identifica con lo straniero. Vittorini, con questa formula, dimostra di aver introiettato perfettamente lo schema letterario della polemica antiliberale del fascismo e di essere disponibile a ingaggiare la 'lotta contro la borghesia' (classe di pochi e senza legame con le masse, perché 'snaturata,' cioè intessuta artificialmente di valori straordinari, mentre il 'popolo' è naturalmente ordinario) nei termini di lotta contro le sopravvivenze e il riformarsi della 'mentalità' borghese" (In this context – fully Malapartian but one that is anticipated stylistically by the xenophobic poetics of the Ronda – Elio Vittorini proposes his first anti-bourgeois politics: The Italian bourgeois is the personification of the extraordinary because it is identified with the foreigner. Vittorini, with this axiom, demonstrates to have internalized perfectly the literary coordinates of fascism's anti-liberal polemics and to be willing to engage in the "fight against the bourgeoisie" (class of the few and without ties to the masses, because "unnatural," that is, artificially imbued with extraordinary values, while the "people" is naturally ordinary) as the fight against survival and reform of the bourgeois "mentality"). All translations of Anna Panicali, *Il primo Vittorini*, are mine. For Vittorini's anti-bourgeois sentiments in the context of the cultural policies of the fascist regime, see Ben-Ghiat, *Fascist Modernities*, particularly the chapter, "Class Dismissed: Fascism's Politics of Youth," 93–122.

21 As in my previous chapter's analysis of Gadda's labouring bodies, I am
indebted here to Karen Pinkus' discussion (*Bodily Regimes*, 119–24) of the
hands' status as "hands" in fascist iconography and advertising which
she sees as the visual translation of Marx's distinction between *Kopf-* and
Handarbeit, albeit operating with the opposite logic, as fascism sought to
separate rigidly the two terms.

22 See, e.g., "Lettera a Togliatti" in *Il Politecnico*, no. 35 (Jan.–March 1947),
where Vittorini seems to subordinate the work and even the existence of
writers to the larger goal of creating a classless society: "Certo noi scrittori
di partito siamo preparati all'eventualità di dover limitare il nostro lavoro,
il giorno che fosse indispensabile per la costruzione della società senza
classi. Direi che siamo preparati all'eventualità di dovervi addirittura ri-
nunciare" (Of course, as party writers, we are prepared for the eventuality
of having to curtail our work, if the day came when it would prove necessary for building a classless society. I would say we are even prepared for
the eventuality of having to give it up). Reprinted in the anthology *Il Politecnico*, ed. Forti and Pautasso, 138. His prewar position was also strongly
anti-classist. In a 1936 article (*Il Bargello*, no. 38, 5 July), titled "Niente
servi!" (No Servants!) Vittorini objected to a proposal to fill undesirable
jobs in Italy with Abyssinian servants, not on anti-racist grounds (for he
was, in fact, opposed to racial mixing), but because he thought it would
transform the unified Italian *popolo* into a class: "E a dire oggi 'gli italiani
hanno di meglio da fare che portar bagagli' non si correrebbe il rischio
di dire domani 'gli italiani hanno di meglio da fare che zappare la terra'?
Non si correrebbe cioè il rischio di contrarre a poco a poco una mentalità
di popolo 'servito' contraria ai fini della nostra civiltà, e di trasformarci con
secoli da popolo in una classe come, per sua disgrazia, capitò al popolo romano del tardo impero?" (In saying that today "Italians have better things
to do than carrying bags" don't we run the risk of saying tomorrow "Italians have better things to do than tilling the soil"? Don't we run the risk of
slowly acquiring a mentality opposed to the goals of our civilization, that
of a "served" people, and transforming ourselves, after centuries of being
a people, into a class, as the Roman people did, to their detriment, during
the Late Empire?). Republished in Raffaella Rodondi, ed., *Elio Vittorini:
Letteratura, arte, società. Articoli e interventi 1926–1937* (Turin: Einaudi, 1997),
944–5; all translations of this work are mine.

23 The cultural and political complexities (and contradictions) of this ambi-
tious editorial project have been explored by a number of scholars, hence,
I will not attempt to do justice to them here. My brief encapsulation of *Il
Politecnico*'s populist positions has the narrower scope of highlighting the

Vittorinian preoccupation with culture as a vehicle for social mobility and in promoting social change. Detailed and informative works on the subject are: Marina Zancan, *Il progetto "Politecnico": Cronaca e strutture di una rivista* (Venice: Marsilio, 1984), and Panicali, *Elio Vittorini*.

24 See the chapter "Il Politecnico," in Gian Carlo Ferretti, *L'editore Vittorini* (Turin: Einaudi, 1992), 69–114, for a good discussion of Vittorini's efforts to render *Il Politecnico* a cultural laboratory eager to establish an active collaboration with the public at large. See in particular Ferretti's comments on Vittorini's insistence on "contatti con the masse" (contacts with the masses), which he saw as a necessary element for creating a culture that would regenerate society (76–8).

25 See Stephen Gundle, *Between Hollywood and Moscow: The Italian Communists and the Challenge of Mass Culture, 1943–1991* (Durham: Duke University Press, 2000).

26 Palmiro Togliatti, "Politica e cultura: Una lettera di Palmiro Togliatti," *Il Politecnico* 2, nos. 33–4 (1946): 3–4; cited in Gundle, *Between Hollywood and Moscow*, 29.

27 Vittorini, "Questione di mela," *Il lavoro illustrato* (July 1952); republished in Vittorini, *Diario in pubblico*, 405; emphasis in original. On the subject of the cultural education of the masses, see also his article, "Scuola e uguaglianza culturale," *Il Politecnico* 2 (Oct. 1945); republished in Vittorini, *Diario in pubblico*, 214–15: "Sul terreno della scuola il problema non può essere altro che quello di fornire a tutti i mezzi della conoscenza, e rendere tutti armati, attrezzati, preparati allo stesso modo per accostarsi ai libri [. . .] e partecipare alle ricerche della cultura. Anche nel promuovere le riforme più provvisorie non si può non tenerlo presente" (With regard to schooling, the problem can only be how to provide everybody with the tools of knowledge and to make everyone equally prepared, equipped, ready to approach books [. . .] and to be a participant in cultural exploration. Even when promoting the most provisional reforms we have to keep this in mind).

28 I doubt that the hypothetical engineer is a direct reference to Gadda here, for Vittorini certainly knew that Gadda's culture extended far beyond technical knowledge. Nevertheless, when we read it as a critique of social values underpinning mechanisms of social mobility, placing Gadda in the shoes of the hypothetical engineer seems to me right on the mark.

29 Vittorini, "Elogio della cultura popolare," *Il Bargello* (17 Jan. 1937), 3, signed with the pseudonym Abulfeda; republished in Rodondi, ed., *Elio Vittorini*, 1027–30; second emphasis added.

30 For detailed analyses of the Italian editorial market and its readership, see Gabriele Turi, ed., *Storia dell'editoria nell'Italia contemporanea* (Florence:

Giunti, 1997); Stefano Mauri, *Il libro in Italia: Geografia, produzione, consumo* (Milan: Hoepli, 1987); Eugenio Garin, *Editori italiani tra Ottocento e Novecento* (Rome: Laterza, 1991); and Giovanni Ragone, *Un secolo di libri: Storia dell'editoria in Italia dall'Unità al post-moderno* (Turin: Einaudi, 1999).

31 Vittorini, "Elogio della cultura popolare"; republished in Rodondi, ed., *Elio Vittorini*, 1028; emphasis in original.

32 Vittorini's belief in "the good old days" of popular demand for culture is not supported by studies of the publishing market. In his essay, "Un panorama in evoluzione," Enrico Decleva points out that while the Italian publishing industry expanded during the years 1900–15, Italian production, diffusion, and demand still lagged far behind those of other nations such as France, England, Germany, and the United States. Edmondo De Amicis' *Cuore* was still the best seller with 420,000 copies printed by 1908 and second only to Carlo Collodi's *Le avventure di Pinocchio* (half-million copies by 1907). A survey conducted in 1905 indicates that the numbers were far lower for other major authors: Antonio Fogazzaro's *Piccolo mondo antico* (44,000 copies), Giovanni Verga's *Storia di una capinera* (20,000 copies), Gabriele D'Annunzio's *Il piacere* (17,000 copies). As Decleva puts it: "Ma si trattava di titoli particolarmente bene accolti. Per gli standard del tempo andava considerato un successo suparare il traguardo dei 10.000 esemplari stampati. E per le opere di cultura costituiva già un buon risultato, secondo testimonianze attendibili, smaltirne un migliaio" (But these were works that met with uncommon favour. For the standards of the time it was a success to exceed 10,000 printed copies. And, according to reliable reports, in the case of works of culture, selling a thousand copies was considered a good result). In Gabriele Turi, ed., *Storia dell'editoria nell'Italia contemporanea*, 226–7.

33 Vittorini, "Dell'andare verso il popolo," *Il Bargello* (16 June 1935), 2; republished in Rodondi, ed., *Elio Vittorini*, 873.

34 Vittorini, "Quaderno '37"; republished in Rodondi, ed., *Elio Vittorini*, 1004–15; emphasis in original. As Rodondi reports: "Il testo è stato edito per la prima volta nel fascicolo del 'Ponte' 31 luglio – 31 agosto 1973 (interamente dedicato a Vittorini), alle pp. 1132–41. In calce una nota redazionale lo qualificava come 'appunti stesi da Vittorini negli anni trenta e dati a Romano Bilenchi nel 1937 perché li lasciasse tra le sue carte'; di qui il titolo, pure redazionale, che con una certa libertà assolutizza al 1937 appunti ascrivibili, genericamente, agli anni precedenti" (The text was edited for the first time for the issue of *Il Ponte* 31 July – 31 August 1973 (dedicated entirely to Vittorini), on pages 1132–41. An editorial comment identified it

as "notes written by Vittorini in the 1930s and given to Romano Bilenchi in 1937 to keep with his documents"; hence, the title given by the editor which establishes, somewhat arbitrarily, 1937 as the date of notes that can generally be attributed to the preceding years).

35 Vittorini, *Il garofano rosso*, in *Solaria*, nos. 5–6 (1934): 65; cited in Panicali, *Elio Vittorini*, 127. As Panicali points out, this excerpt was suppressed in the volume edition of the novel. For critical appraisals of *Il garofano rosso*, see Lorenzo Greco, "La censura del 'Garofano rosso,'" *Censura e scrittura*, 99–132, and Raffaella Rodondi, "Viaggio intorno al 'Garofano,'" in *Il presente vince sempre* (Palermo: Sellerio, 1985), 13–163.

36 Vittorini, "Ragioni dell'azienda collettiva in A.[frica] O.[rientale]," *Il Bargello* (19 and 26 July 1936), 3 and 3–4; republished in Rodondi, ed., *Elio Vittorini*, 952–3; uppercase letters in original.

37 Vittorini, "La rivoluzione culturale," *Il Bargello* (31 Jan. 1937), 3, signed with the pseudonym Omicron; republished in Rodondi, ed., *Elio Vittorini*, 1038; emphasis in original.

38 Vittorini, "Scandalo tra i commercianti d'uova," *Il Bargello* (20 Nov. 1932), 3; republished in Rodondi, ed., *Elio Vittorini*, 618–19.

39 For an analysis of the concept of *bonifica* as a central component of fascism's cultural policies and modernizing strategy, see Ben-Ghiat, *Fascist Modernities*.

40 Jean-Jacques Rousseau, *Emile*, translated by Barbara Foxley (London: Dent, 1993).

41 Jacques Derrida, ". . . That Dangerous Supplement . . .," in *Of Grammatology*, translated by Gayatri Chakravorty Spivak (Baltimore: Johns Hopkins University Press, 1974), 146.

42 As Ferretti notes, in *L'editore Vittorini*, the "lettore popolare" (popular readership) was linked by Vittorini to the motif of "cuore di ragazzo" (young at heart), as if to underscore the reader's naïve, sincere, and passionate approach to culture – an ideal terrain on which to build a project of "cultural elevation" (51).

43 Jacques Derrida, *Of Grammatology*, 145.

44 Achille Starace, memo dated 29 Nov. 1939, Rome, on letterhead "Milizia Volontaria per la Sicurezza Nazionale, Direzione Centrale di Sanità," ACS, MCP, Gabinetto, b. 83, MVSN, f. 568. Recent scholarship has underscored the central role of Starace within the fascist regime. See Antonio Spinosa, *Starace: L'uomo che inventò lo stile fascista* (Milan: Mondadori, 2002), and Roberto Festorazzi, *Starace: Il mastino della rivoluzione fascista* (Milan: Mursia, 2002).

45 Mussolini, "Per l'aviazione italiana," 4 Nov. 1923, in *SD* 3: 246.

46 Mussolini, "Settimo anniversario dei Fasci a Villa Glori," 28 March 1926, in *SD* 5: 298.

47 Mussolini, "Per il terzo anniversario della marcia su Roma," 28 Oct. 1925, in *SD* 5: 158.

48 Mussolini, "Battisti," 12 July 1917, in *SD* 1: 256.

49 "Solo la guerra porta al massimo di tensione tutte le energie umane e imprime un sigillo di nobiltà ai popoli che hanno la virtù di affrontarla" (Only war is capable of bringing all human energies to a point of maximum tension and of conferring a seal of nobility on the peoples virtuous enough to engage in it). From the article written for the entry "Fascismo" in the Treccani Italian Encyclopedia. *SD* 8: 77.

50 Mussolini, "Per lo Stato corporativo," 14 Nov. 1933, in *SD* 8: 272–3.

51 Mussolini, "Al Consiglio di Stato," 22 Dec. 1928, in *SD* 6: 358.

52 Mussolini, "Al popolo di Roma per il XXVIII Ottobre," 28 Oct. 1926, in *SD* 5: 449. A synthetic portrayal of the "harmonizing" function of the fascist state can be found in his commemorative speech, "Michele Bianchi," 3 March 1930, in *OO* 24: 197: "Fascita integrale, uomo della rivoluzione, egli ha il senso, vorrei dire religioso, dello Stato: autorità suprema in cui tutto si accentra e si armonizza: individui e gruppi, passato e futuro, spirito e materia" (Integral fascist, man of the revolution, he has what I would call a religious sense of the State: a supreme authority in which everything is centred and harmonized: individuals and groups, past and future, spirit and matter). See also the speech, "Al Sindaco di Lodi," 4 Oct. 1924, in *OO* 21: 87: "Fare grande il nostro popolo; renderlo consapevole e orgoglioso dei suoi destini; renderlo una unità armonica, organica, nella quale ogni cittadino abbia il proprio posto per l'adempimento di un proprio dovere, ecco le mète, quali prossime, quali remote, del Governo nazionale. Occorre tendere a queste mète con tutte le nostre forze" (To make our people great; to make it aware and proud of its destiny; to transform it into an harmonic, organic whole, in which every citizen has a role in fulfilling his duty – these are the goals, some for the short term, others for the long term, of the national Government. We need to pursue these goals with all of our strength).

53 Mussolini, "Elementi di Storia," *Gerarchia*, no. 10 (Oct. 1925), in *OO* 21: 435.

54 Mussolini, "Sintesi del regime," 18 March 1934, in *OO* 26: 192; emphasis added.

55 Mussolini, "Per la medaglia dei benemeriti del comune di Milano," 28 Oct. 1925, in *OO* 21: 426.

56 Mussolini, "Prefazione a 'Il Gran Consiglio nei primi quindici anni dell'era fascista,'" 1 July 1938,in *OO* 29: 117.
57 Mussolini, "Il discorso di Eboli," 6 July 1935, in *OO* 27: 103.
58 Mussolini, "Alla vecchia guardia," 26 March 1939, in *OO* 29: 250.
59 See, e.g., the Mussolinian speech, "Al popolo di Prato," 25 May 1926: "Mi tardava venire in questa Prato che lavora, che produce, che esporta, che ha masse operaie disciplinate, che applica il principio vitale della collaborazione di classe, perché il principio opposto, della lotta di classe, significa soltanto distruzione di ricchezza e rovina anche del popolo" (I was impatient to come to Prato, a town that works, that produces, that exports, that has disciplined masses of workers, that applies the vital principle of class collaboration, because the opposite principle of class conflict leads only to the destruction of wealth and the ruin of the people). *SD* 5: 349.
60 Mussolini, "Al popolo di Rovigo," 2 June 1923, in *SD* 3: 114.
61 Mussolini, "Agli operai del Monte Amiata," 31 Aug. 1924, in *OO* 21: 56.
62 For a discussion of the 1938 "riforma del costume" in connection to the regime's expansionist policies, see Ben-Ghiat, *Fascist Modernities*, 123–70.
63 Mussolini, "Discorso di Firenze," 17 May 1930, in *OO* 24: 235. The expansionist rhetoric of "superamento dei confini" (overcoming the national borders) is also present in speeches delivered during the early and mid-1920s, hence, cannot, in my view, be considered a by-product of later colonialist policies. See, e.g., the speech, "Al popolo di Firenze," 19 June 1923, in *OO* 19: 278: "Vogliamo che il mare non sia una cintura contro la nostra vitalità, ma invece la strada per la nostra necessaria espansione nel mondo" (We do not want the sea to be a barrier against our vitality but instead a road for our necessary expansion in the world). See also the speech, "Ciò che rimane e ciò che verrà," 13 Nov. 1920, in *OO* 16: 6: "Terzo dato di fatto è questo: che gli italiani non devono ipnotizzarsi nell'Adriatico o in alcune isole o sponde dell'Adriatico. C'è anche – se non ci inganniamo – un vasto mare di cui l'Adriatico è un modesto golfo e che si chiama il Mediterraneo, nel quale le possibilità vive dell'espansione italiana sono fortissime" (This is the third fact: Italians must not be hypnotized by the Adriatic Sea or by some Adriatic islands or shores. If we are not mistaken, there is also a vast sea, of which the Adriatic is only a modest gulf, called the Mediterranean, where the possibilities for Italian expansion are very strong). Italian emigration was portrayed as a physiological necessity of the nation and often conflated with the necessity for expansionist policies: "Bene o male che sia l'emigrazione è una necessità fisiologica del popolo italiano [. . .] Dico espansione: espansione in ogni senso: morale, politico, economico,

demografico" (For better or worse, emigration is a physiological necessity of the Italian people [. . .] I say expansion: expansion in every sense
of the term: moral, political, economic, and demographic). "Il problema
dell'emigrazione," 31 March 1923, in *OO* 19: 191.

64 Mussolini, "Alla nuova sede dei mutilati," 11 March 1923, in *OO* 19: 167.
Labour was also an ennobling factor of the new social hierarchy, a distinguishing activity separating the fascists from other parasitical groups
that had to be eliminated. See the speech, "Al popolo di Ferrara," 22 Sept.
1924, in *OO* 21: 78: "Io rispetto i calli alle mani. Sono un titolo di nobiltà.
Io stesso li ho avuti, poiché nobile è veramente colui che lavora, nobile è
veramente colui che produce, colui che porta il suo sasso anche modesto
all'edificio della patria. E la patria che noi sogniamo è la patria dove tutti
lavorano e dove parassiti non ne esistono più" (I respect calloused hands.
They are an emblem of nobility. I had them myself. True nobility belongs to
the man who works, true nobility belongs to the man who produces, who
carries a stone, even a modest one, to the edifice of the country. The country we dream of is the country where everyone works and where parasites
no longer exist). The origin of the new aristocracy of amputees was linked
discursively to labour by the double valence of *travaglio* (travail), as work
and giving birth: "Voi siete seriamente l'aristocrazia nuova, nata dal travaglio sanguinoso e penoso della guerra" (You are truly the new aristocracy,
born of the bloody and painful travail of war). 19 June 1923, in *OO* 19: 279.

65 Mussolini, "Alle medaglie d'oro," 16 Dec. 1926, in *SD* 5: 475.

66 Mussolini, "Vincolo di sangue," 19 Jan. 1922, in *OO* 18: 13.

67 Mussolini, "Al popolo di Busto Arsizio," 25 Oct. 1924, in *SD* 4: 321. See
also a much later speech delivered in Bologna, 24 Oct. 1936, in *SD* 10:
184: "Tutta la Nazione oggi è su un piano diverso e più elevato: il piano
dell'Impero" (The entire Nation today is on a different and more elevated
plane: the plane of Empire).

68 On *Uomini e no*, see Giacomo Noventa, *Il grande amore* (Milan: Scheiwiller,
1960); Giovanna Falaschi, *La resistenza armata nella narrativa italiana* (Turin:
Einaudi, 1976); Franco Fortini, *Saggi italiani* (Bari: De Donato, 1974); and
Bruno Falcetto, *Storia della narrativa neorealista* (Milan: Mursia, 1992).

69 The preoccupation with defining "man" was already quite evident in
the pages of *Conversazione in Sicilia* (1939), which contains the following
famous passage (114): "Non ogni uomo è uomo, allora. Uno perseguita e
uno è perseguitato; e genere umano non è tutto il genere umano, ma quello
soltanto del perseguitato. Uccidete un uomo; egli sarà più uomo. E così è
più uomo un malato, un affamato; è più genere umano il genere umano
dei morti di fame" ("Not every man then, is a man. One persecutes and

another is persecuted; not all the human race is human, but only the race of the persecuted. Kill a man, and he will be something more than a man. Similarly, a man who is sick or starving is more than a man; and more human is the human race of the starving"; *In Sicily*, 144).

70 Vittorini could not have made the association between dogs and the German occupiers any stronger. The reason for feeding the prisoner to the dogs is that he had killed Greta, the dog of the German captain, albeit in self-defence.

71 Vittorini, *Uomini e no*, 196–7 (*MN*, 164).

72 I am obviously playing here on the title of one of the classic essays on fetishism: Octave Mannoni, "Je sais bien, mais quand meme . . ." *Clefs pour l'imaginaire ou l'autre scene* (Paris: Ed. Du Seuil, 1969). The best collection of critical essays on fetishism remains Emily Apter and William Pietz, eds., *Fetishism as Cultural Discourse* (Ithaca: Cornell University Press, 1993).

73 Vittorini, *Uomini e no*, 202–3 (*MN*, 169–70).

74 Ibid., 223–4 (*MN*, 188); emphasis added.

Abbreviations

ACS	Archivio Centrale dello Stato, Rome
MCP	Ministero della Cultura Popolare
PNF	Partito Nazionale Fascista
AG	Acquainted with Grief
DG	"Discorso del 3 gennaio"
DL	"Discorso alla 'Decima Legio'" ("Discorso del 23 settembre")
MN	Men and Not Men
OO	Opera Omnia di Benito Mussolini
PD	"Primo Discorso per il Decennale"
SD	Scritti e discorsi di Benito Mussolini

Bibliography

Abraham, Nicolas, and Maria Torok. *The Wolf Man's Magic Word: A Cryp-tonymy*. Trans. Nicholas Rand. Minneapolis: University of Minnesota Press, 1986.

Adami, Eugenio. *La lingua di Mussolini*. Modena: Società Tipografica Moden-ese, 1939.

Adamson, Walter L. "The Language of Opposition in Early Twentieth-Century Italy: Rhetorical Continuities between Prewar Florentine Avant-gardism and Mussolini's Fascism." *Journal of Modern History* 64, no. 1 (1992): 22–51. http://dx.doi.org/10.1086/244440.

Agamben, Giorgio. *Means without End: Notes on Politics*. Trans. Vincenzo Binetti and Cesare Casarino. Minneapolis: University of Minnesota Press, 2000.

Althusser, Louis. "Ideology and Ideological State Apparatuses (Notes To-wards an Investigation)." In *Lenin and Philosophy and Other Essays*, trans. Ben Brewster, 127–86. New York: Monthly Review Press, 1971.

Apter, Emily, and William Pietz, eds. *Fetishism as Cultural Discourse*. Ithaca: Cornell University Press, 1993.

Ardau, Giuseppe. *L'eloquenza mussoliniana*. Milan: Mondadori, 1929.

Baird, Jay W. *To Die for Germany: Heroes in the Nazi Pantheon*. Bloomington: Indiana University Press, 1990.

Baker, Margaret. "The Women Characters of Carlo Emilio Gadda." In *Visions and Revisions: Women in Italian Culture*, ed. Mirna Cicioni and Nicole Prunster, 53–69. Providence: Berg, 1993.

Bataille, Georges. *Visions of Excess: Selected Writings, 1927–1939*. Ed. Allan Stoekl. Trans. Allan Stoekl, with Carl R. Lovitt and Donald M. Leslie, Jr. Minneapolis: University of Minnesota Press, 1985.

Benedetti, Carla. "The Enigma of Grief: An Expressionism against the Self." In *Carlo Emilio Gadda: Contemporary Perspectives*, ed. Manuela Bertone and Robert S. Dombroski, 159–76. Toronto: University of Toronto Press, 1997.

Ben-Ghiat, Ruth. *Fascist Modernities: Italy, 1922–1945*. Berkeley: University of California Press, 2001.

Benjamin, Jessica. *The Bonds of Love: Psychoanalysis, Feminism, and the Problems of Domination*. New York: Pantheon, 1988.

Benjamin, Walter. "The Work of Art in the Age of Mechanical Reproduction." [1936]. In *Illuminations*, ed. Hannah Arendt, trans. Harry Zohn, 217–51. New York: Schocken, 1985.

Berezin, Mabel. *Making the Fascist Self: The Political Culture of Interwar Italy*. Ithaca: Cornell University Press, 1997.

Bertone, Manuela. "Murderous Desires: Gaddian Matricides from *Novella seconda* to *La cognizione del dolore*." In *Carlo Emilio Gadda: Contemporary Perspectives*, ed. Manuela Bertone and Robert S. Dombroski, 111–31. Toronto: University of Toronto Press, 1997.

Bertone, Manuela, and Robert S. Dombroski, eds. *Carlo Emilio Gadda: Contemporary Perspectives*. Toronto: University of Toronto Press, 1997.

Bianchi, Lorenzo. *Mussolini scrittore e oratore*. Bologna: Zanichelli, 1937.

Bonsaver, Guido. *Elio Vittorini: The Writer and the Written*. Leeds: Northern Universities Press, 2000.

–––––. "Fascist Censorship on Literature and the Case of Elio Vittorini." *Modern Italy* 8, no. 2 (2003): 165–86. http://dx.doi.org/10.1080/1353294032 000131229.

–––––. *Censorship and Literature in Fascist Italy*. Toronto: University of Toronto Press, 2007.

Bottai, Giuseppe. *Diario 1935–1944*. Milan: Rizzoli, 1989.

Bouchard, Norma. "(Re)considering Gadda and Futurism." *Italica* 79, no. 1 (2002): 23–43. http://dx.doi.org/10.2307/3655970.

Buchignani, Paolo. *La rivoluzione in camicia nera*. Milan: Mondadori, 2006.

Buck-Morss, Susan. "Aesthetics and Anaesthetics: Walter Benjamin's Artwork Essay Reconsidered." *New Formations* 20 (1993): 123–43.

Butler, Judith. *The Psychic Life of Power: Theories in Subjection*. Stanford: Stanford University Press, 1997.

Candeloro, Giorgio. *Storia dell'Italia moderna*. 11 vols. Milan: Feltrinelli, 1960–86.

Catalano, Ettore. *La forma della coscienza: L'ideologia letteraria del primo Vittorini*. Bari: Dedalo, 1977.

Cavarero, Adriana. *A più voci: Filosofia dell'espressione vocale*. Milan: Feltrinelli, 2003.

Chion, Michel. *The Voice in Cinema*. Trans. Claudia Gorbman. New York: Columbia University Press, 1999.

Chytry, Josef. *The Aesthetic State: A Quest in Modern German Thought*. Berkeley: University of California Press, 1989.

Ciarlantini, Franco. *Mussolini immaginario*. Milan: Sonzogno, 1933.

Colarizi, Simona. *La seconda guerra mondiale e la Repubblica*. Turin: UTET, 1984.

Crovi, Raffaele. *Il lungo viaggio di Vittorini: Una biografia critica*. Venice: Marsilio, 1998.

De Felice, Renzo. *Mussolini il fascista*. 2 vols. Turin: Einaudi, 1966–68.

———. *Le interpretazioni del fascismo*. Rome: Laterza, 1974.

———. *Mussolini il duce*. 2 vols. Turin: Einaudi, 1974–81.

———, ed. *Autobiografia del fascismo: Antologia di testi fascisti 1919–1945*. Bergamo: Minerva Italica, 1978.

De Felice, Renzo, and Luigi Goglia. *Mussolini: Il mito*. Rome: Laterza, 1983.

de Man, Paul. *Allegories of Reading: Figural Language in Rousseau, Nietzsche, Rilke, and Proust*. New Haven: Yale University Press, 1979.

———. *Aesthetic Ideology*. Ed. Andrzej Warminski. Minneapolis: University of Minnesota Press, 1996.

de Vries, Hent. "Violence and Testimony: On Sacrificing Sacrifice." In *Violence, Identity, and Self-Determination*, ed. Hent de Vries and Samuel Weber, 15–43. Stanford: Stanford University Press, 1997.

Dean, Kenneth, and Brian Massumi. *First and Last Emperors: The Absolute State and the Body of the Despot*. New York: Autonomedia, 1992. http://dx.doi.org/10.2307/1399750

Derrida, Jacques. *Of Grammatology*. Trans. Gayatri Chakravorty Spivack. Baltimore: Johns Hopkins University Press, 1976.

———. *Dissemination*. Trans. Barbara Johnson. Chicago: University of Chicago Press, 1981.

Dolar, Mladen. "The Object Voice." In *Gaze and Voice as Love Objects*, ed. Renata Salecl and Slavoj Zizek, 7–31. Durham: Duke University Press, 1996.

Dombroski, Robert S. *L'esistenza ubbidiente: Letterati italiani sotto il fascismo*. Naples: Guida, 1984.

———. *Properties of Writing: Ideological Discourse in Modern Italian Fiction*. Baltimore: Johns Hopkins University Press, 1994.

———. *Creative Entanglements: Gadda and the Baroque*. Toronto: University of Toronto Press, 1999.

Eagleton, Terry. *The Ideology of the Aesthetic*. Oxford: Basil Blackwell, 1990.

Ellwanger, Hermann. *Sulla lingua di Mussolini*. Milan: Mondadori, 1941.

Falasca-Zamponi, Simonetta. *Fascist Spectacle: The Aesthetics of Power in Mussolini's Italy*. Berkeley: University of California Press, 1997.

Falaschi, Giovanna. *La resistenza armata nella narrativa italiana*. Turin: Einaudi, 1976.

Falcetto, Bruno. *Storia della narrativa neorealista*. Milan: Mursia, 1992.

Femia, Joseph. "Machiavelli and Italian Fascism." *History of Political Thought* 25, no. 1 (2004): 1–15.

Ferretti, Gian Carlo. *L'editore Vittorini*. Turin: Einaudi, 1992.

Festorazzi, Roberto. *Starace: Il mastino della rivoluzione fascista*. Milan: Mursia, 2002.

Fischer-Lichte, Erika. *Theatre, Sacrifice, Ritual: Exploring Forms of Political Theatre*. New York: Routledge, 2005.

Forti, Marco, and Sergio Pautasso, eds. *Il Politecnico*. Milan: Rizzoli, 1980.

Fortini, Franco. *Saggi italiani*. Bari: De Donato, 1974.

Foscolo, Ugo. *Last Letters of Jacopo Ortis* [*Ultime lettere di Jacopo Ortis*]. Trans. Douglas Radcliff-Umstead. Chapel Hill: University of North Carolina Press, 1970.

Freud, Sigmund. "Fetishism." In *Sexuality and the Psychology of Love*, ed. Philip Rieff, 204–9. New York: Macmillan, 1963.

———. "Mourning and Melancholia." In *The Standard Edition of the Complete Psychological Works of Sigmund Freud*, ed. and trans. James Strachey. 24 vols. London: Hogarth, 1953–74. 14: 237–58.

Gadda, Carlo Emilio. *La cognizione del dolore*. Turin: Einaudi, 1963.

———. *Acquainted with Grief* [*La cognizione del dolore*]. Trans. William Weaver. New York: Braziller, 1969.

———. *Eros e Priapo (da furore a cenere)*. Milan: Garzanti, 1975.

———. *Azoto e altri scritti di divulgazione scientifica*. Ed. Vanni Scheiwiller, Andrea Silvestri, and Dante Isella. Milan: Scheiwiller, 1986.

———. *Opere di Carlo Emilio Gadda*. 5 vols. Ed. Dante Isella. Milan: Garzanti, 1988–93.

———. *Un fulmine sul 220*. Milan: Garzanti, 2000.

———. *I Littoriali del Lavoro e altri scritti giornalistici 1932–1941*. Ed. Manuela Bertone. Pisa: ETS, 2005.

Gallerano, Nicola. "Gli italiani in guerra 1940–43: Appunti per una ricerca." *Italia Contemporanea* no. 160 (1985): 81–93.

Garin, Eugenio. *Editori italiani tra Ottocento e Novecento*. Rome: Laterza, 1991.

Gentile, Emilio. *Il culto del Littorio: La sacralizzazione della politica nell'Italia fascista*. Rome: Laterza, 1993.

———. *Le origini dell'ideologia fascista 1918–1925*. Bologna: Il Mulino, 1996.

———. *The Sacralization of Politics in Fascist Italy* [*Il culto del Littorio*]. Trans. Keith Botsford. Cambridge: Harvard University Press, 1996.

———. *The Struggle for Modernity: Nationalism, Futurism, and Fascism*. Westport: Praeger, 2003.

Gillette, Aaron. *Racial Theories in Fascist Italy*. New York: Routledge, 2002. http://dx.doi.org/10.4324/9780203279212

Girard, René. *Violence and the Sacred*. Trans. Patrick Gregory. Baltimore: Johns Hopkins University Press, 1977.

———. *"To Double Business Bound": Essays on Literature, Mimesis, and Anthropology*. Baltimore: Johns Hopkins University Press, 1978.

Godelier, Maurice. *The Enigma of the Gift*. Trans. Nora Scott. Chicago: University of Chicago Press, 1999.

Goldhammer, Jesse. *The Headless Republic: Sacrificial Violence in Modern French Thought*. Ithaca: Cornell University Press, 2005.

Gori, Gigliola. *Italian Fascism and the Female Body: Sport, Submissive Women, and Strong Mothers*. New York: Routledge, 2004.

Greco, Lorenzo. *Censura e Scrittura: Vittorini, lo pseudo-Malaparte, Gadda*. Milan: Il Saggiatore, 1983.

Gregor, James A. *Interpretations of Fascism*. Morristown, N.J: General Learning Press, 1974.

Griffin, Roger. *Modernism and Fascism: The Sense of a Beginning under Mussolini and Hitler*. London: Palgrave Macmillan, 2007.

———, ed. *International Fascism: Theories, Causes and the New Consensus*. London: Oxford University Press, 1998.

———. *Fascism, Totalitarianism and Political Religion*. New York: Routledge, 2005.

Gundle, Stephen. *Between Hollywood and Moscow: The Italian Communists and the Challenge of Mass Culture, 1943–1991*. Durham: Duke University Press, 2000.

Gustarelli, Andrea. *Mussolini, scrittore ed oratore*. Milan: Vallardi, 1935.

Hainsworth, Peter. "Fascism and Anti-fascism in Gadda." In *Carlo Emilio Gadda: Contemporary Perspectives*, ed. Manuela Bertone and Robert S. Dombroski, 221–41. Toronto: University of Toronto Press, 1997.

Henri, Hubert, and Marcel Mauss. *Sacrifice: Its Nature and Function*. Trans. W.D. Halls. Chicago: University of Chicago Press, 1964.

Horn, David. *Social Bodies: Science, Reproduction, and Italian Modernity*. Princeton: Princeton University Press, 1994.

Hsia, R. Po-chia. *The Myth of Ritual Murder: Jews and Magic in Reformation Germany*. New Haven: Yale University Press, 1988.

Ian, Marcia. *Remembering the Phallic Mother: Psychoanalysis, Modernism, and the Fetish*. Ithaca: Cornell University Press, 1991.

Imbriani, Angelo Michele. *Gli italiani e il Duce: Il mito e l'immagine di Mussolini negli ultimi anni del fascismo (1938–1943)*. Naples: Liguori, 1992.

Isnenghi, Mario. *Il mito della grande guerra*. Bologna: Il Mulino, 1989.

———. "Il corpo del Duce." In *Gli occhi di Alessandro: Potere sovrano e sacralità del corpo da Alessandro Magno à Ceausescu*, ed. Sergio Bertelli and Cristiano Grottanelli, 170–83. Florence: Ponte alle Grazie, 1990.

Jay, Martin. "'The Aesthetic Ideology' as Ideology; or What Does It Mean to Aestheticize Politics?" *Cultural Critique* 21, no. 21 (1992): 41–61. http://dx.doi.org/10.2307/1354116.

Kantorowicz, Ernst. *The King's Two Bodies: A Study in Medieval Political Theology*. Princeton: Princeton University Press, 1957.

Kaplan, Alice Y. *Reproductions of Banality: Fascism, Literature, and French Intellectual Life*. Minneapolis: University of Minnesota Press, 1986.

Keenan, Dennis King. *The Question of Sacrifice*. Bloomington: Indiana University Press, 2005.

Lacan, Jacques. "The Mirror Stage as Formative of the Function of the I as Revealed in Psychoanalytic Experience." In *Écrits: A Selection*. Trans. Alan Sheridan, 1–7. New York: Norton, 1982.

Laclau, Ernesto. "Fascism and Ideology." In *Politics and Ideology in Marxist Theory: Capitalism, Fascism, Populism*, 81–142. London: Verso, 1979.

Lazzaro, Claudia, and Roger J. Crum. *Donatello among the Blackshirts: History and Modernity in the Visual Culture of Fascist Italy*. Ithaca: Cornell University Press, 2005.

Lepre, Aurelio. *Le illusioni, la paura, la rabbia: Il fronte interno italiano 1940–1943*. Naples: Edizioni Scientifiche Italiane, 1989.

Leso, Erasmo, et al., eds. *La lingua italiana e il fascismo*. Bologna: Consorzio Provinciale Pubblica Lettura, 1978.

Lucchini, Guido. "Gadda's Freud." In *Carlo Emilio Gadda: Contemporary Perspectives*, ed. Manuela Bertone and Robert S. Dombroski, 177–94. Toronto: University of Toronto Press, 1997.

Ludwig, Emil. *Talks with Mussolini*. Trans. Eden and Cedar Paul. Boston: Little, Brown, 1933.

———. *Colloqui con Mussolini*. Trans. Tomaso Gnoli. Milan: Mondadori, 1970.

Luzzatto, Sergio. *Il corpo del duce: Un cadavere tra immaginazione, storia e memoria*. Turin: Einaudi, 1998.

———. *L'immagine del duce: Mussolini nelle fotografie dell'Istituto Luce*. Rome: Editori Riuniti-Istituto Luce, 2001.

———. *The Body of Il Duce: Mussolini's Corpse and the Fortunes of Italy* [*Il corpo del duce*]. Trans. Frederika Randall. New York: Metropolitan, 2005.

Madeddu, Anselmo. *Vittorini da Robinson a Gulliver*. Siracusa: Edizioni dell'Ariete, 1997.

Malaparte, Curzio, and Enrico Falqui. *Vita di Pizzo-di-Ferro detto Italo Balbo*. Turin: Libreria del Littorio, 1931.

Malvano, Laura. "The Myth of Youth in Images: Italian Fascism." In *A History of Young People in the West*, vol 2, *Stormy Evolution to Modern Times*, ed. Giovanni Levi and Jean-Claude Schmitt, 232–56. Cambridge: Harvard University Press, 1997.

Mann, Michael. *Fascists*. Cambridge: Cambridge University Press, 2004. http://dx.doi.org/10.1017/CBO9780511806568

Mannoni, Octave. "Je sais bien, mais quand même." In *Clefs pour l'imaginaire ou l'autre scene*. Paris: Ed. Du Seuil, 1969.

Manzotti, Emilio, ed. *Le ragioni del dolore: Carlo Emilio Gadda 1893–1993*. Lugano: Cenobio, 1993.

Marvin, Carolyn, and David W. Ingle. *Blood Sacrifice and the Nation: Totem Rituals and the American Flag*. Cambridge: Cambridge University Press, 1999.

Mauri, Stefano. *Il libro in Italia: Geografia, produzione, consumo*. Milan: Hoepli, 1987.

McKenna, Andrew J. *Violence and Difference: Girard, Derrida, and Deconstruction*. Urbana: University of Illinois Press, 1992.

Mitscherlich, Alexander, and Margarete. *The Inability to Mourn: Principles of Collective Behavior*. Trans. Beverly R. Placzek. New York: Grove Press, 1975.

Mizruchi, Susan L. *The Science of Sacrifice: American Literature and Modern Social Theory*. Princeton: Princeton University Press, 1998.

Mussolini, Benito. *Scritti e discorsi di Benito Mussolini*. 12 vols. Milan: Hoepli, 1934–40.

———. *Opera Omnia di Benito Mussolini*. Ed. Edoardo and Duilio Susmel. 36 vols. Florence: La Fenice, 1951–63.

Nancy, Jean-Luc. "The Unsacrificable." Trans. Richard Livingston. *Yale French Studies* 79 (1991): 20–38. http://dx.doi.org/10.2307/2930245.

Nerenberg, Ellen V. *Prison Terms: Representing Confinement during and after Italian Fascism*. Toronto: University of Toronto Press, 2001.

Noventa, Giacomo. *Il grande amore*. Milan: Scheiwiller, 1960.

Panicali, Anna. *Il primo Vittorini*. Milan: Celuc, 1974.

———, ed. *Elio Vittorini: La narrativa, la saggistica, le traduzioni, le riviste, l'attività editoriale*. Milan: Mursia, 1994.

Papponetti, Giuseppe. *Gadda-D'Annunzio e il lavoro italiano*. Rome: Fondazione Ignazio Silone, 2002.

Payne, Stanley G. *A History of Fascism, 1914–1945*. Madison: University of Wisconsin Press, 1995.

Pedriali, Federica G. *Altre carceri d'invenzione: Studi gaddiani*. Ravenna: Longo, 2007.

Perfetti, Francesco. *Il dibattito sul fascismo*. Rome: Bonacci, 1984.

Perry, Alan R, ed. *Il santo partigiano martire: La retorica del sacrificio nelle biografie commemorative*. Ravenna: Longo, 2001.

Pickering-Iazzi, Robin. *Politics of the Visible: Writing Women, Culture, and Fascism*. Minneapolis: University of Minnesota Press, 1997.

Pinkus, Karen. *Bodily Regimes: Italian Advertising under Fascism*. Minneapolis: University of Minnesota Press, 1995.

Pizzato, Mark. *Theatres of Human Sacrifice: From Ancient Ritual to Screen Violence*. Albany: State University of New York Press, 2005.

Ragone, Giovanni. *Un secolo di libri: Storia dell'editoria in Italia dall'Unità al postmoderno*. Turin: Einaudi, 1999.

Rigotti, Francesca. "Il medico-chirurgo dello Stato nel linguaggio metaforico di Mussolini." In *Cultura e società negli anni del fascismo*, 501–17. Milan: Cordani, 1987.

Rodogno, Davide. *Fascism's European Empire: Italian Occupation during the Second World War*. Trans. Adrian Belton. Cambridge: Cambridge University Press, 2006.

Rodondi, Raffaella. "Viaggio intorno al 'Garofano.'" In *Il presente vince sempre*, ed. Raffaella Rodondi, 13–163. Palermo: Sellerio, 1985.

———, ed. *Elio Vittorini: Letteratura, arte, società. Articoli e interventi 1926–1937*. Turin: Einaudi, 1997.

Rossi, Cesare. *Il delitto Matteotti nei procedimenti giudiziari e nelle polemiche giornalistiche*. Milan: Ceschina, 1965.

Rousseau, Jean-Jacques. *Emile*. Trans. Barbara Foxley. London: Dent, 1993.

Salecl, Renata, and Slavoj Zizek, eds. *Gaze and Voice as Love Objects*. Durham: Duke University Press, 1996.

Santarelli, Enzo. *Storia del fascismo*. 3 vols. Rome: Editori Riuniti, 1973.

Santner, Eric. *Stranded Objects: Mourning, Memory, and Film in Postwar Germany*. Ithaca: Cornell University Press, 1990.

Schmidt, Dennis J. "Ruins and Roses: Hegel and Heidegger on Sacrifice, Mourning, and Memory." In *Endings: Questions of Memory in Hegel and Heidegger*, ed. Rebecca Comay and John McCumber, 97–113. Evanston: Northwestern University Press, 1999.

Schnapp, Jeffrey T. *Staging Fascism: 18BL and the Theater of Masses for Masses*. Stanford: Stanford University Press, 1996.

Scott, Joan W. "Fantasy Echo: History and the Construction of Identity." *Critical Inquiry* 27, no. 2 (2001): 284–304. http://dx.doi.org/10.1086/449009.

Silverman, Kaja. *The Acoustic Mirror: The Female Voice in Psychoanalysis and Cinema*. Bloomington: Indiana University Press, 1988.

Simonini, Augusto. *Il linguaggio di Mussolini*. Milan: Bompiani, 1978.

Sorel, Georges. In *Reflections on Violence*. Ed. Jeremy Jennings. New York: Cambridge University Press, 1999. http://dx.doi.org/10.1017/CBO9780511815614

Spackman, Barbara. "*Il verbo (e)sangue*: Gabriele D'Annunzio and the Ritualization of Violence." *Quaderni d'italianistica* 4, no. 2 (1983): 218–29.

———. *Decadent Genealogies: The Rhetoric of Sickness from Baudelaire to D'Annunzio*. Ithaca: Cornell University Press, 1989.

———. *Fascist Virilities: Rhetoric, Ideology, and Social Fantasy in Italy*. Minneapolis: University of Minnesota Press, 1996.

———. "Fascist Puerility." *Qui Parle* 13, no. 1 (2001): 13–28.

Spinosa, Antonio. *Starace: L'uomo che inventò lo stile fascista*. Milan: Mondadori, 2002.

Stone, Marla. *The Patron State: Culture and Politics in Fascist Italy*. Princeton: Princeton University Press, 1998.

Strenski, Ivan. *Contesting Sacrifice: Religion, Nationalism, and Social Thought in France*. Chicago: University of Chicago Press, 2002.

Tedeschi, E., ed. *Il "Duce" visto da Mussolini*. Milan: Bietti, 1965.

Turi, Gabriele, ed. *Storia dell'editoria nell'Italia contemporanea*. Florence: Giunti, 1997.

Turner, Victor. "Sacrifice as Quintessential Process: Prophylaxis or Abandonment?" *History of Religions* 16, no. 3 (1977): 189–215. http://dx.doi.org/10.1086/462765.

Valesio, Paolo. *Novantiqua: Rhetorics as a Contemporary Theory*. Bloomington: Indiana University Press, 1980.

Vittorini, Elio. *Il garofano rosso*. Milan: Mondadori, 1948.

———. *In Sicily* [*Conversazione in Sicilia*]. Trans. Wilfrid David. New York: New Directions, 1949.

———. *Diario in pubblico (1929–1956)*. Milan: Bompiani, 1970.

———. *Uomini e no*. Milan: Mondadori, 1973.

———. *Conversazione in Sicilia*. Manchester: Manchester University Press, 1978.

———. *Men and Not Men* [*Uomini e no*]. Trans. Sarah Henry. Marlboro: Marlboro Press, 1985.

Wanrooij, Bruno. "The Rise and Fall of Italian Fascism as a Generational Revolt." *Journal of Contemporary History* 22, no. 3 (1987): 401–18. http://dx.doi.org/10.1177/002200948702200303.

Winkler, Emil. *Grundlegung der Stilistik*. Bielefeld: Velhagen and Klasing, 1929.

———. *Sprachtheoretische studien*. Leipzig: Wilhelm Gronaü, 1933.

Witt, Mary Ann Frese. *The Search for Modern Tragedy: Aesthetic Fascism in Italy and France*. Ithaca: Cornell University Press, 2001.

Wyschogrod, Edith, Jean-Joseph Goux, and Eric Boynton, eds. *The Enigma of Grief and Sacrifice*. New York: Fordham University Press, 2002.

Zancan, Marina. *Il progetto "Politecnico": Cronaca e strutture di una rivista*. Venice: Marsilio, 1984.

Zizek, Slavoj. *The Sublime Object of Ideology*. London: Verso, 1989.

———. "The Spectre of Ideology." In *Mapping Ideology*, ed. Slavoj Zizek, 1–33. London: Verso, 1994.

Zunino, Pier Giorgio. *L'ideologia del fascismo: Miti, credenze e valori nella stabilizzazione del regime*. Bologna: Il Mulino, 1985.

Index